A COCKNEY SOLI

The true story of a boy's poor upbring. London from the days of the First World War. His broken home, causing him to be raised by his grandmother, and the conditions of the times leading to the Second World War make poignant reading.

Having joined the Army to better his living conditions, service life in peace and in war is related in graphic detail — as is his existence as a prisoner of war until the war's conclusion in 1945.

This insight into what must be, for many now, a different way of life can only make the reader value more the world in which we live today.

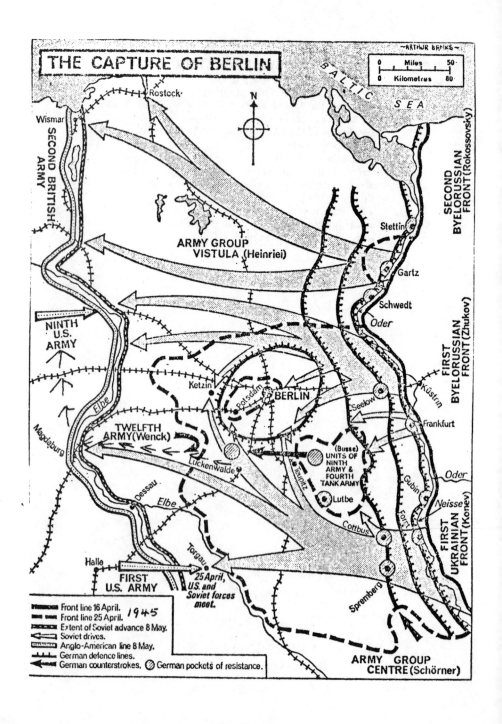

THE CAPTURE OF BERLIN

~ARTHUR BANKS~

Miles 50
Kilometres 80

BALTIC SEA

Rostock

Wismar

N

SECOND BRITISH ARMY

SECOND BYELORUSSIAN FRONT (Rokossovsky)

ARMY GROUP VISTULA (Heinriei)

Stettin

Gartz

Schwedt

Oder

NINTH U.S. ARMY

FIRST BYELORUSSIAN FRONT (Zhukov)

Ketzin

Potsdam

BERLIN

Seelow

Küstrin

Frankfurt

Elbe

Magdeburg

TWELFTH ARMY (Wenck)

Luckenwalde

Teupitz

(Busse) UNITS OF NINTH ARMY & FOURTH TANK ARMY

Gubin

Oder

Neisse (Konev)

FIRST UKRAINIAN FRONT (Konev)

Dessau

Elbe

Lutbe

Cottbus

Forst

Halle

Torgau

FIRST U.S. ARMY

25 April, U.S. and Soviet forces meet.

Spremberg

Front line 16 April. *1945*
Front line 25 April.
Extent of Soviet advance 8 May.
Soviet drives.
Anglo-American line 8 May.
German defence lines.
German counterstrokes. ⊘ German pockets of resistance.

ARMY GROUP CENTRE (Schörner)

A COCKNEY SOLDIER
'DUTY BEFORE PLEASURE'

An
Autobiography
1918-46
by
William Harding

MERLIN BOOKS LTD.
Braunton   **Devon**

To
the poor and unwanted,
and to all ex-prisoners of war
who may forgive, but never forget

ISBN 0 86303 452-7
Printed in England by Antony Rowe Ltd., Chippenham, Wilts.

CONTENTS

ILLUSTRATIONS

ACKNOWLEDGEMENTS

Some events from my prisoner of war accounts have previously been published in *Rough Ride from Trier,* Books I and II.

My grateful thanks to Anne and Syd Dodds for their help in the production of this book.

PART I

CHAPTER ONE

The good old days

My young life started on the 20th April, 1918, in a side street which led to the Hoxton Market in Shoreditch.

After several house moves, the family settled in Redvers Street, which linked Hoxton Street to Kingsland Road — a short distance from Shoreditch Church, centuries old, with a beautiful spire, which was mentioned by Shakespeare.

Shoreditch is adjacent to the Borough of Hackney, and not far from Bethnal Green, in the East End of London, all having a large Jewish population. Hoxton being within hearing distance of Bow Bells gave me claim to being a 'true Cockney', but nowadays anyone from London is referred to as a cockney. The dialect then was distinct from any other in London, but through better education has now faded into extinction.

I was a sickly child, having survived several near fatal illnesses, such as scarlet fever, diphtheria, pneumonia, and minor ones such as whooping cough, measles, etc. Finally my appendix and tonsils were removed, but on reaching the age of seven I had no more illnesses and became much stronger. I recall the very bitter medicine I had to take, and having my nose held, forcing me to swallow it.

My family consisted of my father and mother, my grandparents, my mother's sisters and brother, namely Emmy, Nan and Albert, living in a two up and two down small house at No. 9, the front door opening on to the pavement. My gran had borne seventeen children, of whom seven survived, five girls and two boys. Her family was originally from Tunbridge Wells. Her father became a London policeman, one of four brothers, who on the death of their father, sold the farm, known then as 'Wenham's Farm' and went their separate ways.

At seventeen years of age my gran married a young labourer, which upset her father so much that he would have nothing more to do with her. As a child, I remember seeing his oval sepia photograph in police uniform, with a row of silver buttons down the front. He had mutton chop whiskers and a very stern look; no matter where I was in the room, his eyes always seemed to follow me.

Grandad was happy enough when in work, but when out of it (which was often) he became unbearable and abusive, making life unpleasant in the house. I have known him when arriving home, if he didn't like the meal laid ready for him, to tip the table over, with rows and fights to follow. He was known in the street as 'Mad Waller' and I can remember him coming home the worse for drink, and when my gran asked for money he threw a handful of loose money across the room, shouting, "There you are, you old cow, what I pick up is mine." With them both on their hands and knees picking it up, I made a quick exit!

It was not a happy household, with constant bickering between the women, and when Grandad had no money for baccy and beer, he would be constantly demanding and being abusive until he got some.

Emmy worked at the Mannikin Cigar factory, and as a result of licking cigar leaves, her teeth all went black and she had to have them extracted.

Nan worked at Peak Freans biscuit factory in Bermondsey, south of the river, and was always complaining of burnt fingertips, caused by picking up the hot biscuits as they left the ovens.

Albert worked in a bakery, and it was his practice in the early hours to wake me and in the dark, place a piece of pastry in my hand. This he did regularly, as far back as I can remember. What a kind-hearted chap he was.

My mother would work well into the night by candle-light in the kitchen, pasting together gramophone record covers, for which, I learned later on in life, she was paid one shilling and sixpence for 500! She had to wear glasses as a result of doing this work.

My gran took in washing, using a brick built wash copper in the kitchen, which, when filled with water and a fire lit underneath would boil the clothes. Then after many hours of hard work at the wash board, followed by rinsing and wringing, all the clothes lines in the back yard would be filled, or in wet weather, the washing was draped in front of the large hob, fire and oven combined, which gave off a good heat. This always annoyed Grandad, because he wasn't able to spit, whilst smoking, at the fire bars, and he rarely missed. When the washing was dry, it would be neatly ironed and I would take it to the various houses, collecting a shilling here and a shilling there.

My memories in the main are happy ones. There was a small back garden to dig about in, and chicken run with hens and a cock, so that we always had eggs, and a chicken for Sunday dinner once in a while. I grew up in the exciting atmosphere of Hoxton market, which catered for everybody, with the 'in and out' shops full of cheap clothes, the many stalls where, if funds permitted, one could buy almost anything, including live poultry, rabbits, puppies, kittens, goldfish and all kinds of caged birds. The flare lamps on the stalls would light up the whole market, and one could hear the shouts and calls of the coster and fishmongers. Haddocks, kippers and bloaters would hang in rows on rods and every kind of fish, including crabs and shellfish would be on sale. There were huge conger eels, from which pieces were chopped off to order, and people would eat shell fish and jellied eels on the spot.

There were the entertainers trying to make a few coppers, such as jugglers, the ones performing balancing acts with bicycles, the Punch and Judy shows in an odd corner, crowded with laughing children, then the 'Bing Boys', who, with a barrel-organ playing and a rolled out slatted mat would give good entertainment. There would be tap dancers dressed in ragged evening dress, with tails and top hats, the lids flapping. They would do somersaults in time to the music, whilst one played old popular songs on the barrel-organ. Plastered over it were cuttings from programmes and newspapers showing pictures of their past stage successes and experiences.

When the hat came round, the watching crowds would melt away. They needed their pennies too. Small groups of Welsh miners carrying miners' lamps would be singing in harmony, caps on the ground, hoping for donations, but with so many trying the same thing and Hoxton in the main being very poor, I wouldn't think that they had come to the right place or had much success, even allowing for the old saying that 'It's the poor that helps the poor.'

The odd group of musicians with trombone, accordion, trumpet and banjo would all add to the market noise. It was common for men with concertinas to stand playing in pub doorways, swinging the instrument in a circle to good effect. One thing that I liked to hear was a small harp on a folding stand which was played by striking the wires with tiny hammers. Then there were the tin whistles.

Through the market were scattered the blind men, standing holding cans with a notice 'Please help the blind'. My gran used to say, "If you dropped a farthing they would bloody soon see it." Then there would be the ex-servicemen on crutches wearing medal ribbons selling matches (they were too proud to beg) with a board 'Wife and children to support'. The street singers were the worst. They would stand in one spot making a terrible noise until irate people would throw them a penny to make them move on. The eel stalls used to fascinate me, watching the eels slithering around in trays, and when a buyer chose one, it would be chopped up and the pieces, still wriggling, wrapped in paper.

One pleasant memory I have is of the bakers' shops, the smell of freshly baked bread from the ovens would make my mouth water. In time I became familiar with every shop and stall. I would enjoy watching men, one playing a mouth-organ and the other clicking a pair of mutton bones or spoons over his body in rhythm.

At the market end of Redvers Street was a large old building, the music hall 'Britannia', where many famous entertainers made their names, including, I believe, Marie Lloyd and Florrie Ford. The period had arrived when silent films were displacing the stage acts and the old 'Brit' being no exception, had to move with the times. Sometimes my gran would take me to see the half programme of stage turns and half silent films. The piano playing always sounded eerie to me and the lighting not adjusted properly in those days meant sitting in total darkness. It was great fun when, in tense moments, with villains creeping up behind the unsuspecting hero the crowd would roar, "Look out, he's behind you," etc. Also, if the film broke down, shouts of ripe old language would almost lift the roof off!

The butcher's shop next door to the old 'Brit' did a good trade selling cooked pig's trotters, and a stall outside sold peanuts in the shells and sweets. Opposite was the fried fish and chip shop, so most people went in eating something, with the vinegary smell of fish and chips wafting everywhere, combined with the non-stop cracking of peanut shells. Bones from the pig's trotters, screwed up chip papers and other rubbish was thown about in the dark, causing uproars, and louts in the front row of the circle would at times urinate over the edge, causing many protests from the ones on the receiving end in the stalls below.

Stink bombs were favourites, but if the 'chucker out' ever caught any of the culprits they would land outside on the pavement, often with a black eye.

Just before it was demolished, I saw a show at the London Music Hall, situated near Shoreditch Church, and watched 'Samson' bend iron bars around his neck and lift a girder off the stage with his teeth and a strap, having six members of the audience sitting on it, three at each end. This giant of a man finished his act by bending underneath a horse, and with arms locked around the horse's legs, lifted it clear of the stage. The silent films were great and gave lots of pleasure, with comics such as Charlie Chaplin, Harold Lloyd, the Keystone Cops and so many others. Then there were the cowboy films, with names like Buck Jones and Tom Mix, with a host of others who influenced us kids into playing cowboys and Indians, rather than cops and robbers.

It was an era of great pleasure, where for a few coppers people could go and forget their troubles for two or three hours, and be lost in a different world. Films of the war seemed very realistic to me, and I loved them, being too young to appreciate the real suffering which war brings.

Some of the old cries of London still survived. The fly-paper man in his top hat, carrying a tray, from which hung sticky fly-papers would shout, "Catch them all alive." There was the chimney sweep, with his barrow of brushes who would cry, "Chimneys to sweep," while his boy knocked on doors, seeking customers, also the knife grinder, who was always around with his call of, "Knives to grind." I remember in the summer time Gran would pin a fly-paper to the ceiling over the table, when flies would build up in layers on top of each other, buzzing away, only to slide off on to the table and sometimes on to the food. Sunday afternoon would bring the cry of the muffin man ringing his handbell with his trays of muffins and crumpets balancing on his head. There were also the various boys selling winkles, shell fish, cockles and prawns, celery and water-cress from small hand barrows. The children's favourite was the toffee barrows, selling plain or coconut toffee, home-made, in trays, broken up with tiny hammers. There was also 'stickjaw', a glutinous toffee, very popular. Also the large 'gob-stoppers', which would last ages, constantly changing colour. The ice-cream tricycle was always around, with the seller in straw boater shouting, "Assenheims, they're lovely, the more you eat the more you jump and all for a penny a lump."

These were not days of boredom; there was something going on all the time. Albert had bought and fixed up a 'cat's whisker' crystal set, which we all thought was great.

I recall one day, as the Salvation Army marched by, playing noisily, when the dust-cart horse tugged the heavy cart round and galloped after them. Fortunately the dustmen caught it in time, thus avoiding an accident. I was shown the army number stamped in one of the horse's front hoofs, proving why he liked the bands, being an ex-army horse.

My school was situated at the market end of the street, so I was lucky, as it combined infants and juniors, boys and girls. I grew to love that school and apart from some sadistic teachers, my memories are happy ones.

My family's fortunes started to deteriorate when my grandad died at his night-watchman's job on road repairs. This followed a few months after a fight between him and his son, who broke his walking stick over his head and threw him into the coal cellar. Albert was severely provoked, as Grandad could be extremely nasty at times. He was laid in his coffin on trestles in the front room for a week before the funeral, and the smell of that coffin remains with me to this day.

There were distressing scenes when people kept coming and going to pay their last respects. I was compelled to kiss his forehead, which I didn't like, as apart from the touch of the dead body, my grandad never liked me. Often when passing his chair, he would grab hold of some skin on my upper arm and twist it, making me cry out in pain. I recall once when my younger sister Rosina stood between his knees holding a bag of sweets. He said to her, "See him over there, don't give him any."

Everybody saw that he had a grand funeral, according to what could be afforded from the 'penny' insurances, plus a clear out of everything to the pawnshops, leaving the house almost bare. Four jet black plumed horses pulled the elaborate ornamented glass hearse, with the bereaved following in black coaches, also pulled by black horses. There were distressing scenes at the graveside, especially Gran, and looking into the deep grave, I saw the coffin at the bottom sink into water. I thought at the time that it didn't seem right for such a polished shiny box with nice handles and my grandad inside should be covered in water. It was customary in those days on the day of the funeral for most people in the street to gather around the door as the coffin was carried out, and when passing the local pub and shops, everybody would stand on the pavement showing their respects. I didn't have to run to buy his clay pipes and tobacco any more, and I felt free of his presence.

A firm called Hayes and English were the predominant undertakers in Hoxton, and I had often stood and watched the joiners making the coffins in the shop windows of their premises, with brass fitments and name plates on view. Most people in the area only went to church for three reasons in their lives, christenings, weddings and funerals. The firm had a good name and the poor of Hoxton would be provided with a funeral of dignity. Very often the cost meant a long drag of rent arrears, with goods bought on the never-never, and instantly sold or pawned for ready cash. The 'tallyman' calling for his weekly payment would often face a hostile family at the door, and be sent away with nothing.

Shortly after Grandad's funeral another calamity occurred, when Albert lost his job at the baker's, thus joining the many unemployed in Shoreditch. It happened one night when preparing for baking. The boss's son started passing insulting remarks about the British in the war. The boss was a German named Anspach, and Albert's brother had served during the war in the Royal Marine Light Infantry and early in 1918 lost his life when his ship was torpedoed and sunk in the North Irish Sea. Albert, in his rage, tipped the boss's son head-first into a vat of dough, so he was sacked, and try as he could to find work, he remained one of the unemployed. In those days, if one couldn't produce a testimonial from a previous employer, it usually meant no chance of employment elsewhere. The extras Albert used to bring home ceased, including my little feasts in bed each night, and sure enough, no matter how much he tried, he was never able to find another job. The Labour Exchange was situated just around the corner of Redvers Street in Mail Coach Yard and on signing-on days, the large crowds had to be controlled by the police and often there would be protesting individuals thrown out from the counters inside.

Albert had been progressing well at the Polytechnic in Pitfield Street, learning the art of making tiered wedding cakes, entirely by hand, and had already won several medals and was doing well in his exams. This came to a stop because he couldn't pay the fees, and after walking many miles seeking work, the time came when he had to cut and fit cardboard into his shoes to cover the holes in the soles. He must have been pretty hungry each day, because Gran used to complain that he was eating her out of house and home!

During the long summer school holidays Albert used to take me on the long walk to Victoria Park, where we would kick a ball about, and after a drink at the water fountain, there would be the tiring walk back. I always looked forward to the thick slices of bread and jam, 'doorsteps' Gran called them, and the hot, strong tea, laced with condensed milk. Now and again there would be the spicy bread pudding, full of mixed fruit, at which Gran excelled. Bread and dripping was a favourite, and also tinned milk spread on bread and sprinkled with sugar. I never went hungry but Gran would say, "What won't fatten will fill." A regular drink was hot cabbage water, quite nice, laced with salt and pepper. Stalls and shops sold sarsaparilla, a lovely drink, also milk and cream soda, if the pennies were available. The Italian café round the corner did a good trade selling tea to the unemployed and would never refuse a halfpenny.

Provided one was early enough at a baker's shop, three stale cakes could be bought for a penny. Large pieces of bread pudding were sold for a penny. Nothing was ever wasted by anyone. For a halfpenny we kids could buy a good helping of crackling skimmed from the top of the fish frying vats in fish and chip shops. In winter, one could buy roast chestnuts and baked potatoes from mobile ovens and hot cordial drinks.

In the long, hot summer evenings, it was the custom for people to bring chairs out on to the pavement, and have a good natter, while the streets would be filled with children playing games, or whipping tops. I liked the peg tops, also the iron ring hoops and the thing which most boys had, four pram wheels on their axles to which a board had been fixed and a soap box on top to sit on. They were great fun, but also a danger to life and limb, with boys whizzing along shouting their heads off. We all had our share of coloured marbles and the glass ones, with nice patterns inside, which we called 'glarnies'.

We played with these along the gutters on a win or lose basis, and if our pockets were bulging out with too many, teachers at school would often confiscate them. We would pester men for their cigarette cards, which we boys would flick against walls, the nearest would take all. These simple games required skill and I would end up with wads of cigarette cards, which when set into series, doubles would be swopped around. The cards were very educational, on almost every subject, including sport, and were helpful in school lessons to many children. On warm dry evenings children would draw pictures on the pavements with coloured chalks, making grottoes with coloured stones set in different designs, competitions being held for the best ones.

Boys rarely played with girls, it being considered cissy, so girls played hopscotch and sang, dancing to the rhythm of the skipping ropes.

Emmy was courting a sailor named Walter, who visited her from Portsmouth whenever possible, and one day, whilst playing in the street I saw a sailor turn the corner on his hands and knees, with a woman saying, "This is Redvers Street, and I will show you number nine." It was Walter, drunk and incapable, so I ran indoors, and told them. Poor as people were, things like this happening were not welcome for neighbours to see. Eventually they married, Emmy renting two rooms in her sister's house in East Ham, London. This now meant less money coming into the house, so life became harder for Gran, trying to make ends meet.

I spent a lot of time collecting orange boxes from the market to use as fuel for the wash copper fire and when road repairs were being done, I would steal the old tar blocks for the front room fire. It was interesting to see how the concrete road was broken up. One man would hold a large point steady in heavy tongs, whilst navvies in a circle would, with sledge-hammers commence hitting the point lightly until it pierced the surface, then with regular rhythm they would swing the heavy hammers and never miss the point top, soon breaking up the concrete.

There were regular visits on Monday mornings before school to 'Ponds', the main pawn shop in Hoxton, one of several that always did a good trade. Gran would clear the house out of any linen, sheets off the beds, all curtains and spare clothing, to make up one large bundle for her to carry and a smaller one for me. Old coats of Grandad's would cover me at night. We used to join the queue at the pawn shop and inside there would be arguments over money offered for bundles and pennies would often be the bone of contention, also some would be rejected if bugs were found inside. I liked watching the man writing out the pawn tickets with three pens, dipping into three ink wells simultaneously as he wrote on three tickets, all done with a light framework. The money Gran received helped pay the rent and buy food until Friday, when with Nan's wages we would go back and redeem the bundles, thus having sheets on the beds and curtains at the windows for the weekend, until Monday came round again.

Nan, often in tears, would complain when Gran would force almost every penny out of her, leaving just her bus fares for work, the end result being that clothes would just have to be mended and altered continuously, because of lack of money.

I have memories of the 1926 General Strike, of police and soldiers riding on trams and buses, army lorries picking up people who tried to get to work, come what may. I recall the hoarse cries of men fighting police who were stopping them from dragging baulk timbers on to the tram lines, and throwing stones through the windows; of mounted police breaking up large groups and the unemployed being arrested, some with bloody heads. These are scattered memories, but there just the same. Hoxton was a hard place, and in general, police went around in pairs. They were detested. It wasn't easy for them either. I recall one night when, on hearing police whistles, I ran to Kingsland Road to see a policeman, minus his helmet and tunic, his shirt in bloody tatters, frogmarching a man along the tramlines being whacked by a bunch of screaming women. For all that, although staggering, he still got his prisoner to Old Street police station. Also on odd occasions, I have seen the single policeman, back to a wall, wielding his rolled up waterproof cape, a blow from which would lay out an ox, defending himself against attacking gangs. It was quite common at night, after the pubs emptied, to hear cries of 'stop thief', when gold watches and chains with Alberts (jewelled ornaments) would be snatched from waistcoats of the unwary. Most of the police were hard cases anyway, as they wore medal ribbons of the Great War, and when going on duty they would form up outside the police station in line, to be inspected by the sergeant, who would then march them off in single file, like soldiers, with their food bags hanging on their belts. At each beat point, the last man would drop off and the relieving man join the column, thus the sergeant would arrive back at the station with the same number of men that he had started out with.

Servicemen walked about very smart in their uniforms, especially the Artillery men in riding dress and bandoliers, also the Guards, in scarlet and blue with peaked caps. Going back to my early childhood, I now come to my father, who was a leading stoker in the Royal Navy, and had taken part in the Battle of Jutland in 1916. He served on after the war, and when he came home on leave, the top front room would be used by my mother and him to sleep in. I was always told to keep out of his way, and at times I would wake up in the night hearing them rowing and once I heard my mother cry out, "Don't hit me Bill," and I've seen her with black eyes and split lips. He was a broad stocky man, and something of a boxer, with a broken nose, a real Hoxtonite.

In the course of their married life, she obtained nine police court summonses for assault, and two legal separations, but in those days, burdened with children, a woman was invariably forced back to a brutal husband because she had no money or nowhere to go. I was told years later that during the hearing of an assault charge, a magistrate told my mother that she must have asked for it, or he wouldn't have hit her. How lucky women are today, if only they realized it.

My father would go on a 2½ to 3 years commission, serving on battleships, mostly in the Far East, and when he did come home on leave, I would see a sailor and be told this is your dad, but I cannot remember him once showing any affection or feeling towards me. I recall him bringing home the long torpedo-shaped 'pricks' of tobacco which he would make on board ship by soaking whole leaves with water, then when doused with rum, roll them together, then tie the roll tightly from end to end with cord. After some months they would cure, and on removing the cord, he would cut off pieces and sell them in the pubs. This was much sought after by pipe smokers. My mother had seven children in all, seven children and several miscarriages, so she never had an easy life.

When I was eight years old, my father was granted married quarters in Portsmouth, a furniture van came to the house, and my mother's home was packed in it. My young sister and brother, with Mother, waved goodbye as the van drove off, leaving me standing on the pavement, so it was left to my gran to bring me up, and I always called her Mum. I was known to everyone as 'Billy Waller', and only became used to my real name when I left school, Waller being Gran's surname.

Tramps and gypsies were always part of the Hoxton scene, and were constantly knocking on the door for something. If Gran saw them through the window, she would ignore them, but if she was caught out, she would never refuse the penny sprig of white heather, mindful of gypsies' curse, saying, "There's enough bad luck in the house already without adding to it." Tramps would usually hold out a can and ask for a spoonful of tea, then to each house in turn for sugar, some milk, then hot water and they would end up with a can of tea. Tramps would also hover in food shop doorways, when they would be given something to make them go away.

Times became harder, so Albert killed off all the chickens for the table, Gran being unable to buy the corn, bran and grit, also the run was dismantled and used as fuel for the wash copper, but Albert, for all his efforts, had no luck in finding work, and became so depressed that he went to Finsbury Barracks just off the City Road in September 1928 and enlisted with the Royal Field Artillery, aged 20 years. He went to the Woolwich Depot, home of the Gunners, making one less in the house, and how I missed him, he was always kind to me. I had, at times, when wandering around the streets, stood at the railings of Finsbury Barracks of an evening, watching the men wearing medals and their ladies in long dresses, going in for some function or other.

The Sunday dinner was mostly mutton stew, with cow heel and tripe, accompanied by large dumplings rolled in barley, which I loved to eat. Gran always made a marvellous stew in the huge iron pot on the hob, and there was always enough for Monday. She always made plenty of dumplings which, when cold, would make a nice supper, cut up with jam spread on them. I often went to the market with a large bag, and would crawl underneath greengrocers' stalls, taking the best of what had been thrown away, including oranges and apples, but when the bad parts were cut off, they were quite nice to eat. If I couldn't find enough to fill the bag, I would have to buy twopennyworth of 'hot pot', namely onions, carrots, turnip, a stick of celery and a few tomatoes.

The school was well organized, with discipline maintained at all times in the class-room, sports and playground. Fighting was strictly forbidden, so the challenge 'see you outside', meant boys forming a circle in the street, whilst two boys would fight until one gave in. The Elementary system meant a fast and a slow side, with Standard X7 being the highest one could go.

Playing truant was a serious offence, and anyone found absent without a sick note soon had the school-board man at the door, and continued absence brought a summons for the parents to attend court.

I found most subjects interesting, but English history was my favourite. We were taught the correct way to start and finish a letter, and also how to address people from all walks of life. Spelling was drummed into us and pronunciation helped along by each reading a paragraph from books regularly. To write correctly was considered important and arithmetic was a must, and had to be learned thoroughly, even to the extent of staying in during school playtime or dinner break doing some of the harder sums. Unruly classes were unheard of and some teachers were sadistic when at the slightest excuse one would be called out, receiving a stinging cut across the hand with the cane.

One teacher I didn't like, and who was feared by all was a ginger-haired man, Mr Trump, the Maths teacher. Any excuse was enough to have one out with first a verbal blasting, when he would swish the cane through the air first, then a cut across each hand with force. I could never get my thumbs right back, so the bone took a whack, and would hurt for days after. He would set out a sum on the blackboard and fully explain it all, then give the class one to do. He would walk around the class-room looking over our shoulders at our progress, and if he saw someone in difficulties, as I was once, it resulted in a slap across the ear from behind, and be straightened up with a good slap on the other.

Once a month a visiting nurse would examine all children in the school for lice and flea bites. I always had a 'tuppenny all-off' at the barber's shop but I took a note home from the nurse regarding flea bites on my body, making Gran go into a flaming temper, but when I said that my teacher had passed remarks about my patched clothes, that did it, setting me off crying. Then she would go to school and have a bust up the next day. Gran had a very strong will, and once she made up her mind, nothing would change it. Next morning I was terrified when she came into the class-room, shouting at the teacher that if my clothes were old and patched, they were clean. They went outside and I heard a slanging match, after which, the teacher returned red-faced. It set the boys off after me in the playground and in the street, calling 'Ragshop' among other things, ending in several fights in the ring of boys, causing me to go home with my clothes ripped and torn, and bruises to go with it. Gran would go mad on seeing the state I was in, so a few more clouts was my reward. One morning, the teacher gave me a parcel of clothes and insisted I tell my gran not to take offence, as they were from his own children. On arriving home, Gran was delighted to see a suit, jersey, shirts and underwear, which all fitted me, but I never wore them. She took them to the pawn shop! The teacher received no thanks, Gran saying, "He's got plenty," and he said nothing to me, but I felt awful when he looked at me.

I always liked singing lessons and the teacher used to start off with a tuning fork, and with good effect, sang patriotic songs of the British Isles, sea shanties, folk songs and many others. To sing is to be happy, but I fell foul of the music teacher one day when, during a singing session he caught me laughing, so I was caned on each hand. As I stood with a hand under each arm in agony he said, "Not laughing now, eh, stay in at playtime and at 12 o'clock, and write fifty lines . . . 'I must not laugh during singing lessons'." When 1 o'clock came I was trying to get through my fifty lines when Gran charged into the class-room, saying to me, "You, out," and to the teacher, "don't keep him in again, he has errands to run; if he does something wrong, cane him." I'm afraid it was accepted that if one was caned, it was deserved and serve you right.

I recall a set to after school, when a classmate — Johnny Hooper and myself ended up fighting in the 'ring'. His mother brought him to my house and was arguing with Emmy. I showed myself when Mrs Hooper made a dive into the passage after me. A fight ensued, with her and Emmy having it out in the street, like two wild cats, and they had to be dragged apart by passers-by. On another occasion, I arrived home tearful, having had the worst of a fight. Albert opened the door, saying, "Been fighting again? Did you beat him?" I said "No" and he gave me a stinging slap and said, "Don't come back until you have." I went round to the other boy's street and waited. He came out and I grabbed him and then beat him. Arriving home, Albert asked, "Did you beat him?" and when I said yes, he let me in. I only mention these events to show that Hoxton was no place for softees.

My happiest memories are of school friends, in the playgrounds, around the streets, and the good times spent in each other's houses. Swapping was exciting, and I ended up with a mixture of lead soldiers, a fort, puzzles and comics, which I would not otherwise have had. One good friend was Emrys Williams, whose parents owned the dairy round the corner. Another was Sammy Benysh — a Jewish family owning a haberdashery shop in Hoxton. Others were very poor, like Alfie Hines, who, I heard years later, ended up in prison. In a Jewish friend's house one night, keeping an eye on very young children while the parents went out, I was given a meal of pickled herring, bagels and bread with seeds on it. I always remember how tasty that simple meal was.

CHAPTER TWO

God helps those who help themselves

I went to Shoreditch Church for Sunday morning service, and attended Sunday-school at Hoxton House School, opened for the occasion in the afternoon. I would sometimes attend an evening church service if a magic lantern show was on. On Tuesday evenings I used to attend scripture lessons, and on Wednesday evenings, the Band of Hope. Friday evenings would be a trip to the Baptist Tabernacle. The main attraction, other than Sundays, was the bowl of soup and sandwiches, but I took things in my stride, and was quite happy wherever I went. Also, when Christmas came round, there were the children's parties to look forward to, with the usual orange, apple, bag of sweets, and a bright new penny. Some even gave a toy as well. I remember one Christmas Eve saying to Gran, "Can I hang my socks up on the mantelpiece?" To which she replied, "You can if you like, but you will find sod-all in them." Next morning I ran downstairs to find nothing, as she said.

The Band of Hope was a small mission, situated in a cul-de-sac close by. It holds special memories for me as a child. The meetings would be packed with children, as it was so popular, we being made so welcome, with kindness and happiness within the four walls. The staff would make sandwiches and tea, sometimes fairy cakes, and there was always the delicious aroma of soup cooking.

The grey-haired man in charge was a wonderful person. He would get us singing at the tops of our voices various hymns, one of my favourites being 'Dare to be a Daniel', and the stories of Daniel in the Lion's Den and standing in the fires without getting burned. We took part in biblical sketches on the stage, then in the interval it was time for soup and sandwiches, after which, we had simple lessons on how to combat the 'demon drink' and a questionnaire, which we would return the following week with some answers. I won a prize, an illustrated book which I treasured; also, in time, I signed the pledge never to take alcoholic drink. The framed certificate was hung in the passage at home, but as the house was constantly full of steam from the wash copper, it eventually fell to pieces. There used to be good sing-a-longs organized by the Master and his staff. The dedication of those kind and generous people knew no bounds, and sometimes a special treat would be a magic lantern show, given by a visiting missionary, showing strange looking people from far off lands. I'm afraid that years later I broke the pledge, but I was quite familiar with the 'demon drink' in my own home and in Hoxton, but I never was much of a drinker anyway, so the seed never fell on stony ground entirely.

I can remember times when my father would be on leave, and I would stand for hours outside the pub doors until he and my mother would come out and row all the way home. Also Grandad, in drunken tempers would come home later, and in bed I would hear screams and shouts from downstairs, with the sound of glass and furniture being smashed. I used to lie there feeling very frightened. The Band of Hope tried to educate the children about the miseries drink can bring, but many of us had first hand experience of this in our own homes.

Bad news came from India to say that Albert was ill, and would soon be on his way back to England. I learned later in life, that Albert had been found, after many hours, lying dead drunk in the sun at Christmas, with no helmet on, and from then on, became mentally ill. It was said that Gran had received a letter from one of his soldier friends in India, stating that this was how Albert became ill, but the army medical authorities maintained that in their opinion, he must have been mentally unwell before he enlisted. I had received some photographs and an anna, he always thought of me. One day a large trunk arrived containing his khaki drill and boots, with other items of kit, but no personal possessions, and my imagination ran wild as I held the stuff. I was determined that no one would touch it, being Albert's, but like everything in that house, it eventually went, the trunk as well.

Albert arrived at Southampton and became a patient in Netley hospital. Letters passed to and fro, but as Nan could not afford the fare to Southampton, it wasn't until he was medically discharged from the army and became an in-patient and certified that she was able to see him. Nan took me on the visit, and I felt bewildered and hurt on seeing Albert, vacant, showing no recognition of us, then raving and shouting orders . . . "They're coming, look out, fire," then throwing himself on the floor. He had been my idol when home on leave, and I thought something terrible must have happened to him.

He had a badly bruised face and chest, with some teeth missing. Nan was shocked and very upset, and demanded to see a doctor, who confronting her, insisted that his injuries were caused whilst being constrained when violent. Nan said, "Are you saying that in order to restrain him he had to be knocked about and lose his teeth?" She received no satisfaction from the doctor, and apart from remembering the conversation, it had been talked about enough at home.

On another occasion when visiting him, Albert was in bed ill, and a patient near by said that four attendants had grabbed him, one on each arm and leg, then folded him up and crashed him on to the stone floor. No one would take notice of another patient, but when he was up, he walked with a stoop and had no teeth, and if he ever started to shout, I saw him looking frightened when an attendant came towards him, when he would immediately go quiet. To date, Albert has been in the hospital near 60 years, and is a quiet, vacant old man, with crunchy eyes, caused, I believe, by punches, but the creation of the NHS in 1948 put a stop to a lot of the attendants carrying on their brutal work.

Gran, Albert's mother, tried very hard to obtain some compensation or pension from the authorities, but the answer was always the same, that his illness was not considered to have been caused by his army service, so therefore he could not be given any monetary award. His other sisters did visit him once or twice, but soon lost interest. On one visit, Emmy, Nan and myself caused Emmy to laugh until she was too weak to stand, watching the antics of some of the inmates, and for her it was a good day out.

From the age of nine, I had always run errands in the street, and as I had the habit of running most of the time, I was always in demand. I used to win lots of races in the school sports, as I loved running and would get a wonderful feeling of exhilaration as my feet sped over the ground. The pennies I earned I always gave to Gran, and I would often be out until 11 p.m., eventually going to bed tired out. The things people wanted in the evenings would be cigarettes, tobacco, beer, or spirits, gin being the favourite. Faggots, pease-pudding or large saveloys could be obtained hot from the butcher in the market, who stayed open until the pubs closed after 11 p.m. He also cooked half pig's heads and trotters, ox tongues and tails, and half sheep's heads, complete with eyeball, taken out of the boiling vat. Everybody wanted an eyeball and Gran loved them, but I couldn't stand the look of them.

There was the usual fish and chips, hot pies and mash to be had from 'Fortune's' eel and pie shop, and when finished I would buy some supper for Gran, Nan and myself. In the school lunch break I would do some errands to earn threepence, then run to 'Fortune's' and buy my dinner — a tuppeny pie, a penn'orth of mash with parsley liquor, as it was called then. It was a lovely meal and I would walk out wishing I could buy another one, and judging by the queues at the door, I think 'Fortune's' must have fed most of the poor in Hoxton, and their name was known for miles around.

I also took a hand at window cleaning for part-time on Saturdays for two shillings, going up the ladder a bit gingerly at first, but I soon got used to it. The money I earned went a long way towards buying groceries for the home, and Gran made sure that I did, and it was my pleasure to take a shopping bag late on Saturday and spend every penny I had earned buying bacon, eggs, tea, sugar, tinned milk and margarine with other things, as far as the money would go. Gran used to be delighted when it was placed on the table, and I would feel very proud. The rent was £1 a week, a lot in those days, when so many people were out of work, or receiving starvation wages.

While Gran was bringing me up, she was always worried that the school would find out that she was not my legal guardian and have me put in a home. There had already been some callers enquiring about my mother, but Gran would always say that my mother was away visiting someone. Gran's joints were seizing up with arthritis from years of slaving at the wash tub, and this resulted in her stopping taking in washing, she was in so much pain. 'The Land of Promise' was carved over the entrance to the workhouse in Hoxton. It was next door to St Leonard's Hospital, and the thought of going into hospital struck terror in the old people, who would say that once in there, you either came out feet first, or went into the workhouse. Nothing would induce Gran to call the doctor in. For one thing, it would cost 7/6d, and another, there was the fear of the hospital, so when I was able I would buy in the chemist a box of rheumatism pills, to try to ease her pain, but they never seemed to work.

All the year round my clothing consisted in the main of a jersey, short trousers, underclothes and canvas plimsolls. These I wore come rain or shine, summer or winter, and I never once had a coat or boots to wear. The plimsolls were the cheapest form of footwear at 11½d a pair and when the canvas uppers wore away, Gran would sew them over and over with thread until they could be mended no more. My clothes were always bought on second-hand stalls for a few coppers. I used to get chilblains in the winter, so Gran would make me soak my feet in a jerry, half filled with urine, and if I had coughs and colds, it meant a good rubbing in with camphorated oil, and a bowl of onions laced with pepper, then to bed and sweat it out. The biggest curse in the house were the bugs, which crawled up the bedroom walls at night, so Gran would sprinkle Keating's powder on the bed joints and the mattress to keep them off the bed. The powder had a pungent smell and I could never get used to it. Also at night, mice would be squeaking and scampering under the bed, but Gran would say, "They are wasting their time, they will find nothing here."

One day a large piece of the ceiling fell down in Gran's bedroom, and some rotten floor boards collapsed in the passage, near the front door. When asked about repairs, the landlord said that if he did them, he would have to double the rent, so the ceiling stayed as it was, and I nailed some boards from orange boxes over the holes in the passage. There never was any lino on the floor, but rugs were made from thin strips of cloth, cut from old coats and threaded in small pieces into sacking.

It was my job, once a week, with a sack tied round me, with bucket, soap, cloth and brush, to scrub out all the rooms, floors up and down, the staircase and passage. I had to wash out the kitchen and the outside toilet, white hearthstone the steps back and front, and blacklead the hob and oven with 'Zebra' polish and shine it until it gleamed. As Gran would say, "It shines like a new sixpence up a sweep's arse." The kitchen and front room fire grates would then be cleaned out and laid ready for lighting. The staircase treads had worn hollow through the years, and to a knife edge, and protruding nails would often catch the foot, making it dangerous.

Nan was constantly ill with a painful back and chest, resulting in spells in bed and time off work, with consequent loss of wages. The fear of eviction when the rent couldn't be paid forced Gran to apply to the Poor Relief Office for assistance. It was arranged with the school that I should be present, and I recall the argument which went on between a woman official and Gran. She told Gran that as she was almost housebound, she could be better looked after in the workhouse, and as it appeared that my mother wasn't interested in me it would be arranged for me to go into a council home. Gran exploded, I started crying, terrified at the thought of it all as I listened to the bust up. Gran eventually convinced her that I was in good hands with herself and Nan, so the official gave in, telling Gran to sell all surplus furniture and chattels and keep just three chairs and so on. It was arranged that we would be left alone, and that the Poor Relief would pay the rent and grant weekly vouchers for groceries, coal and some meat, the amounts were small but very welcome. I had bad dreams for nights after of being in a home, of weird fantasies and Gran was hopping mad to find that one night I had wet the bed and being unable to dry it, she covered it in cloths, so eventually it dried out with me sleeping on it!

About this time, Walter had completed his twelve years in the Navy and was out as a civilian on reserve, finding employment with the GPO at Mount Pleasant sorting office. The old widow next door let her upstairs rooms to Emmy and him. Emmy furnished it out on HP and after some weeks bailiffs came to take it away as she had not kept up the weekly payments. Whenever I ran an errand for the old widow, a Mrs Ford, she always gave me a small china ornament, of which she had many, and also glass cases of stuffed birds standing on twigs. I had my eye though on her late husband's Boer War rifle, hanging on the wall, I would have loved to have that.

Emmy now had two children, both boys, to keep her occupied.

A tragedy happened at home when Nan became very ill, so Gran painted her back with iodine again, but I saw Nan crying because she was in so much pain. I was sent to get the doctor to call, but at his house I was told that he was out and my name and address was taken for him to come later. By the evening, Nan was crying in a very bad way, so I was sent again to the doctor, only to be told he would come round in the morning. A terrible night followed, with poor Nan screaming and groaning and delirious so Gran told me to get into bed with her to keep her warm, but she was already very hot. The night passed, with Nan twisting and turning and suffering a lot of pain. Gran looked very worried and during the night the walls showed distorted flickering shadows from the naked gas light and I began to see faces and figures, adding to the general misery of the night. When daylight came I was again sent to the doctor, who appeared at his door very angry and it was only when I insisted that Nan was very ill all night that he said he would come right away. I ran home and as I arrived the doctor turned up. He took one look at Nan and rushed to the corner to telephone for an ambulance. Gran looked very worried as Nan was taken away to Tottenham Hospital, a long journey. Walter went with her, but it was too late and Nan died that night. A policeman brought the sad news and Gran was devastated, saying over and over again that the doctor was to blame.

Emmy, Gran and myself went by tram to the hospital and saw Nan on a plinth, covered with a sheet, her face looking waxen and I noticed some red splashes around the throat part. There were some distressing scenes when Gran had to be restrained from trying to hold Nan, and as Gran was in a state of collapse, we helped her out to the tram and eventually arrived home.

Poor Gran should never have gone, as she was almost crippled with arthritis and it was very hard getting her on and off the trams. As tradition had it in those days, Nan was brought home and the coffin rested upon trestles in the front room. Hayes and English were the undertakers and everyone in the family contributed towards the cost of the funeral, as Gran only had one penny insurance. There were many comings and goings of neighbours and work colleagues to see Nan, also her sisters Alice and Lil from East Ham. I was kept away from school for the week to do any running about needed. My mother came up from Portsmouth the day before the funeral and stayed the night, comforting Gran, saying little to me, and seemed just like my other aunts. On the morning of the funeral the house seemed full of people, aunts, uncles and friends, everyone saying last goodbyes to Nan and crying when the lid was screwed down, and as with Grandad, there was the coffin smell, mixed with the scent of the wreaths. At the graveside, Gran had tried to throw herself into the grave. Nan had died from pleurisy. When we returned, a tea had been laid on by some neighbours and afterwards, with tearful farewells, everyone left to go home, including my mother, who returned to Portsmouth.

The house seemed deserted with Gran now quiet, and up to then, with all the upset during the previous week, I had not shed a tear, but now I went to my bedroom and it finally sunk in that Nan had gone, a very dear friend, who I would sadly miss.

To try and make up the loss of Nan's wages, Gran asked Emmy and Walter if they would rent the two downstairs rooms and pay half the rent, i.e. ten shillings. This in the long run turned out to be a disaster. A kind neighbour fixed Gran up with an old gas stove in her bedroom, piped to the house gas meter downstairs. We already had a large china jug and basin, so it was now my job continually to bring water upstairs and take slop buckets down. Gran couldn't manage the stairs and she should really have stayed downstairs.

I well recall a happy memory of Nan when she was given two complimentary tickets to see the *Queen of Hearts* at the Drury Lane theatre. With much tidying up and mending, and a neighbour lending me a jacket and shoes for the night, shining from a good wash and brush up, off went Nan and I. I was completely taken aback with amazement on entering the brightly lit entrance to the theatre, with the stairs covered in beautiful carpeting and the shiny brass handrails. I was really awestruck at the sight of the walls, in colour and gold, the toffs sitting in the side boxes, the plush seats and the smart ladies in neat black uniforms with little aprons selling programmes.

The magnificent velvet curtains on the stage, with hanging gold tassels, the jumbled sounds of the orchestra tuning up in the pit, all together made for me one word, 'Magic', because that is what I seemed to have walked into. The lights dimmed, the orchestra started to play and the show for me was fantastic and full of laughs, and I thoroughly enjoyed the antics of the actors.

Nan was like that, if it was only a bus ride to St James's Park on a summer

Sunday afternoon to listen to the military band or anything else she could afford, she would often take me. One marvellous Christmas, armed with two complimentary tickets, she took me to see the World's Fair, which was held in the Agricultural Hall, Islington. Yes, I was going to miss her very much.

One special event in my young life occurred when I was about ten years old. I was at Sunday-school, when a Miss Newland, an old lady dressed in long Victorian style clothes called me over and asked, "Billy, have you ever had a holiday?" I replied that I had not and when asked if I would like one I replied, "Yes please, Miss." The holiday on offer was two weeks on a farm during the school summer break, which was soon approaching. I was to get written permission from Gran by signing a form. This was done by Gran, with the comment, "I shall be glad to see the bloody back of you for two weeks." I then took home a form, stating the date, time and place pick-up point, and a list of clothing items to take with me, plus a pair of strong boots. The day came, with me so excited that I couldn't sleep the night before. I had told all my neighbours in the street why, for two weeks, I couldn't do their errands and I ended up with nearly two shillings in pennies, with many good wishes to "Have a good time, Billy."

I took my clothes parcel and some sandwiches and made my way to the pick-up point, where I found six others waiting, two of them girls, and all of us about the same age. Accompanied by a Sunday-school teacher, who was spending the two weeks with us, we went by tram to a main line station, the hustle and bustle, whistles and steam all adding to the excitement. She bought us some tea and we ate some sandwiches, then boarded the train and off we went. As the train was rushing through the countryside, which I was seeing for the first time in my life, we were singing lots of songs, such as 'Shepherd of the Hills, I hear you calling' and 'Show me the way to go home' with the old favourite 'Ten green bottles, hanging on the wall'.

We arrived at Newbury Station to find a horse and cart waiting for us, our final destination being a large house, where we were warmly welcomed by a nice looking man and his wife into the house, which smelled of floor polish and was spotlessly clean.

After being checked, we stripped and had hot baths in a huge bathroom, and were told to open our parcels and put our pyjamas on. I told the lady that I had none and never had had any. My opened parcel revealed a clean jersey, vest, pants and socks, so I was taken upstairs and from a large cupboard the kind lady fitted me out with a suit, shirt, boots and pyjamas. I was somewhat overawed on being given all these things, especially the boots, as they were the first I had ever owned. I felt like a king and after a good supper, with a cup of cocoa, we all said a short prayer and went to bed in such luxury that I had never known, and were soon asleep.

That holiday turned out to be the happiest experience of my young life and whilst the others played around the farm, I seemed to be attracted to the mucky areas where the animals were, especially the pigs, and the old man in charge told me, "You seem to get on well with the animals," and showed me how, by scratching a pig's back with a stick he could make it go to sleep.

The master used to take us out on rambles through the woods and on nature trails, learning signs made by small animals. I loved the paper chase, and with various other activities it was all great fun, and I hoped it would never end. We went to church on Sunday for the beautifully laid out Harvest Festival, and to the evening service. The master noticed that I knew some of the hymns and was familiar with church routine. The meals were very tasty and plentiful, and in the evenings there were plenty of games to play and books to read. The time passed all too quickly for me, but all good things have to end, and on the last day, I changed back into my old clothes and plimsolls, said our goodbyes and regretfully made our journey home. On arriving home I found nothing had changed, and people were saying how well I looked and I had put on some weight.

Shortly after that, old Mrs Ford next door poured paraffin over herself and set light to it, dying a horrible death and burning the kitchen out.

CHAPTER THREE

In the jungle

At school, I seemed to be developing into something of a mini artist. I was encouraged by Mr Cooper, my teacher, to spend more time on water-colour painting and he showed me how to mix different paints to produce various shades for blending in. In time, some of my paintings were framed and hung in the main hall — a hidden talent, perhaps? I took to painting and enjoyed every minute of it. I loved taking part in school plays, the Christmas period being the best. One I liked was with a school choir singing sea shanties and doing the sailor's hornpipe with all its sequences, as part of a maritime play.

Weather permitting, Empire Day would be something rather special. The playground would be marked out in chalk for guidelines for the events, and chairs and tables laid out for school staff and visiting guests, one of whom was the Mayor of Shoreditch. Having perfected our presentation after much rehearsing, we would give our displays, with the infants in rows, holding up lettered and numbered cards at given times, forming short sentences, etc. Music was provided by the piano, and coupled with our singing it must have sounded great, with traditional songs of the British Isles. The boys and girls used to be dressed up as members of the Forces of the war, with 'nurses' helping wounded 'soldiers' on sticks, with bandages stained with red ink, which was not very complimentary to the crippled ex-servicemen in the market selling matches. To conclude, the infants would, with their coloured cards form a large Union Jack, while we all sang 'Land of Hope and Glory', 'Jerusalem', 'Three cheers for the red, white and blue', then the National Anthem. The VIPs would give patriotic speeches, and would in turn receive three rousing cheers, and our reward would be a half day's holiday. Plenty of mums and dads used to stand in the roped off area in the playground as, being unemployed, they had nothing else to do.

November the 11th, Armistice Day, was also a ceremony in which the whole school would participate. At 10.30 a.m., the headmaster would have the whole school assembled in the main hall, with the teachers standing down the sides to keep an eye on us. He would then remove from a glass case on the wall a large book with 1914-1918 in gold numbers marked on the cover, open it and read various parts appertaining to the sacrifices in casualties made in the Great War to end wars. He would also read out the names of boys from the school who had lost their lives for their country. Then the piano was played and we sang the hymn 'O God our help in ages past'. At 11 a.m. the sirens sounded and we would stand silent for two minutes. I remember how hard it was to keep still for that time, after which we would troop back to our class-rooms.

I had an uncle, Alf, my grandad's brother, who was as different to him as chalk from cheese. He had enlisted in the Middlesex Regiment (the Diehards) in 1886 at the age of 18, and completed twelve years' service, being discharged with exemplary character in 1898. He rejoined in 1901 to 1903, then enlisted in the Middlesex Regiment Militia from 1903 to 1907, then joined the Rifle Brigade Militia from 1907 to 1913. He then rejoined his old regiment to be part of the British Expeditionary Force, in which he was involved in the retreat from Mons in 1914. He served through the war up to 1917, when he was medically discharged, then immediately joined the Labour Corps in France, but served 141 days, only to be discharged for good. He had served his country over 27 years. He never married, and lived in lodgings in Bermondsey, south of the river, working as a docker. It was very hard work loading and unloading ships and uncertain because of the system of casual labour, whereby the foreman at the gates would let through only the ones he wanted, always leaving a disappointed crowd outside.

When Alf was down on his luck he would visit us and get Gran to pawn his medals and any other little treasures he brought along, but with a good run of work behind him and a few pounds in his pocket, he would come and redeem his medals, etc., and being the generous man he was, he would bring in lots of beer, bags of cakes, and give me a sixpence. He and Gran used to sing all the old songs, including barrack room ditties, and he would make me a cocked hat out of newspaper, and thumping the wall, would march me up and down, singing marches until it drove Gran nearly crazy, when he would stop and then tell me some old soldiers' stories. My favourite was 'The Angel of Mons', when in a terrible attack by the Germans, the gallant British Army were being beaten back by sheer weight of numbers. The sky came over black and an angel appeared, pointing a finger at the Germans, causing them to turn and run, throwing down their weapons, terrified in thousands, thus giving the hard pressed British Army a great victory. I loved this story so much that I would ask him to repeat it over and over again, until in the end I think he got so fed up with me he wished he had never started it! One of his medals portrayed the 'Angel of Peace', but he wrongfully told me that it was the 'Angel of Mons' and I believed this for years after. He used to leave in a cheerful mood, with Gran tipsy and no doubt with a few extra shillings in her pocket.

In time, my uncle became too old to stand the punishing hard work on the docks, so he had to give up and not being able to pay for lodgings, he sought refuge in a 'Rowton House', an establishment for down and outs, where he could get a bed for a few coppers a night, and find what he could for food during the day in order to survive. What a sorry end for an old soldier, who in Lloyd George's words during the war had told the men that they would come home to a land 'Fit for heroes to live in'. What with the 1939 war, and myself being away for six years, I lost touch and have no idea what happened to him.

Once, as usual, I was running down our street when someone threw a mat out and catching my feet in it I crashed to the ground, and remember coming round in hospital with a busted nose and jaw. After a week, I became an out-patient, and for some time I was unable to eat without my teeth nipping my tongue and I could only breathe through one side of my nose, which has caused problems all my life.

There were, at that period, two rival bus companies, namely Thomas Tillings and the General Omnibus Company. Competition was so fierce that in between bus stops, buses would stop and pick up passengers, both rival buses going at breakneck speed down Kingsland Road to beat each other to the next stop for passengers, whose only benefit was to arrive at their destinations in record time. In the end, Thomas Tillings were bought out, leaving the General Omnibus Company master of the roads. I recall the solid tyred buses, which on wet days would slide on the cobble-stones when stopping and bump into the kerb. Also still in use were the open-top buses and in wet weather the passengers used to travel on top with umbrellas up. Drivers on the buses and trams had to face all kinds of weather with a protective sheet and goggles.

Redvers Street had its full share of unemployed and the more fortunate could be distinguished by the decent curtains at the windows and the better clothing of their children.

The end of the street was blocked off with an alleyway on each corner, leading into Hoxton Market. One alley had a row of small houses which were occupied by prostitutes, who could be seen getting off trams with seamen from the river ships, and they would walk down the street, one on each side making out they didn't know each other, but everybody knew what was going on. The other alley started from the school wall adjacent to a block of flats, which led to a large pub. Running through at night I would, at times see men and women standing against the wall having sexual intercourse, and to annoy them I would stand and watch. Then a stream of abuse would be forthcoming and I would run off, making sure that I jumped over the puddles of urine.

In between the alleys was a general and sweet shop which closed on Sunday afternoons. It was regularly used as a gambling school, and one Sunday afternoon on returning home from Sunday-school through an alley, I saw a police raid, with the gamblers being chased down the street. I saw a pile of pound notes and coins, with cards and dice so I quickly picked up all the money and ran home, giving it to Gran, whose only comment was, "Are you sure you picked up all of it?" It was lucky for me that nobody saw me take the money as later our house would have been under attack from the gamblers. Redvers Street, like the rest of Hoxton, was rough and tough. Street betting was illegal, but one house in the street was run as a betting shop and touts were everywhere, furtively taking bets and quite often I had seen policemen standing back in the passage holding pints of beer, and small time moneylenders would be constantly persecuting people for repayment.

I think the most notorious street in Hoxton was Essex Street, which consisted of three storey houses with basements, and if you were passing through early in the morning it was wise to keep a wary eye aloft, as there would be the occasional shout of 'below' when a bucket would be tipped out on to the street from the top windows. The houses only had one outside toilet each, and with lots of children, people wouldn't bother to carry buckets down the stairs.

Occasionally the sanitary inspector would order a house to be fumigated, and as the families were usually interrelated, a house could be emptied of people, then the mattresses from the beds taken away for treatment while the house and rooms were sealed and sulphur candles lit in every room, the fumes killing off the bugs and cockroaches, but the infestation soon returned, from the houses next door.

I well remember one day hearing multiple police whistles from the direction of Essex Street, so as always, when there was trouble, I went running along, to find the whole street full of people fighting, with women rolling on the ground nearly naked, screaming and tugging out handfuls of hair, and a certain amount of blood was in evidence. Men were being chased by the police in and out of the houses and some policemen were running for their lives, chased by groups of men, then a commandeered bus arrived full of policemen from Old Street, and they waded in with truncheons, soon restoring order and then using the bus to take the prisoners and injured back to Old Street.

I was on the spot one Sunday at pub closing time in Hoxton when two families started fighting. A forced wedding had taken place that morning, with the girl heavily pregnant. Large numbers of the two families, furious with hate were fighting it out so the police sent for the fire brigade, who, with high powered hoses soon had the situation under control, with people still trying to fight and losing their balance, then like drowned rats they made off with many threats and somewhat ripe language!

A trick played in the market on single stall holders would be for a boy to steal something from the front, causing the stall holder to dash there to catch him, leaving his takings unguarded, when another boy would grab some money and run. It was usually Jewish stalls that were picked on, and if a boy was ever caught, an unsympathetic crowd would bash the stall holder and tip the stall over. Pickpockets were always active in the market and the cry of people who had been robbed was often heard. In the main, rough and ready as the people of Hoxton were, whenever illness struck a family, the neighbours were always first to help, without being asked. They would wash the kids and get them off to school, do shopping and washing. The streets were small communities of their own and everybody more or less knew each other's business.

The most common theft was breaking open the coin gas meters, so houses were fitted with pull-to shutters over the windows, bolted on the inside. It is common these days to hear of troubles between various Irish factions and Redvers Street had its own. At the far end were the O'Connors, with windows full of 'bleeding hearts' and plaster saints, and at my end was a Protestant Irish family, the Barnets, and there was occasionally a Saturday night smash up between them, in which they would all be involved, from grandmothers to schoolchildren. No one interfered, but just watched from the windows and Gran would say, "Let them get on with it and lose some of their mad blood," and they did.

I lived fairly close to the Geffrye Museum in Kingsland Road, a little gem of a place, showing beautiful period furniture in a park setting, with nicely laid out gardens. The centre-piece was a bandstand, where in the summer months, visiting brass bands would give concerts, and it says much for the downtrodden people of Hoxton that at these performances the place was packed with people standing enjoying the music, with lots of children running happily around.

CHAPTER FOUR

Being exploited

In Redvers Street was an old shack, in which I noticed a man working on his own. I was 12 years old and he called me over, saying he was looking for a boy to work after school hours in his shop at the far end of Hoxton, to where he was moving, called the 'Acme Valet Service', which would do hat cleaning and blocking, dry cleaning and hand pressing. He offered me half a crown a week, so I thought that with my errands and window cleaning, it would be very welcome to Gran, so I accepted and I was to work very hard for that half-crown.

I noticed that at one end of the shop a man was pressing clothes with a large iron and at the other end, alongside a steamer and a large assortment of wooden blocks, Mrs Reid was stitching new bands and leathers on trilby hats. Mr Reid explained what he wanted me to do, and my first job was to take two piles of three hat boxes containing thirty renovated hats to Brick Lane, through to Commercial Road, round to Whitechapel to Aldgate, delivering to shops on the way. This involved undoing boxes and replacing renovated hats with dirty ones, ending up with more weight than when I started out. I left the shop with two pennies for my fare and with my forearms tucked between the box and the string, I found that as I wasn't a tall lad, I had to lift the boxes to clear the ground and try not to catch my legs on them. It was a long walk to the tram stop and already my arms were aching badly. Also it was difficult to board a tram with both arms locked. Brick Lane onwards was mostly Jewish, as were my list of shops. One thing which annoyed me was that at each shop I had to untie the boxes, then retie, and being oval, sometimes they would slip out of the string and scatter on the pavement. My long trek ended at Aldgate, being pushed aside by a crowd when I tried to get on the tram, but I held onto the handrail when the tram started. It went very fast and I hung on, shouting my head off as my hands slid down with my legs and boxes dragging on the ground. Passengers pulled me in, but I had received a terrible fright and in future, I pushed on to the trams, not caring about other people, receiving many curses in the process.

When I arrived at the shop, my arms, shoulders and back would be in a state of numbed pain, and my skinny arms were chafed sore by the string, but Gran would rub salt margarine in them. I'd be ravenously hungry, but I was never offered a cup of tea in that shop. Mr Reid would, on my return, try to keep me as long as possible but I would be off and run home about 1½ miles for tea and 'doorsteps' of bread and jam, then do my neighbours' errands.

The hat deliveries were two nights a week and the other three were spent down in the basement, working at a bench on which was placed an enamel bowl of petrol, a hat block and a nail brush, plus a pile of greasy hats to scrub clean, one at a time on a hat block with brush and petrol, then place them on stands to dry off. Ventilation was a pavement grill, which gave a little light, plus an electric light bulb.

I used to be in a state of tension over the numerous black beetles crawling around the floor and I couldn't bring myself to tread on them the way Mr Reid did, and I was constantly looking round to see if any were coming my way. Several times I found myself in the back yard sitting on a chair with Mrs Reid patting my face and calling my name, having found me on the floor passed out from the petrol fumes. Mr Reid though it was a great joke, 'a cheap drunk' he called it, and I was told to carry on. Now and again one of them would call down the stairs to see if I answered. I used to get bad headaches, but I never told Gran because the money was needed. I used to get into hot water at school for not concentrating, and be livened up with the cane, but I still had these bad headaches.

One old lady in the street used to have a half quartern of whisky regularly every night, and her grown-up son had comics, which he gave to me when he had finished with them. I averaged about sixpence each day by running errands, which was very good, considering that at dinner-times, when I earned threepence, I bought my pie and mash. I always gave every penny I earned to Gran, or bought groceries with it.

Problems arose at home with Emmy, because of her drunken husband. She was kept so short of money that she would order items of clothing, etc., and take them to the pawn shop in order to have some ready cash. Then she would let the agent 'take it out of the knocker' when he called for the weekly payments. I found that the two children spent most of the time upstairs in our part of the house, and whatever food I bought, plus the voucher groceries for the week were disappearing and all I was having to eat was bread and jam and tea, with a little extra when I could, and by this time I was 13 years of age.

Young as I was, I had an eye for a bargain, and on the second-hand stalls I would buy items of clothing for a couple of pence. I could not however, buy the second-hand shoes, as my toes had grown so spread from constantly wearing plimsolls. At home there was always something needed, such as pennies for the gas meter, which was downstairs and communal. Emmy would often call up, "Gas gone, your turn Billy." Gran was almost housebound, being unable to manage the stairs.

I had now extended my hat round to Dalston, famous for the Sir Oswald Mosley marches and demonstrations. It was another market for Saturdays only and unlike Hoxton, a more specialized area, where one could buy parts for clocks and watches, radios or DIY wireless. Gramophones and records were in great demand, DIY furniture of all kinds ready for assembly, and so many other things of interest and people came from miles around to shop.

The winters were very hard on my legs, as it was the fashion then for boys to wear short trousers and my thighs would be red raw with chaps, and it was cheer agony when the salt margarine was rubbed in.

At the age of 13½ years I was transferred to nearby St John's Road School to learn something in the workshops there and on my first day, assembled in the woodwork class, the teacher instructor gave us basic uses of tools. Then on the blackboard was written a poem which we all said aloud, parrot fashion, and it went like this: 'Don't plane against the grain, spoil the wood spoil the plane, spoil the plane, get the cane. Don't plane against the grain'.

I enjoyed the work and was quite proud of the things I made, but after taking them home, they were used as firewood for Gran's fire.

A couple of weeks before my birthday I returned to my old school, when the headmaster sent for me and said, "Soon, Harding, you will be going out into the world to earn your living. Have you found work yet?" I replied, "No sir." He then said, "Get looking lad, get looking," and that was it. The time arrived for me to leave school and I was handed my school leaving certificate, an excellent testimonial from Mr Cooper and a short one from St John's Road school. I had reached Standard X7, the top class on the fast side at Redvers Street school. Mr Cooper told me that whoever my future employer might be, to give of my best, be truthful and honest and not let the school or myself down. He then shook hands and said goodbye, so in 1932 I walked out of that school wondering what on earth I was going to do. I was excited and rushed home to show my testimonial, as I was rather proud of it, but Gran wasn't interested. She just told me to go out and find work and bring some bloody money into the house. Emmy also had a go at me, and in the past she had always been free with giving me cuffs around the ears.

I ran an errand for a Mrs Weir, who asked me if I had left school, and when I replied that I had, she then asked if I had found work. Almost in tears I said, "How can I, in short trousers?" She then took me to the market and bought me my first pair of long trousers. I had to change into them in the shop, as she knew about Gran and the pawn shops. When I thanked her, the kind old lady would have none of it.

Some of the fathers of my mates had paid for their sons to have an apprenticeship, others worked on family stalls in the market, but I had no father to ask for guidance, only the two grumpy women, and a man who was drunk most of the time. In desperation, all I could think of was to ask Mr Reid to take me on full time, which he did for ten shillings for a 52 hour week. I wasn't happy about it, but at the time it was all I could do.

I was in a no win situation because the Poor Relief stopped paying the rent and ceased giving the vouchers for coal and groceries, stating that there was now a wage earner in the house. Gran had kept it quiet about letting the downstairs rooms, or the relief would have ended sooner. I also lost out on the window cleaning and the errands on Saturday. Also, conforming to market custom, the shop was open on Sundays from 9 a.m. until 1 p.m., as were all shops. I worked from 9 a.m. until 6 p.m. Monday to Wednesday, 9 a.m. to 1 p.m. on Thursdays and 9 a.m. to 8 p.m. Fridays and Saturdays. To balance things out a bit Gran now received 7/6d a week old age pension, but times were not easy, my wages going for rent, so I had to try harder each night on my errand runs, but people were good, they were so used to me.

All I was able to keep for myself was sixpence a week, and I never had my pie and mash in Fortune's at dinner-time any more, so I would run home at dinner break and Gran would always scrape up something for me to eat. During my first week I was so hungry that I would come over faint, but I brought bread and jam slices and Jim, the presser, always gave me a sandwich. Sometimes I would buy a penny piece of bread pudding in the baker's, and this was a good filler.

I soon realized that school days were the happiest days. John Knott, a former school pal was working for a cabinet maker, learning to carve ball and claw legs, having half an hour break each day, but only working a half-day on Saturday. Another pal was learning french-polishing, but Shoreditch and Hoxton was full of small woodwork sweat shops, all cutting each other's throats for business.

My hat rounds now extended to places in the City with which I was familiar, such as Leadenhall Street, Cheapside and Eastcheap, where Homburgs, bowler hats and silk toppers were predominant. I would also go to Harrods and Barkers, which opened up a new world to me, even though I looked scruffy with my hat boxes. I now learned how to steam and block hats, steam and brush bowlers, also to brush and iron silk toppers after Mrs Reid had fixed in the new linings and sewn in new bands. That woman never stopped working all day. The City shops were small and posh, with boys of my age dressed like proper gents.

As I progressed Mr Gillies (Jim) taught me hand pressing with a wet cloth and I had to stand on a box and lift the 14 lb electric iron with both hands. Jim was always smartly dressed, with knife edged creased trousers. He told me that he had been wounded at Paschendaele in France and was saved from drowning in the mud. He asked me about my family so I told him how things were. He fixed me up with a pair of trousers, altered to fit me, and I did manage a pair of shoes from a second-hand stall, as I had to be tidy in the shop, so eventually my appearance improved somewhat, with a shirt, tie and jacket.

I learned to use the treadle sewing-machine and succeeded in running the needle through my finger a couple of times. I also started doing small repairs. Christmas was close, making us very busy and the lead up to it meant working late on Fridays and Saturdays until 10 p.m., also Thursday half day for two shillings.

On Christmas Eve, about 10.30 p.m. the shop was closed. Jim had gone earlier and Mr Reid gave me £1, half wages, half Christmas box. He had a knack of making me feel like a beggar, but I had worked long hours for that ten shillings Christmas box.

On leaving the shop with my £1 + 2s, a half for the rent, I hung around the butcher's shops, who were having their last fling selling off meat and poultry at knock down prices, with the poorest in Hoxton crowding round, hoping to get something for their Christmas dinner. I bought some belly of pork and a shoulder of lamb, plus extras such as vegetables, etc. I still had to take some money home. I had, two weeks earlier, made my annual visits to the local shops for our Christmas box, which they gave to regular customers. The dairy gave eggs and butter, the 'Jew Shop', so-called, gave some tea, sugar and biscuits, the butcher a standard gift of a pound of sausages and some lard. The paper shop would give some snuff for Gran and two comics for me, and she would look at it all and complain that she was given less than last year, and tried to make me go back and ask for more, but I wouldn't stand for that, my name wasn't Oliver. In the late evening I used to go over to the pub and ask for Granny Waller's Christmas box. On one occasion it was a glass quart jug engraved 'Merry Christmas and a Happy New Year from Jim Hensman, The Star and Woolpack'. The jug was filled with ale so Gran had her Christmas drink. Far different today, when shops have staff boxes on their counters expecting customers to make a contribution for the privilege of spending their money there.

At this time of year, someone in Hoxton would always do a bunk with the loan club money, leaving people who totally relied on it upset, with nothing to spend for Christmas.

The market and shops were truly a picture at Christmas, with decorations and coloured lights, the flare lamps showing up their garlands and packed with toys of every description, making it all look like fairyland, with the pubs trying to outdo each other with decorations and tinsel. People generally struggled hard all through the year paying into loan clubs to help provide the Christmas dinner, toys for the children and a knees up on Christmas Eve, when the pubs were packed out, letting themselves go singing and dancing as only cockneys do, no animosity, rows or fights, and the Salvation Army bands dotted about playing carols, with good humour all round.

As I made my way home with the meat and groceries, the market almost closed down, I would pause by the pubs, longing to be in there and join in the fun and I would feel very lonely, thinking of what I was going back to. Gran was, for once, delighted with what I had brought home, which pleased me, but life was awful in the house when Walter came home paralytic drunk. On opening the door he fell full length into the passage, out like a light, with Emmy screaming and her two children crying. Emmy and I had to drag Walter further down the passage so as to close the front door and leave him there all night. It was more like bedlam than Christmas, as he had provided nothing for Christmas and what money he did give in the morning was no use, with all the shops closed. The kids had no toys, but I had memories of Christmases like that, and presents were totally unknown, and even cards were very few.

Emmy was always scrounging from us and as our food began to disappear very rapidly I became alarmed, so I hid in my bedroom all the tins and packets that I could, but Gran seemed to have lost the will to reprimand Emmy. However, Emmy had her uses in helping her mother doing things which I couldn't bear to do. I was always fetching water from downstairs and carrying smelly slop buckets down until it got bad, when I would come home to find no water and our buckets filled with children's washing soaking. I told Emmy not to do it, but a 14-year-old telling her off set her into screaming rages and she vented her own misfortunes on me because the more she screamed at Walter, the more he drank. In the kitchen downstairs, Emmy hung a large frying pan on a nail over the gas stove and through constant use, dripping fat had run down the wall and hardened to an inch thick! Towels for toiletry purposes, almost black, were also used to dry the plates and cups, etc., often unwashed first.

CHAPTER FIVE

No place like home

On the corner of Essex Street was an old factory converted into a cinema, called the 'Gainsborough', and fitted out with most uncomfortable seats. It was a rough house and a flea pit, and in the dark, boys and girls were always skylarking about, but the talking pictures were good, with lots of thrillers, which I loved, and the Hollywood spectaculars, with such beautiful girls, convinced me that America was a fabulous place compared to dirty old Hoxton. There was still the inevitable eating of peanuts with the crunching of shells as they were trodden on. Many of the latest songs came from the films and we all had our favourites, the words being printed on penny song sheets in the market.

My pals had all managed to buy bicycles — every boy's dream in those days — and for a very long time I had looked longingly at a new Hercules bicycle in a shop window, complete with tools and saddle bag for £3.19.6d., but for me, it was impossible, as I could not even afford HP terms. I wanted that bike badly, but it wasn't to be. In time, however, after much rummaging from rubbish dumps, we found a frame and wheels and put together a bike of sorts, so I was happy, and apart from riding to Victoria Park for a kick around with a ball, I used to go home at dinner-times, to and from work. I had reached the age when running through the market was looked upon with suspicion, though wherever I happened to be out walking, if no one was around I would run my heart out for the sheer joy of it.

I was now well past my 15th birthday, and having become quite proficient at work, my wages increased to 12s/6d per week. It was the hardest thing trying to get a rise from Mr Reid. I would ask, and a few weeks later he would sense when I was about to ask again, then give something. There was little change in the routine at home, with another Christmas come and gone, with Gran incarcerated upstairs, every movement bringing a groan of pain, and she often said, "Don't ever leave me Billy, as I will surely be put into the workhouse." I considered that Emmy was now bordering on insanity, the way she constantly shouted and screamed at Walter and the children, to whom she was quite brutal. One day some neighbours told her to stop it or they would send for the police, and this resulted in a terrible slanging match, but she did ease off from hitting them so much. I also received considerable verbal abuse from her, unprintable here, but I refused to speak to her unless I had to.

My errand running had long since come to a halt, but it was surprising how occasionally a neighbour would stop me and holding a shirt or other item of clothing would ask me to see if it would fit me and I was very grateful to them. I managed to get hold of a cheap wireless for Gran, run off a battery, and this brought a little cheer into her life. I also had a try at painting, but Emmy's kids were everywhere, nothing being safe, so I had to give it up. There was no communication from my mother nor the aunts, and it was as if we didn't exist as far as they were concerned and I was now 16 years old.

There was an unfortunate flare-up one morning, when having put a penny in the meter I was heating a kettle of water when Emmy came up. She was just about to take it when I stopped her and said, "No you don't, that's my washing water." With her face distorted and screaming, she grabbed a carving knife shouting, "I'll gut you, you bastard." She was pressing the knife to my stomach, so on a reflex action I punched her in the mouth sending her sprawling on to the floor with her mouth bleeding. I was very upset over this and wished I hadn't done it, but I knew that the knife nearly went in. This set Gran off, and with Emmy calling me filthy names, I walked out of the house, to find groups of neighbours at their doors. Then I saw a policeman at the corner, so I asked him to come to the house, and explained to him what had taken place.

When he came upstairs Emmy started shouting again and he told her to shut up. When Gran told him that she was always upstairs causing trouble, and that she had threatened to kill me with a knife when I hit her in self-defence, he wrote it all down and told Emmy to go downstairs and only to come up when invited, also she was to stop pestering me. He asked me for Mr Reid's phone number and told me to try and avoid her as much as possible, and he would return later in the day. I couldn't go to work, as I was too worried about the situation with Gran. Emmy was quiet for a while but started shouting up the stairs again, saying among other things that when Walter came home he would smash my face in. The prospect of fighting him made me feel very nervous. Early in the afternoon the policeman returned, accompanied by a sergeant. They came upstairs and asked a lot of questions, then called Emmy up and warned her that if she assaulted me again there would be charges, and she would most certainly get six months in prison. To me he said the neighbours had given me a good character, saying that I worked hard and looked after my gran, and my employer spoke very well of me. He said that if I was ever threatened or attacked again, to report it to the station.

I sat upstairs, dreading the thought of facing Walter, and Gran told me to go out and come back late, when they were asleep, but I couldn't do that. I had to face him some time so whatever happened, I thought it best to get it over and done with. Eventually he came in and Emmy shouted, "Look what that bastard's done to my face, what are you going to do about it?"

I heard some talking, then Walter shouted up the stairs, "Come down here, you."

With a racing heart I went down, and facing him I said, "She came upstairs to take my kettle of water, then pushed a knife at my stomach, so I hit her in self-defence. She comes up eating all our food because you don't give her enough money. The police have been here, so if you touch me, I'll go straight to the police station and have you arrested." He stared at me, and without a word, turned and went into his room. Emmy went completely berserk and hell on earth is putting it mildly.

When Gran saw that I was all right she calmed down, and Walter could take no more and went out, to come back late and blind drunk.

I hardly slept that night, and I went to work next morning feeling somewhat washed out. Various neighbours stopped me but I never said much, there was no point. Mr Reid knew from the police what had happened and Jim very kindly offered me a spare room in his house, but thanking him I declined, saying that I couldn't desert my gran, as my aunt would put her into the workhouse, having hinted that she would like the whole house, with two children and another on the way.

The old routine of work and home carried on much the same, and to keep out of Emmy's way I would often go out for long walks at night and I enjoyed walking for miles. Because Emmy never stopped harassing me, I couldn't make use of our bath in the kitchen, and had to make do with a late night once a week at the local baths. I totally ignored her now, but her abuse never ceased, and Gran was now confined to bed, so it was very difficult.

Another Christmas came and went, with Gran's two daughters paying a rare visit, which was very welcome, with their chatter livening the place up a little. I scraped up enough for my fare and some fruit, and straight from work one Sunday, with much rushing about, I managed to visit Albert, but the poor man was no different at all, and showed no sign of recognition. I left him and that depressing place with a heavy heart.

Mr Reid had bought a tradesman's bicycle and I did pretty well with tips when delivering parcels. Easter came and I thought I might ride to Portsmouth on my old bone shaker to see my parents. After making sure Gran was fixed up OK, and having got the address from her, I set off on Easter Sunday morning. I had only the vaguest idea how to find the Portsmouth Road but once on it, I discovered what a task I had set myself, with a single speed bicycle and steep hills to climb. By the afternoon I had reached the Devil's Punch-Bowl and being very tired I rested on the grass verge and soon fell asleep and on awakening, saw the stars. I carried on and finally reached Portsmouth, and after some searching found the address. I knocked on the door and eventually my father opened it and looking at me said, "What do you want?" Standing there a bit embarrassed, my mother appeared, so I was given a meal, had a wash and fixed up on the couch to sleep. In the morning my mother said she could not imagine how I had ridden from London on that bike.

My brother and sister didn't know me and said little. After a meal, my father said bring your bike, so saying goodbye, my father took me to the coach station, and with the bike stowed away on a rack he paid a single fare and at 9 a.m. we drove off. My father didn't speak, except to say 'cheerio' as I left. I noticed that my mother had twins. I felt an emptiness inside and realized how foolish I had been to tear my heart out riding all that way for nothing, and it was to be years before I was to see my family again.

Emmy meanwhile gave birth to a little girl, which she called Evelyn, and this kept her occupied and there was a bit of peace in the house. Sadly it died a year later, and the tiny coffin was kept in the front room for a week.

Some weeks later I was passing a large parked furniture van in Kingsland Road on my bicycle. I had time to pass hearing a tram behind me, when a door at the back of the van swung open and I hit it, landing on the lines when the tram hit me. I came round in the casualty department of St Leonard's hospital, when a nurse told me to stay still and she would bring me a cup of tea. I hated hospitals and the smell of ether, so I moved off the plinth, but my legs folded up and I crawled out into the market and sat against the wall concussed, my legs in a mess with my trousers in shreds. Apparently the grille at the front of the tram had rolled me along the lines, thus saving my life. As I sat there dazed, a neighbour passing by stopped and after ensuring that I wouldn't return to the hospital and that my legs were good enough to stand on, he gave me a pick-a-back home. I was only a flyweight, but by the time he got me to my bedroom he was worn out. He collected my unmendable twisted bike and went to the shop for me to tell Mr Reid what had happened. In trouble, good neighbours helped without asking and I was quite well known.

Taking stock, I saw that I was in a bit of a mess, but had no regrets about leaving the hospital. My legs were badly bruised and grazed and one knee appeared to be twisted. My arms were skinned in places and there were bumps all over my head. Gran came in and washed me and ripping up an old sheet to use as bandages, she tightly bound up my rapidly swelling knee. I had to fend for myself, hobbling painfully about for a week, eking out what food we had, then after ten days I was forced back to work, there being an empty food cupboard and no money forthcoming from Mr Reid. Also, as there was nothing left for her to plunder, Emmy began shouting up the stairs, "When are you going back to work, you lazy bastard?"

I managed to hobble back to work, and as I had to stay all day I needed food, but could only afford a little bread. Mr Reid was quite grumpy when he found that my stiff leg would prevent me using the sewing-machine and riding the shop bike. For several weeks I lived on a shoe-string, as Mr Reid paid me only one week sick pay, not ten days. Though by now my wages were increased to £1.10s.0d, the rent was also increased to £1.10s.0d but somehow I managed, my dinner consisting of a bowl of Quaker Oats, bread and tea.

Mr Reid was doing so well with his business that he opened another shop in Hackney Road and also bought a light van, a Jowett, engaging a driver to do a greatly enlarged hat business. He and myself in turns got through mountains of hats, using a spin dryer to dry them faster. He used to pack it so tight that if he didn't lie across it, the machine would dance along the floor. When my head ached or I was dizzy, I would go into the back yard, ignoring Mr Reid until it cleared. Looking back, it was a miracle that the shop wasn't blown sky high, as both Mr Reid and Jim were heavy smokers. The new shop had been freshly painted inside and out, and looked very smart, its manager was a live wire man called Len Byatt, about thirty, and highly skilled in tailoring work and the use of the steam Hoffman press. I expect Mr Reid had to pay a good salary for a man of his qualifications.

I was sent to assist Len during the first three weeks after the opening, including my half-day, and I got along very well with him. He persuaded Mr Reid to increase my wages to £1.12s.6d a week, plus 5/– for working my half-day. Although painful to bend, my knee allowed me to use the sewing-machine when helping Len. I also bought a bicycle very cheap in the market, old but well taken care of, with a three-speed gear, so I was content. Len used to bring extra sandwiches and always gave me some, although I would never ask. He also tried to keep me with him but was not allowed. An old man was engaged part-time. He told me that in 1917 he worked as a tailor in a prisoner of war camp in Germany. I was to think of him years later. The shop in Hackney didn't open on Sundays like the Hoxton one, so for three Sunday mornings I rode to Len's new house in Enfield, a very long ride that aggravated my knee condition, and whilst there I helped Len in digging over and clearing his front and back gardens, for which I had dinner with him and his wife, and was given a pound. At dusk, I used to have a long ride back home.

One morning, Len told me to go down to the basement and turn on the stopcock for the Hoffman press, so down I went, and on opening the door, I was confronted by a nude teenage girl with long black hair, washing herself down in a tin bath. I stood watching her, then she looked up, and gave a piercing scream on seeing me, so I bolted back up into the shop! Her very fat mother came in and chased me round the counter until Len calmed her down, explaining that I had opened the wrong door by mistake, whereupon the mother smiled and called me a 'cheeky bugger'.

I noticed that she had a blue bristly chin, which thick make-up failed to conceal, denoting that she shaved like a man every day. As for the girl, I thought that she was beautiful and for that minute I enjoyed looking at her. I went down again, found the right door and went in and could hear a sort of rustling sound. In the torchlight, I saw the walls and floor covered in cockroaches, so once again, I was off and told Len that I wouldn't go down there again, so good humouredly he went down and did it thereafter. I also have a thing about beetles, and I remember when I was very young, my Gran picked up a black beetle from the hearth, put it on her arm and held it near my face, and I screamed my head off.

CHAPTER SIX

Reaping one's reward

During the good weather at holiday periods, five of us would go for long bike rides to the river Lea and reservoirs, Victoria Park being the favourite. It was a treat to get away from the dingy back streets of Hoxton. We did a run to Windsor once and I was very impressed with the castle, the grounds, the guards and the beautiful town and the river. This was a period of large cycling clubs, which were well organized and rode long distances in batches of about twenty, some up to fifty, spread out thinly and causing lots of shouting from passing motorists. On returning from Windsor a group cut in front of me, and my front wheel caught in the wing nut of a bike in front and over the top I went with my mates singing 'he flew through the air with the greatest of ease' . . . . My bike was damaged but just rideable, with bent handlebars and a wobbly front wheel with some broken spokes. I had a few bruises, but for all of it I had enjoyed my day out to Windsor.

Time was passing, with no change in the home situation. Walter was constantly drunk and I suppose if Emmy had not married an alcoholic, she may have been a different person, but as she was constantly short of money, with two children, she became slovenly and full of hate, whereas life could have been so much easier for us all. But for all of Emmy's screaming rages, Walter never once struck her and he was by no means a soft type of man. I had now reached my eighteenth birthday and Emmy tended to lay off me a bit now, except when I went to the kitchen for water, when she would call me filthy names, etc. She never realized how deeply she hurt me with this behaviour. I would feel tightened up inside and wonder at times if life was worth living, but whatever happened, I couldn't desert Gran. I felt that I was held by invisible chains.

Some of my mates had moved away, their parents seeking a better life; some started taking girls out, and we were reduced to three and in time, because of shortage of money, I tended to spend more time on my own, reading a lot, some of my favourite books being by Edgar Wallace. Some evenings I would hear the sound of drums and see Sir Oswald Mosley and his blackshirts march by along the Kingsland Road on the way to Dalston, where they would clash with crowds of Jews, and police trying to keep them apart. The blackshirts always marched in impressive ranks, flanked by foot and mounted police, and I felt that Hoxton people had a lot of sympathy with them, judging by the comments I heard, as the 'sweat shops' were run by Jews and were not popular.

My next door neighbours were a nice family, with two sons and a daughter. She was roughly my age and we more or less grew up together at the same school, and whenever I was in the back garden, Frances would be there too and we always liked talking to each other. She was an attractive girl and I wanted to ask her out, but the mother always called her inside when I would hear Frances protesting. Her mother need not have worried, because it was usual, when you took a girl out, to have good seats in the cinema, with chocolates or ice-cream, etc., and the man was expected to pay. As I had nothing, I didn't ask, though I dearly wanted to. We just seemed to click. I suppose constantly hearing shouting and swearing from Emmy, and Walter always rolling down the street drunk turned the mother off. Also, they all knew about Albert and in those days, any family with a history of mental illness was avoided like the plague. The attitude was that if one was mad, the whole family was contaminated. With this in mind, I was always embarrassed when neighbours stopped and asked questions about my family, when I would say very little.

One day I was approached by Mr McGee whilst I was at work. He owned the men's outfitters shop opposite and via Jim, he told me that if I cared to pay him one shilling a week until he thought I had paid sufficient money, he would allow me to choose a jacket, trousers, shirt and tie, shoes, socks and underwear, and let me have them at cost price as a favour to me. I had earlier seen Mr McGee and Jim talking and looking in my direction, so I guessed that it was Jim's idea. Although I was always tidy, I never wore anything new, as all my clothes came from second-hand stalls. However, I jumped at the chance, and thanked him for the offer. I was excited about this and paid my shilling regularly. Time went by and on my 38th payment, Mr McGee asked me over and I chose my clothes, a navy blue blazer and grey flannel trousers, brown shoes and other things to match. Mr McGee told me they were good clothes, and the shop price would be double what I had paid, but he kept his word and didn't make a penny profit. I thanked him and took my parcel and showed Jim, who could see how pleased I was. I felt I could hardly believe my good luck and Sunday couldn't come quickly enough to show my mates, and I also wanted to dash home and show Gran. On arriving home, I quickly changed into my new clothes and said to Gran, "Well, how do I look?"

"Very nice," she replied, then I parcelled them up and put them in my bedroom cupboard.

Rushing home from work on Sunday I was eager to change and get out with my pals, so after some stew for dinner, I went to my bedroom cupboard, when an icy hand seemed to grip me. The parcel had gone, and was nowhere to be seen. I went into Gran's and asked her what had happened to my clothes. She threw a pawn ticket on to the table and said, "If you want them, go and get them out."

I looked at her stunned and said, "How could you do this to me?"

She replied, "Money is more important than your bloody clothes." Then I heard Emmy laughing at the foot of the stairs and I knew that it was revenge and hate, as Gran couldn't get out, but she too was a thief and I didn't deserve this dirty trick played on me. I saw on the pawn ticket 30/– and knew that it was goodbye to my clothes. Looking at Gran I saw that what I ought to do was walk out for good, but that was what Emmy wanted, so feeling crushed, I went into my bedroom.

I had told one of my pals about my new clothes, so I wouldn't go out now. I kept brooding over the way that no matter what I did, there was no gratitude and my own family didn't want me. Next morning at work, Jim and Mr McGee asked me how were the clothes. I replied, "Fine, but I'm keeping them for Sundays." Mr McGee seemed to accept it, but Jim gave me a hard look and I knew he hadn't been taken in. He had seen the hurt in my eyes. When I left for work each morning Emmy would shout after me, jeering about the clothes, and I wouldn't let her see I was bothered, but I never forgave Gran. I wouldn't desert her, but I hardly stayed indoors any more.

My 19th Christmas came, and with a few shillings in my pocket I went with some pals and had a few drinks in a cheerful pub in Hoxton, but it was fatal to stay too long because if someone bought you a drink, woe betide you if you went out without returning it, and I was in no position to do that. It was a bad winter, very cold, and to keep the room warm I used to buy coke; a waste product remaining after gas was extracted from coal, and at a giveaway price — twopence a sack — but it gave off very smelly fumes so a little mixed with coal would last for hours. It gave a terrific heat and kept Gran warm, because she was always complaining of the cold.

Mr Reid had an attack on the nerves of his face, causing the lower lid of one eye and his upper lip under it to tighten up towards each other, exposing his back teeth and half his eyeball, making him look hideous and this prevented him from serving customers. I never saw it get any better, and when he smoked a cigarette, it caused him to dribble from the mouth, and was not a pretty sight.

I was in the habit of wearing a collar and tie in the shop, but when out with my mates I wore a white silky type muffler pinned with a penny brass tie pin, which one could almost claim to be a Hoxton trade mark, and made us all feel really flash.

The weather broke into spring and I thought of riding to Epsom to visit Albert, but the route seemed full of twists and turns and I knew it would take me too long to get there, so with scrimping and scraping I managed to go by train to Epsom, with a very long walk to the hospital. However, there was no change in his condition and no sign of recognition, so once more I left Albert, feeling so helpless that there was nothing I could do. When I returned home and told Gran she merely remarked that what is bred in the bone comes out in the flesh.

Gran was now totally riddled with arthritis, with every movement bringing a groan of pain, and Emmy was upstairs most of the time now, so I kept to my bedroom. It was during this period that I had a spate of boils on my neck, shoulder and a thigh, and it was extremely painful to work and ride my bike, so

I saw a doctor who asked what kind of meals I was having. I told him — a bowl of porridge at midday, tea and bread with jam or cheese, and stew on Sundays. He said it was a poor diet and not sufficient and I must eat a variety of better food. I was given a tonic and told that I was also underweight, but there was nothing I could do about that.

I began going on long walks after work on my own. I felt that I couldn't stand that dismal house much longer. The weather never bothered me, for if it was raining I still went out and my favourite route was past Shoreditch Church to Bishopsgate, then through the City to the Embankment, along there to Westminster, down Whitehall to the Strand, past Waterloo Bridge, back to the Embankment, then on to home — quite a few miles in all. This would make me very tired and I would sleep like a log. Sometimes I would see a detachment of Guards on their way along the Embankment to do duty at the Bank of England. If they were English regiments or Welsh, they would be led by a drummer-bugler, but if they were Scottish or Irish they were led by a lone piper. A man in the rear used to carry a lighted lantern.

In the Strand, I would look in well lit windows of the shops, marvelling at the exhorbitant prices being charged. I noticed the well-dressed men in evening dress and their ladies in expensive clothes and jewellery, getting in or out of chauffeur-driven cars outside hotels that looked like palaces. What really caught my eye were the window exhibitions of the Commonwealth countries, with their offers of emigration. Australia and South Africa appealed to me most and I wouldn't miss a word. I felt very tempted and felt myself weakening, comparing in my mind the chances of a better life to the one I had. Work never worried me, and it seemed to me that a worker was well rewarded for his efforts in those countries.

My 20th birthday came and went and out of the blue one morning, just before I left for work, John Knott, my pal, called and said he would wait until I was ready to leave, as he had something to discuss with me. Eventually he told me that he was absolutely fed up with his situation at home, with his father unemployed and with several younger brothers and sisters; he was giving up all the wages he earned, so in a way, we were in a similar situation. Knowing my position anyway, he came round to tell me that he was going to join the Army, and would I go with him and join up. We were almost the same age, and had grown up together in the school and the streets, and I thought quickly it was a way out. Emmy was upstairs all the time now, and Gran was bedridden, so I felt that she would have to come to terms without my wages carrying all of them. I had done more than enough, with no thanks whatsoever so I said to John, "Righto, let's go and join up."

We walked to Whitehall to the Central London Recruiting Centre, an old impressive stone building which had posters and enamel plaques on the walls outside, portraying colourful pictures of the various regiments in which to enlist. It all looked very impressive, and as we were discussing it, a very smart recruiting sergeant appeared in the doorway and, looking at us, asked if we were thinking of joining the Army. We replied that we were, and on entering the building were taken to an officer, who asked various questions related to work and seemed satisfied that we were employed. Then the obvious question: Why? So we said it was mainly because of a bad home life. Other points were cleared up, then we were taken for hot showers prior to a medical examination. During the medical with several doctors, one of them told me that I was very thin, but that the Army food would soon fatten me up. He told me to get dressed and then take a letter over to the military hospital in Millbank to have a chest X-ray and then bring the result back to him. I did this quickly while John waited, telling the sergeant that he would do nothing until I came back.

I returned and the answer gave me the all clear, so back to the officer, who told us that we were passed medically fit (A1). Next he asked which regiment we had decided on, so remembering Albert, I said the Royal Artillery and John agreed, so after being told the terms of service, etc., and with the sergeant as witness, we took the oath to serve His Majesty, his heirs and successors, etc., signed some papers and that was it. We were given some ration money, our fare home and a travel warrant and told to be at London Bridge in ten days' time. The date was the 9th June 1938 that I decided and became a member of His Majesty's Armed Forces. On leaving the recruiting centre I had a feeling of elation, of being free, but there was the nagging thought about Gran. She would be upset and I felt it would be like desertion, but Emmy had sponged on me long enough. John and I had a drink in a nearby pub, and in a very happy frame of mind made off to our respective homes — John's in Essex Street in the basement.

As I entered, through the front door, Emmy came at me, seeing my bike in the back yard and me not working. She started her insulting remarks so I told her to shut up, and that I had joined the Army. She stared at me in disbelief then started shouting, "What about us, how are we going to manage?"

I just laughed and said, "That's your worry, not mine," then went upstairs to Gran.

As I told her she started crying, saying, "What's to become of me? How will I live? 'They' will put me in the workhouse!" It was at that moment when I felt a tug at my heart, so I told her that I would make her an allotment out of my pay. That it was now up to Emmy to start giving instead of always taking and that she would pay all the rent from now on, and the workhouse wouldn't come into it. When Gran calmed down, with a cup of tea, she looked at me and said, "I don't blame you Billy. You've had a rotten life and you've always stood by me." After explaining everything I asked to have my bedroom left as it was, in case I came home on leave. I told her that I hoped my ultimate destination would be India and the sooner the better, which set her off again, no doubt with thoughts of what happened to Albert in mind. I then made my way to Fortune's and tucked in to two pies and mash, then went on to the shop.

When Mr Reid saw me he exploded, saying, "What time do you call this? You will have to pull your socks up." I looked at him, thinking to myself you tight-fisted old skinflint, then I told him that as from Monday next to take a week's notice, as I had joined the Army. He turned purple spluttering, "You bloody fool, I was preparing you to be manager of my third shop. If it was a question of money, I would have increased your wages. I can get you out of it by telling them you are indispensable and you have an invalid grandmother to support." I told him not to do that, it was my life and I had decided on a clean break. Then I went home.

In the shop the next day Jim shook hands with me and told me I had done the right thing. He said I wouldn't regret it as the Army life was a good life, provided I 'kept my nose clean'.

The period of my notice passed rather uncomfortably with Mr and Mrs Reid speaking curtly and only in relation to the work, and I was glad when it had ended. I told Len of my plans, but he already knew, and gave me his address and told me if ever I wanted anything, not to be afraid to ask. We finally shook hands and he wished me good luck and goodbye.

On the Saturday I asked Mr Reid for a work testimonial. He hesitated and remarked that I would not need one in the Army, but I told him that I had worked for him for a long time and I would like one. He wrote a very short sparing one, but I was glad to have it, in case I needed it at some time in the future. I was paid my one week's wages and said goodbye. Jim shook hands and wished me well, but Mr Reid hardly spoke. I looked around the shop and the basement stairs and thought of how at 12 years of age I went down there and encountered the beetles; now after eight years of hard work I turned back and walked out of the shop with a spring in my step, glad to see the back of it. I sold my bike for thirty shillings and then the day of departure arrived. There was an emotional goodbye from Gran, her old face wet with tears. Emmy stood by silent and as I passed I muttered to her, "Look after Mum, and no workhouse," at which she flushed, but said nothing. Walter gave me a limp handshake, then with John at the front door, I was gone.

We arrived at London Bridge to find a very smart sergeant with a clipboard ticking off the names of about twenty men, who we joined and then handed over our travel warrants. We boarded the train for Woolwich, all strangers, yet there was already a feeling of camaraderie, all with one thing in common, we were on our way to start a new life. I felt a thrill and excitement and looked forward to whatever the future held for me.

PART II

CHAPTER SEVEN

For King and Country

My first sight of the Woolwich Depot was of a run of very high walls, looking rather grim and more like a prison and I realized that my life was going to be drastically changed during the next three months. Apart from my group, quite a large number of men such as ourselves were assembled, and with the precision born of practice, we were shepherded from place to place, until we had been shorn of most of our hair, been to the showers, had a meal and a good one it was too. That alone made me feel good, plus the marvellous atmosphere of large barrack blocks and dining-rooms, then the kitting out, passing along a long stores counter, where the storesmen miraculously doled out the right sizes. By the time all this was done, I felt pretty whacked, with both arms stretched out packed with kit so that I could hardly see where I was going. A sergeant bellowed for silence and announced that we had received and signed for a full kit, and anything lost would have to be paid for. Then he took us to our barrack rooms, beds and lockers to take at choice. With our kit on the beds, looking an impossible mess, we each signed for a locker key, and were then shown how to pack our kit away. We were then taken to another stores and collected sheets, pillows, and blankets, together with three 'biscuits' for a mattress.

After this, we were formed up with knife, fork, spoon and mug and taken for tea, which to me was a dinner, after which we were shown how to make the bed Army style by a bombardier guiding us along, having numerous questions thrown at him. I went to sleep that night, tired but contented, trying to digest what seemed to me a mountain of things to remember, most of all my regimental number.

The next day was crammed with not a spare minute, drawing a rifle from stores, getting everything wood and metal stamped with my regimental number and clothing stencilled with indelible ink. There was a session in a class-room on regimental history, which I found very interesting, then we were briefed by an officer on our pay and how it was divided up. Out of fourteen shillings a week we received ten shillings. One shilling was taken for barrack room damages, another shilling for kit replacements when lost, one for savings and the last for widows and orphans. Out of the ten shillings one paid for laundry, and had to pay for blanco, metal polish, black and brown leather polish and all toilet requisites, so the meagre pay didn't leave much for pleasure, but I kept my word and arranged for an allotment of 3/6d a week to be made to my gran immediately. I was used to being without and I didn't smoke, so with care I would get by on my 6/6d quite happy in the knowledge that Gran's food would get a boost, small as it was. I did manage to have the usual threepenny 'char and wad' in the NAAFI at night. This was the focal point of all recruits and staff and I found it great fun listening to the barrack room ballads sung by the older soldiers, with seemingly endless verses. Some of the songs were rather crude, but the Orderly Sergeant maintained the no swearing rule, as there were women serving. There would always be someone around to play the piano and good rough and ready singalongs. The NAAFI furnishings at that time would be considered as garden furniture today, rough wooden folding type chairs, nothing like today, with armchairs, etc.

My barrack block was named Shrapnel Barracks, and I was situated over stables. Barrack room duties comprised shining the huge fire grate and accessories, all inspected by eagle-eyed sergeants. The floor was quite a performance, with soft polish being splashed everywhere, then spread with large bumpers by two men, with one crouched on it to give weight, so as eventually to produce a mirror shine, no doubt done by thousands of recruits before us, since the Crimean War and before. The idea was to keep going flat out all day on every kind of drill and so eventually be brainwashed from civilians into soldiers. It was hard and tough but I enjoyed it, always hungry, given good main meals, breakfast, dinner and tea, then supper at 6.30 p.m. To me, the breakfast was like a dinner, with porridge, egg, bacon, sausage and fried bread with unlimited bread, butter and marmalade. I had never known anything like it, and the doctor was right when he told me that the Army food would soon fatten me up, though I never became really fat.

I don't think the average man had much to complain about, but there were always the odd ones. The Scots were the worst, wanting the porridge cooked with salt in it, but we mostly wanted it clear, and put milk and sugar on it. I was content, with good food, a nice clean bed and my pal (John Knott) next to me, coupled with lots of fresh air and hard training. I had never felt so good, but as always, there was just one fly in the ointment — the gymnasium. When I first went there and watched the antics of the recruits, I was certain I would never be able to do what they were doing. I had never seen the inside of a gym before and the shouting of the physical training instructors with their rippling muscles filled me with apprehension.

If we were unlucky enough to have our gym session late in the afternoon, being tired after hours of foot drill on the Front Parade — where as many as thirty squads would be training at once — the PTIs would give us a real hard time until they had dragged out the last reserves of energy, which we thought we never had. Going over the 'horse' was very hard indeed, as we had no springboards, and our PTI would place a long form in front, making our jump begin well back. We jumped straight off the floor, and one day my foot caught in the form and I hit the 'horse' at full speed, falling dazed. The PTI said, "If you want a hole made to go through, I will effing-well get one made for you." I had to keep going until I did get over. Being a natural runner helped, as I would go flat out for the 'horse' and strain every ounce to get over. Climbing the ropes was also hard, getting up to the roof their way, and one chap crashed from the top, fracturing his skull and ending up in the Royal Herbert Hospital. Anybody who was not very good had to do an hour extra PT in the evening, likewise men slow on foot, rifle or gun drull did extra time in the evening, with tough, unrelenting drill instructors.

During one session in the gym, a flurry of a line of us all went flying over the 'horse' at speed, doing head rolls on landing, and crashing into each other, when a foot gave me a vicious kick in the groin, bringing up a large purple lump which locked one leg in agony. The next morning I fell in on sick parade, the purple swelling now very much larger and looking ugly. The MO looked at it and said one week's extra drill, that will loosen it up, and gritting my teeth I had to do my day's drill dragging one leg behind me, also having to face the fury of the PTI when it was beyond me to run or jump. When the evening came, I showed the PTI my injury, and he told me to sit down, but to stay there the whole time. I discovered that going sick was virtually looked upon as a crime, hence the call 'outside the sick, the lame and the lazy.'

But I found the gun drill most interesting. It was a clever system of calculations, and the Gun Park was sacred ground — once over the perimeter white line, it was at the double and anyone forgetting had to drag a limber round the Gun Park, losing half a stone in the process. Once, the drill sergeant was explaining during gun drill on an eighteen-pounder gun and stressing where it was dangerous to put your hand on the trail. In order to demonstrate, he ordered, 'load with a training round, fire and open breech,' upon which the extracted round flew out and the sergeant, not quick enough, lost the top of a finger as the round hit the trail, so we had a grandstand view of what not to do.

When the hard sweaty day came to an end, we would march with towel and soap to the showers, a long place with a pipe running full length overhead supplying the water. One time in the shower an Irishman from Eire was next to me, a man over six feet tall, well built, when someone shouted, "Blimey Paddy, ain't you got a little one!" causing us all to look and seeing a little boy's penis, which set up a roar of laughter. Poor Paddy, very embarrassed, dressed quickly and told the sergeant that he refused to shower again with the squad, so it was arranged that henceforth he could bath alone, but it didn't end there, and Paddy had a rough time with ribald remarks in the barrack room coming from all directions. Paddy was a religious man, and oblivious to all he would kneel by his bed and say his prayers every night, which seemed to me to show a special kind of courage.

There were two sessions a week in the class-room and I easily obtained my 3rd class certificate of education. I settled down to gaining my 2nd class certificate of education; and having achieved 80% marks on map reading, it was stamped and signed by the Colonel. One catch question was to give the estimated width and height of the gates in the west wall of the barracks. My answer was that I couldn't recall seeing any gates, but most gave all kinds of sizes for their answers. There were no such gates.

The drill instructors were real professionals and our sergeant gave a demonstration one day. With the parade ground full of squads training, he stood at one end, letting us march on to the other then amid the clamour he threw his voice, giving the order, "Squad will turn about, about turn!" which reached us on the correct foot and was carried out to perfection. I've heard much about the Guards and the Royal Marines being the best at drill, but allowing some differences between infantry and gunners, I consider that our training and performance ranked with the best. Every aspect was hard graft, designed to toughen us up and I truly enjoyed the life, but I didn't like the gym, the PTIs went too far I thought. My squad PTI forced each of us to hold a halfpenny on edge between the shoulder blades and those who didn't were given karate chops, bringing the shoulders back until they did.

One day a spot of bother occurred in the gym, with the next squad sitting down and refusing to budge, and their PTI bellowing at them, so an officer was sent for. He first asked the squad, who had never moved, to stand, then a spokesman for the squad told the officer (who was holding a large book 'King's Rules and Regulations') that the PTI was brutal, etc., and that they would not take orders from him. Other moves were suggested by the officer, with no response, so he read out a paragraph from the book appertaining to mutinous conduct with the dire consequences for the ringleaders, who would face long terms of imprisonment. But if they agreed to obey orders and take his punishment, he would overlook the incident and not look for ringleaders. They slowly stood up, accepting his terms, and as far as my memory serves me, I believe they had to do head rolls on a long gravel road. Then after that, their PTI treated them shamefully, he was a brutal sadistic man.

The PTIs, rippling with muscles, would bounce around showing how to do a movement over the horse and so on, then go mad when blokes were falling all over the place. My PTI had a rope's end, thick with a turk's head, which he wielded freely. In one instance, when a chap couldn't jump the horse with feet between hands, he whacked him with the turk's head again and again, until he stood blubbering like a child. My one failure was pulling myself over and under the beam and over again, so in exasperation the PTI pulled my hair hard, so that I crashed down. The PTI shouted, "I hope you break your effing neck. Get back and do it again." I never did manage it, yet I had no problem walking the beam (their way) when many kept falling off.

A bad patch was at outside PT late one afternoon. The PTI had two, long, heavily-constructed hurdling timbers dragged close enough together to prevent a run between them, so on jumping from the first to the second, most people came a cropper, including myself. I landed awkwardly on my left hand and hearing a crack, realized that my wrist was broken. I just sat there with the pain building up when the PTI shouted at me to get up. I told him my wrist was broken and was told that it served me effing-well right! He then tried to make me do handstands, on which I fell sideways. I was doubled over to the MI room and after a considerable wait, the MO came in, in his Mess dress, none too pleased at being disturbed at his dinner. He wiggled my hand, causing me almost to pass out and told the orderly to put on a cold bandage, and ordered me, medicine and duty. I protested, saying that I couldn't do guard with a broken wrist, as I couldn't hold a rifle at the slope, to which he replied, "You should be more bloody careful."

I went on guard duty holding my rifle at the slope with both hands. I did no sentry duty, being in so much pain, as the guard sergeant had seen my left hand swollen up. Next morning, I saw the same doctor, who said I was to go to the Royal Herbert Hospital, which entailed putting all bedding and kit into store one handed, then walking to the hospital with small kit, where my wrist was X-rayed and put into plaster. The hospital doctor asked me, "What's going on in the Depot? Most of the patients here have broken bones." I was kept in barracks for three weeks, and realized that my squad was close to passing out parade, and knowing that I would lose many friends, including John Knott. I was sent home on sick leave for three weeks, kicking my heels in Redvers Street until the fracture set, when with a week to go, John came home on passing out parade leave, so we were company for each other.

Gran was receiving my 3/6d each week, which was drawn by Emmy at the Post Office, and I could see that she was deteriorating.

John and I paid a visit to the school to see our old teacher, Mr Cooper, who insisted on us all going to a Lyons tea-shop in Bishopsgate, where he paid for tea and cakes. When the time came for him to leave and board his tram, he gave us a warm handshake and with moist eyes, wished us good luck and said goodbye. John had been posted to Lichfield, so I hoped to be sent there too.

I returned to Woolwich, had the plaster removed, and was relegated to another squad. I had to make new friends, and as time passed, all went well, except for one barrack room incident. A recruit named Doyle, older than most, was obviously an old soldier who said and admitted nothing. He could play tricks with a rifle that only a trained infantryman could, but stayed a mystery man. He was a bully, and several times had clouted a recruit in the next bed. Gunner Hills, a cheerful man with a wife and six kids, who told us he had joined the Army to dodge debtors, told Doyle to leave the 'young fella' alone, whereupon Doyle hit Hills and a serious fight took place. Doyle was a tough bull of an individual, while Hills brought up in the slums of London, was used to roughhouse fights. They punched it out to the staircase, when Doyle tried to lift Hills over the iron rail, where he could fall two floors and get killed. Some NCOs arrived in time to separate them, they were bloody and pretty well knocked about by this time. On report an officer told the pair of them that fighting was a serious offence and they could receive severe punishment, unless they fought it out with gloves on in the ring until one gave in. This took place, and after a hammering, Hills gave best. The officer asked them to shake hands, whereas Hills offered but Doyle swore and refused, upsetting the officer. Doyle left the squad next day and we heard no more.

Christmas came and I asked to stay in barracks, as I couldn't bear the thought of spending another one in Redvers Street. It was quite good actually, with the Christmas dinner served to us by officers and NCOs. 'Janker Wallahs', the ones on punishment, did the washing-up, etc.

The weather turned bitterly cold but we were still not allowed to wear our gym vests so we doubled as a squad in just shorts and plimsolls to the gym, blue with the cold. Also, for a spell, the hot water was turned off, so we all had a sore cold water shave. Someone in the planning department had a brainwave with a way to toughen us up by sending us to Woolwich Common, supplied with 20 cwt. 3-inch anti-aircraft guns, and tents with no tent boards. There was snow on the common. We pitched tents on cleared ground and laid our groundsheets down inside to lie on. The guns and command post were set up and gun drill was started on these unfamiliar guns. The weather turned to heavy rain, but in greatcoats, the training went on all day, with whistles blowing, and us slithering in the mud. At the shouted order 'Take Posts', we would jump on the gun platforms in our studded boots, heavily coated with mud. On one mad dash, Gunner Robinson jumped in front of me and skidded on the steel platform, breaking one of his shins in two. When his trouser leg was cut open, I saw the jagged splintered bone showing through the skin. Six of us cradled him, sitting in a truck, which took him to the Royal Herbert Hospital. The doctors there had plenty of experience in mending broken bones!

At daylight, officers and NCOs would have squads of men running around the common, then have food brought in containers from the Depot, all of us enjoying the hot sweet tea at which the Army excels. The conditions became bad, with mud covering the groundsheets in the tents from our boots, which had been covered with issued dubbin. We were packed into the tents, causing us to lay our feet uncomfortably on top of each other by the centre pole. Of course, it wasn't possible to undress and nobody wanted to anyway. There was a rum issue every night, but with so many men being ferried out with chest and back problems, the exercise was finally called off, and on my return to barracks, I needed help to undress as I had a seized up back and shoulders, To add insult to injury, we were given a thorough telling off for not getting a shine on our dubbin-soaked boots. I personally didn't mind the spell on the common, uncomfortable as it was for to me it had been an experience.

My time in the Depot was nearing its end. I had been there quite a time due to being relegated back, and I was feeling very confident, having done so many things twice over.

It was announced that General Sir Edmund Ironside would be visiting the Depot soon, so it was all hustle and bustle, with ceremonial drill being practised, the emphasis being on formation drill. We had all done the ground work anyway for the Sunday church parades, which were held on front parade, where hundreds of recruits took part, with the RA Band and also the boys' trumpet band from their small depot. Many moaned about it, but I loved it, with all the soldiers gleaming, with shining buttons, brasses and spurs, boots and belts with a mirror finish, everybody perfectly turned out as a result of many hours of polishing and boning boots.

We had to train very hard for this event on formation 'fours' drill, also marching and wheeling lines, straight lines, not bent or crooked such as is seen these days on ceremonial parades. It was good training and brought out the best in us, sweating 'blood' until everything was performed exactly right. We were told how to avoid fainting on parade, what not to eat and drink, and how to stand for long spells; as one NCO put it, "We don't want any silly bloody guards antics here."

The big day arrived when the front parade filled with lines of immaculate gunners, the Regimental Band playing incidental music. We waited for a considerable time and then General Sir Edmund Ironside arrived with his entourage. As he alighted from his car, the band played 'General Salute', then after formalities were made by the Commandant, the Grand Depot, the general inspection took place. The General was a tall, broad man, looking every inch a soldier and passing through the ranks stopped and spoke to various men. With the inspection over, he stood on a raised dais, whilst with the band static next to the rostrum, the parade went through the drill manoeuvres which we had been trained to do, in time with marches played by the band. It all went without a hitch, the last move consisting of us being paraded in front of the whole assembly and the General, whereupon he gave us a very complimentary speech on our turn-out, placing much emphasis on our drill performance. I could see that the Commandant and his staff were very pleased and I felt very happy with the results of all our hard grind during the last three weeks. The parade then marched to the end of the parade ground, reformed, and with the band, marched past the General to the regimental march 'The British Grenadiers'. He took the salute and we then carried on to our individual barracks to be dismissed. Apparently the visit of a General was not a very common thing and everybody from the top down appeared very pleased with the outcome, and some 'bouquets' must have been handed out because even the NCOs started to behave like human beings!

A week later, my big day arrived — passing out parade, so it was a real hard bash for the squad, doing everything over and over again, it being impressed on us that if we failed as a squad to achieve a certain percentage of marks, we would be relegated. So with that in mind on the day, we gave of our best in gun drill, marching and rifle drill, the gymnasium and finally, after a full day, dressed in our No. 1 uniforms, we finished off with a drill display and fell in in front of the inspecting officers, who gave the good news that we had passed out well above average. Then with the band leading, we marched past to the playing of our regimental march, when the salute was taken.

Back in barracks, we were all shaking hands with each other, pleased as punch, and our drill instructors congratulated us as well. On the parade ground, prior to the march past, the tailor with a template and cloth punch pierced two holes in both collar fronts, on which we were handed two grenades with pins. When these were fixed into place, it denoted that we were no longer recruits, but were now trained soldiers.

There was much speculation regarding where we would be posted, but all was revealed next morning on regimental orders. I was to go to 6th battery, 2nd HAA regiment, stationed at Whittington Barracks, Lichfield, Staffs, but first, ten days' leave, and we were to go after dinner. In a way, I did have a pang of regret at leaving the Depot, as apart from the hard times, I had enjoyed myself. I liked Army life, the comradeship, and the good food, apart from the PTIs. I never did see why they had such twisted minds and were hell bent on hurting people. We handed in all bedding, rifle and equipment, cleaned the room, had our dinner and then received travel warrants from the pay office, as well as pay and ration allowances. Then, dressed in our best uniforms, hand shakes all round, we all left and walked to Woolwich Station on the way home. As I walked down the hill to the station carrying my kitbag, with a spring in my step, I knew that I was glowing with health, a good weight and not the skinny individual I was when I first came to Woolwich, best of all, I felt hard and alert. I felt that the Army had somehow rescued me and given me a new lease of life when I most needed it, I had a lot to look forward to and be thankful for, and I was eagerly looking forward to Lichfield.

On reaching the station platform a vicar came up to me and said, "Excuse me soldier, is the Army issuing patent leather boots now?" I smiled and replied that they were Army boots, brought to a mirror finish by myself. He was astonished, to say the least.

Recapping, back at the Depot, time serving men from all over the world, mainly India, would return to Woolwich for discharge or reserve, and items could be bought from them for next to nothing. I managed to get a brass cap badge with a moving gun wheel, used in India, but illegal here and an offence to wear other than issued, made of gun-metal. One such gunner was temporarily placed in my barrack room until his discharge came through. He had been shot by a sniper on the North-West Frontier of India, the bullet taking off a big toe. Many a yarn he would spin. I doubt if they were all true, but a full kit inspection was on orders for the next morning, and as the 'old soldier' only had cleaning and shaving kit, having sold everything else, he went to everyone in the room and borrowed something, cleaning it to his standard. When the inspection took place, the Colonel addressed us all, complimenting us, then concluded by saying, "Take note, you young soldiers, of this man's kit layout, it is perfect and sets an example to you all." The old soldier's face beamed with pleasure, the Colonel being unaware that he had been conned. We all made a dash and retrieved our own items of kit, in case he sold them too!

On my way home, I reflected about my forthcoming ten days' leave. My ration allowance would never compensate for the good regular meals I had been having, so I could only keep it to myself and give nothing to Gran. I would have to manage, that's all there would be, so Fortune's pie shop would supply my dinner and supper every day, with what I could bring indoors, and I had a good healthy appetite. With the travel warrant from the station to my home, I had no fares to pay and on arriving at Redvers Street, the memories flooded back, and in a way, apart from seeing Gran, I would much rather have been somewhere else.

Emmy opened the door, not expecting me, and I said. "Hallo." She was quiet, but friendly. Gran looked waxen and was pleased to see me. I explained to her that my ration allowance was very small, and that I could give nothing up, as I would have a job keeping myself for ten days. She understood, and I thanked Emmy, who was standing by, for looking after Gran, and said how hard it must be, with two children. I got to grips with the dusty bedroom and when satisfied, laid my kit out with everything to hand. I searched for bugs, but only found plenty of dead ones, night-time was when they became active.

I went out to make my way to Fortune's and in the street, met with and spoke to several neighbours who all commented on how well I looked, and filled out. I told them that Army life was great and suited me, but I wished the pay was higher. In the course of my leave, I visited the shop and there was a young fellow serving, but I guessed he didn't do half of what I had done. Mr and Mrs Reid showed no desire to speak, but Jim was delighted, quietly saying that judging by the way I looked, I had done the right thing. He then suggested that I should leave, as he was getting dirty looks! I spent a whole afternoon in the Hackney shop with Len and he told me that the van driver had robbed Mr Reid by using the van for his own use and charging the petrol to Mr Reid's account and was therefore sacked. I made a point of going to every street and alley for memory's sake, and slowly my leave slipped by.

Various friends seemed to have moved away or disappeared, but I had some happy conversations with Frances next door, who seemed more than willing to speak to me, but her mother would call her in and a slanging match would ensue. I was longing to ask her out, but a hard up soldier is no different to a hard up civilian. In the pub I had a beer or two and the company of old soldiers from the First World War, recalling their experiences. The time came to leave so it was goodbye to poor old Gran; for better or worse, she was the only family I had known. Leaving my Lichfield address with Emmy, and obtaining her promise to keep in touch with regard to Gran I left, pleased to go and looking forward to my future.

I had worn my uniform throughout my leave, as I had no civvies to wear, but I had others with me, so that I kept myself immaculate. There was one thing burning inside me, I wanted to go to India, but I was yet to come to terms with the Army mentality.

CHAPTER EIGHT

A man's army

I was pleased to meet up with a few of my squad on the train, two of whom were having regrets after ten days of home life. On arrival at Lichfield Station I found a truck waiting to board as our names were accounted for, and we soon sped on our way to Whittington Barracks. Seeing the countryside with its various scented smells reminded me of my farm holiday when I was a kid, and I had very happy feelings indeed.

The barracks were pleasantly laid out, with plenty of space, and some single storey buildings attractively covered by red creeper. I was soon settled in an occupied barrack room of 6th Battery regular soldiers, some already having served abroad. There was an amiable mixture of ages, providing a good balance for conversation. Here were the professional soldiers, some of whom had served in other branches of the regiment, such as garrison, and field. In the main, they were decent helpful fellows and it was best to take note and follow their examples from day to day. We were given a hot meal in the dining-room, which was more spacious in layout than at the Depot, with no need for pushing and shoving. I found the men in my barrack room always ready to help and suggest the easiest ways of doing things, point out pitfalls and how to avoid them, but the thing I appreciated most was that we were treated as equals.

That evening, I found my way round to the NAAFI, the canteen, a library, recreation rooms with billiard tables and other indoor games. There was a quiet room with armchairs for reading and also a writing room. Baths and showers were available at any time, with privacy, and I liked all that I saw, but the Unit, I had to discover as time went by. I went to bed that night in a contented frame of mind, glad to be at Lichfield, glad to be a gunner.

I soon settled in to the routine of 'rise and shine', morning parades, and the time spent mainly on the gun park. A bombardier PTI would, several mornings a week, take early morning PT, in the main, exercises in which everybody took part, and which was quite enjoyable. The same bombardier was in charge of athletics, but a sports sergeant took charge of all sports for the Battery.

Everybody had a job to do, from menial tasks in the barracks and cookhouse to being trained and welded into a proficient fighting unit. There was the MT section, who ran and maintained all the Battery transport with well-equipped workshops. The whole regiment of six batteries was stationed here, with plenty going on all the time. Whittington Barracks was also the

Regimental Depot for the North Stafford and South Staffordshire Regiments, and when seeing recruits training on the square, I noticed that the drill was faster than at Woolwich.

I made many friends, and slipped into place like a piece of a jigsaw puzzle. We newer members of the Battery had it impressed on us to remember the names of the CO and RSM, etc., but one of my weaknesses is in remembering names, it was then and still is now. RSM Quarterly was a tall, broad, Devon man, who lived by the rule book as regards everything. He had a waxed moustache and in Army slang was as 'regimental as a button stick'.

Discipline was very strict, and On Parade meant just that, with Battery movements controlled by our trumpeter. I had once taken a chance and shaved the night before, but on parade next morning, TSM Nicholls asked me if I had shaved. I said that I had and his reply was, "Stand closer to the razor next time." Morning Parade was the main event of the day, with all officers present, including the Battery Commander. This was the time to be really on one's toes, volunteer for nothing, because a sergeant might ask for example, "Anyone here read music?" and anyone stepping forward could end up on coal fatigues. These little so-called jokes suited the warped sense of humour some of the NCOs had. Men reported sick, some fell out on minor charges to report to the Major, others already on punishment called 'Janker Wallahs' would be marched off to do the most unsavoury jobs. The rest of us marched off for daily routine training sessions that went on irrespective of the weather, and there were also guard mounting refreshers and fire drill. According to rank, NCOs and Warrant Officers had their own Messes and it was frowned on for NCOs to be seen associating with gunners, on the grounds that it undermined discipline.

The most important parade of the week was pay, when we were called by name, rank, and number, to march and salute at the table to hear the best or the worst, i.e., in debt or in credit, then salute and march off. I had to scrape through, week by week, but I was never a penny in debt. Some of the men were a pain in the neck, being paid Friday, broke Saturday and forever scrounging for a cigarette or the price of a cup of tea in the NAAFI.

The Battery had received delivery of new 3.7-inch heavy anti-aircraft guns, relieving us of the 3-inch QF mobile guns. These new guns were the latest design, and were electronically controlled from the Sperry Predictor in conjunction with the height and range finder. Information transmitted from the predictor via cables to each gun enabled the gun teams to lay on targets fairly accurately at a great height. There was only one way to be successful in action against a target, and that was speed and efficiency. Fumbling could cause disorder, achieving nothing, so persistent training, working as a team, was essential. 1939 for me, and in fact for everyone, meant two years' work crammed into one, with little time to spare for anything. It was go all the way, so that we all got to know each other very well.

I was sent for in February and offered the appointment of unpaid, temporary Lance-Bombardier, which I accepted with some trepidation, as junior NCOs took the brunt of slanging both ways, but I was keen and willing to have a go. Surprisingly, this followed an incident which I thought would have prevented me from even being considered for promotion. There was a rule on Wednesday afternoons, a half day off commencing at 2 p.m., it was 'into bed or out of barracks'. From 2 to 4 p.m. the NCOs would prowl around, and anyone they caught walking about was put on a charge. I had planned to go into Lichfield that afternoon so, properly dressed, I made my way in time to catch the 1.20 p.m. bus for Lichfield, when the sports sergeant called me, saying, "Be on the sports field at 2.30 p.m. in football gear," taking my name.

I replied, "Sorry Sergeant, I'm on my way to Lichfield, where I have an appointment."

His answer was, "I'm a man short and this Battery is playing 5th Battery, so be there." Annoyed, I reminded him that sport was a voluntary activity, but his final remark was, "Be there, or I shall put you on a charge." I was fuming over this, as sports lists were fixed a day before, including reserves, so I was picked on to cover his mistakes, so I decided to teach this cocky sergeant a lesson.

I was on the field at 2.30 p.m. and placed at half back. I was so angry, I stood still throughout the match until half time, with lines of men shouting their heads off. I had been knocked over a few times during play, but already 6th Battery were two goals down, with ten men playing. At the interval the sports sergeant came over and was sarcastic. It was the same in the second half, I stood fast. After it was over, I found that I wasn't too popular, when a Captain asked me if I was ill. I told him that I wasn't and that I played football regularly, but the sports sergeant had forced me here when I was on my way out of barracks at 1 p.m., and that I never intended to play. He made no comment when the sergeant came up, and among other things, sneering, asked me if I was a sport. I replied, "You can lead a horse to water but you cannot make him drink." He never bothered me again. But the Army takes sport very seriously, and I had often played football and cricket, so in the barrack room I had some explaining to do. But as some other men had been caught like me by the sports sergeant, I was vindicated.

One evening, during a boxing match, it was apparent to the Colonel that the fight was too tame, so he jumped into the ring saying, "Now look here you two men, stop pussyfooting about and fight, I want to see blood." Blood he got, and the fight should have been stopped, as both men were in a mess, fighting to a stop, ending with sawdust being spread on the floor of the ring. I had two bashes in the ring, but both times from the first tap, my nose streamed with blood, so I volunteered no more. I met John Knott, and we had a happy time talking over the events of the last few months. He liked it in 5th Battery but as events in the future were to show it made little difference, for fate had it worked out for us. Whilst at Woolwich, John, Jack Wright and myself had a photograph taken in the Strand, and it turned out very good. Wright was a Canadian lumberjack who, from boredom and the desire to see the world, came over and joined the British Army, he had also gone to 5th Battery with John.

I had palled up with a man called 'Darkie' Burns who was in the bed next to mine. He was a man who had served for some time, and whose jet black hair earned him his nickname. Although of a reserved nature, he was a man I could easily get along with, and we became firm friends. He had a weakness for the girls, and being good looking, he always attracted them. One day, on a trip to Lichfield and in the local park, Darkie said, "There's two girls on a seat, let's go over." His charm soon had us all talking and laughing, so we walked a bit and the girls led us to a spot by a small waterfall. We parted in pairs and settling down, soon started playing about. Nature being what it is, I soon had her dress up and in great ecstasy, we exhausted ourselves. Lying back talking, she told me she was seventeen, then startled me by saying, "You know Billy, I'm pregnant." I stared at her stomach and thought she did look rather plump.

I said, "Why didn't you tell me?"

She replied, "I didn't want to, but I have been going out with a fireman."

We dressed and got tidy but when I bid her goodbye, it was with alarm bells ringing in my head. We all knew that if a young soldier put a girl in the family way, and the mother brought her to the barracks making a real fuss, it meant a show-down with the Colonel and Padre involved, and the young soldier, conscience stricken, agreeing to marry her. It could be a trap; I hoped not, she was a nice girl but I didn't want to be blamed for another man's child.

I had foolishly told her my name and battery, so when I told Darkie, he said keep away from Lichfield, just in case. It so happened that on two occasions she did enquire at the barrack gate for me, but Darkie told me that in seeing his girl, he made it known that I had gone on a draft to India. My outside trips were to Tamworth, a nice little town in the opposite direction. After some time, on Saturday evenings, a bus load of us would have a drink up in Lichfield and return on the last bus.

CHAPTER NINE

Exalted heights

I expected my temporary promotion to be adverse to me in the barrack room. In the main it wasn't, a few men showed resentment, but they did anyway to all NCOs. However, apart from the usual training duties, I was led into contact with the BSM and two TSMs, as well as the Battery Office where I gained an insight into how the system of running a unit worked. I was really a battery runner, carrying messages and papers all over the place, but I was learning a lot and gained confidence as the weeks went by. I was on good terms with the men and was not stupid enough to try throwing my weight about, as it only made enemies, besides I was temporary, so I had to be careful.

After a period I was established Lance-Bombardier with pay, so I immediately went to the pay clerk and had my increase of sixpence a day added on to Gran's allotment, doubling it to seven shillings a week, knowing that she badly needed it; even though I denied myself a few extras, she was the only mother I had ever known.

Darkie couldn't see enough of his girl and she was under age, so I warned him that if her mother found out, he would have a hell of a time, as I knew that in Hoxton, some blokes had to flee for their lives. He applied for the MT section and was accepted, then he was taught to drive. I thought Lichfield was a nice country town, with its beautiful cathedral, and I had spent many happy hours wandering around its small streets and shops.

Although we young soldiers had a job to make ends meet, the 'old sweats' never seemed short of a bob or two. Thieving was a serious crime in the Army, which would invoke severe punishment if a culprit was caught. But the skill and craftiness of some, resulted in hardly anyone ever being caught. It came home to me one day, following pay parade, changing my clothes by my locker, I emptied my pockets on to my bed and turned away, but on looking back, there were two half-crowns missing. I angrily asked if anyone was seen near my bed, but it was the code never to 'shop' anyone, so receiving stony glances, I learned the hard way, having to manage on one and sixpence for the week. There was an incident in the washhouse when a man with his face wet with washing would find his soap missing, but on the second occasion he decided to catch the thief, so he pushed two needles into his soap and washed with another, when there was a yell, and there was a man with his hands bleeding. The thief was caught and received two black eyes for his trouble, plus a badly bruised face, and from then on he was a marked man. The motto was to steal as much as you could from the Army, but never from a comrade.

Barrack room life had its humorous side, as whilst cleaning and polishing kit on our beds, older and much travelled soldiers would sing songs and ballads which we all enjoyed, learning the words and joining in, songs which had been sung many times through the years and passed down. Some were very sentimental, with many verses, others quite vulgar, but very funny. Some of the older soldiers were expert at poetry and it was quite an education to us younger ones. I was so impressed that I acquired a small ledger and wrote down everything I could, almost filling it. I regarded it as a treasure, but alas it was lost during the war, some of the items being inevitably forgotten for ever. Men coming back from weekend leave would jump into bed and then to the accompaniment of much cursing, have to re-make it as it was a 'French bed'.

Tales were my favourites, and I could listen for hours to the experiences related by men who had served abroad, some very enlightening in regard to the details of their sexual antics in the brothels of India. In this day and age, they would be referred to as 'super studs'. Some men had enlisted as the only means of escaping the debt collectors, and immediately pressed hard for a posting abroad.

My gun was designated No. 1 Gun, and it was my misfortune to have as No. 1 Sergeant Morgan, a Welshman who, for reasons best known to himself, took an instant dislike to me and showed his ignorance by calling me a cockney bastard, sometimes in front of the men. I knew that if I complained, it wouldn't look good for me, so I let it ride, hoping that in time he would drop the insulting habit. I also had to keep my temper, as, out of uniform, it would mean a fight. On the gun his word was law, but he had a chip on his shoulder and a set sneer on his face. We had to get along duty-wise on the gun, as good teamwork was essential, spending hours each day taking a turn at each other's jobs. The other NCOs were friendly enough, so I ignored Sergeant Morgan as much as I could, as I was still new at my job, and didn't want to lose my stripe and reduce Gran's pension by half.

TSM Crotty stopped me one day and asked how I would go about filling the gun hydraulic recoil system if it was necessary. I rattled off the correct procedure, as per maintenance manual, when he said, "No need for that, just pour oil in the filler hole until it runs out of the levelling hole," then walked away. Now if I had said that, he would have told me to swot it up in the gun manual and report to him in the morning. Fuse keys hung round our necks for practice familiarizing ourselves with ammunition on gun drill, concluding by swabbing out barrels, then oiling, the whole gun cleaned without so much as a speck on it. Grease nipples were painted red, so that they wouldn't be missed, so on the whole, a hard day's work was put in, with night guards to follow on a rota system. Boots, belts and leather chin straps came in for special attention every night. We now had two pairs of trousers issued to go with our service tunics and wore riding dress on ceremonial only.

Early in the spring of 1939 we went *en route* to the firing ranges at Manobier, in South Wales, where training with live ammunition brought some reality to us. We bedded down in tents and I thought this is the life for me. It seemed to have a holiday atmosphere about it, with huge marquees for use as dining-rooms, the rough and ready ablutions and our having to familiarize ourselves with the field kitchens spreading smoke everywhere. I saw my first 'Aldershot Oven', made from clay and bricks, an improvisation to cook in the field, but pretty useless to depend on feeding large numbers of men. As in barracks, the early morning cry of come and get your 'gunfire' half an hour before reveille at 6.30 a.m. meant a mug of 'Sergeant-Major's' tea, strong, with lashings of milk and sugar, also giving me the chance to wash and shave early before the rush.

When approaching Manobier, I saw what I thought was all sky with a line across. It was the horizon and at 20 years of age, my first sight of the sea. Our firing sessions with live ammunition were timed to drive us to the limit with speed, and our targets were towed sleeves from biplanes just over the sea. I enjoyed every minute, the guns seemed like live monsters gushing flame and smoke and I used to think of the pilot in the plane, one error and that would be his lot.

The RAF would operate a radio controlled plane, no sleeve, with a chap working a control panel for the plane's movements. The plane was called the 'Queen Bee' and it was 6th Battery's turn to fire at it. Allowance in distance was to be made for the four shells to explode behind the plane, but something went wrong because on our first salvo the 'Queen Bee' was hit and dived into the sea. There was all hell let loose, with RAF officers shouting at the umpires, who were checking each battery's efficiency. An RAF launch went out to see if salvage was possible, but I don't know what happened after that, except that our shoot was finished for the day. In a roundabout way, we heard that our CO was highly amused at the incident.

On my time off I visited nearby Tenby, a pretty town, its pubs being private houses. I had a pint in the parlour but never found the people talkative. They spoke to each other in Welsh, which to me was disconcerting, as they kept looking at me, causing me to wonder whether their comments were complimentary or otherwise!

The standard of cleanliness in our tent area was such that it would have been virtually impossible to find a matchstick lying around. An incident took place during a full kit inspection, laid out in lines by the tents, when the Battery Commander found fault with a man fresh from the Depot, for having a dirty kit. The Major made him turn out his kitbag, to find dirty washing and some sandwiches turned green. He was made to strip on the spot, with the Major in a terrible temper. He ordered two NCOs to strip to bathing trunks and scrub him clean under a shower, which they did with relish, using a large scrubbing brush and kitchen soap. He returned looking like a Red Indian, skinned, with all of us hearing his shouts from the bath house. He then had to wash every stitch of clothing he had, including kitbag, and walk around in denims, but a warm sun soon dried them out. His punishment was to lay his kit out every evening for inspection by TSM Crotty, who found fault, tossing his kit all over the place. This went on for a week, and thereafter he had to empty his kitbag on every inspection. This obviously made us more vigilant.

Our spare time was occupied with impromptu games of football, which kept many of the men happy, but I think that card schools took pride of place as No. 1 entertainment, as at every bit of rest time, out came a pack of cards. Now I never learned to play cards because in the main, pennies were the stakes and I couldn't afford the pennies, so I would be an observer, not a player. I took my duties seriously, but with common sense and apart from one or two fools, who would try to resist a given order automatically, I got on well with everybody. Gunner Smith was one such person, a fool to himself and slovenly in carrying out his duties, but I always kept a sharp eye on him and let him get away with nothing. There was a sprinkling of reservists called up with us, and they had settled down and were quite friendly.

Our period under canvas drew to a close and after tidying up the camp area, we loaded the trucks, limbered up the guns and were soon on the journey back to Lichfield, feeling richer in experience, knowing each other better and all the happier for having done it. One interesting fact was coping with meals on convoy. There were prepared sandwiches, two hard-boiled eggs per man and hot tea brought in air-tight containers, issued during a ten minute leg stretch, and all eggshells collected in a rubbish bag. The Scammell trucks were large and powerful, pulling our heavy guns with ease up steep inclines, with the gun teams sitting in the back. One thing I didn't like was when on the road, the air swirl would drive diesel fumes from the exhaust into the covered top where we sat, causing headaches and sore eyes.

In Whittington Barracks was a section of the Army Education Corps, in charge of a small school. I was sent for one day by an AEC Sergeant who said, "I have looked at your records and I see that you did well in your Second Class Certificate. I think you have the potential to better yourself." He then asked if I would be prepared to work hard to achieve my First Class Certificate. It would mean very intensive study to learn one language, among other things, and if I passed, it would be equal to a college degree and instant promotion to Sergeant. Then the future would be up to me. He would help and guide me all the way if I was prepared to give it a try. I said that I would, and do my best. I was to be notified of my date to commence, but the preparations for war and the start of the war killed it, and I never got started.

There was in my barrack room a tall mouthy chap who kept picking on a short stocky man. He went too far one day, when the short man hit the mouthy one twice in the mouth, tearing it at both ends. The scars made his mouth look wider than it was already. The little chap received twenty-eight days' punishment and it turned out that he was an amateur boxer in civilian life.

The period was June 1939, when more drafts of reservists came in.

Volunteers were asked to put their names down for a Singapore posting, so I put mine down and very soon, half of the battery complement were notified, inoculated and kitted out for the Far East. All men were picked out by the OC, and I was not one of them, much to my disappointment, though I hoped that another chance would come along. John Knott and Jack Wright plus other pals from my old Woolwich Squad in 5th Battery went on the same draft, so a few sad handshakes and farewells took place.

Battery strength was made up with reservists and most seemed to me not to take too readily to discipline again, their main gripe being leaving their families and jobs. Training was started virtually from scratch, with some not showing a lot of interest, but during the course of time they became resigned to it and settled down to the daily routine, following threats and warnings from TSM Crotty, a hard man. A case in point was on a morning parade. TSM Crotty was giving a pep talk about smartening up, when he rebuked a reservist, Gunner Turner, and called him out to the front. Turner shambled forward and the TSM roared at him to double, but Turner walked to him and received a dressing down. So Turner shouted at him, "I did 256 days in the glasshouse in Hong Kong. They didn't break me and you won't either." He was then doubled to the guardroom and charged.

We were soon moved to Oswestry, Shropshire, again under canvas, to find an army of civilian workmen building long rows of latrines in rough timber structures, showing that large numbers of men were expected. Sure enough they came by the train load, conscripts called Militiamen, dressed in issued blue blazers, grey flannel trousers, shirts, ties and brown shoes, because of a shortage of uniforms. Territorial Army units also arrived for further training with the Regular Army. It certainly was a busy time getting organized, with messing in giant marquees, and provision for showers a masterpiece of organization considering the numbers involved, especially with it being such a hot summer. With so many men drilling on grass, dust was everywhere and mixed with sweat soon made everybody most uncomfortable. Junior NCOs had to take a week's turn with a squad of 'Janker Wallahs' on the unpleasant task of emptying rows of latrine buckets and swabbing seats with disinfectant water.

My turn came and I was in charge of ten men for this task. When the carrier was full, with its accompanying stench, it was emptied into large dug pits and limed. Toilet paper was distributed as we went along. At one time an officer, looking very concerned, came to me and asked me to place extra toilet paper in the officers' toilets, but I pointed out that the regulation issue was five sheets per man per day. He replied that he couldn't possibly manage on that and would I please place some extra sheets in. I obliged, with a huge box of paper, enough to satisfy anyone with the loosest of bowels!

In a job such as this, something was bound to happen, and sure enough, there was an outbreak of what in soldiers' vernacular was known as 'crabs', a highly irritating inflamed area around the private parts, necessitating non-stop scratching. I caught it, and joined a long queue at the MO tent. Medical orderlies were smearing a mauve coloured lotion on to the affected parts, setting the men dancing as it stung rather smartly. My turn came, and after treatment, I was told to wait half an hour then shower and put on clean clothes. All laundry was to be marked infectious. The shower queues were long and this time all lavatory seats had to be scrubbed with strong disinfectant, but awkward as it was, I tried to avoid sitting on seats in future.

The reservists in the main turned out to be decent blokes. They were really smart on the guns, which was to be expected, having spent years on guns during their service years. It seemed as if they had never left the Army. There were quite a few comedians among them, which helped to make my job easier, as a good sense of humour is necessary at times. Some of our time was spent training TA units on the guns, as they had none of their own, also foot drill and the rudiments of guard mounting. This was, in the circumstances, good training all round, because at least everyone learned something. But as it turned out in the future, it was too late for some. All round guard was maintained to cover the many loopholes in this type of area, and extra vigilance was called for to prevent absconding or getting out to the nearest pub. I noticed some Guards drill sergeants about, who I believe had the task of licking the Militiamen into shape. These Guards sergeants could often be heard to shout, "You may break your mother's heart, but you won't break mine."

Some of my Battery officers were posted elsewhere and in return, replacements were young Army reserve officers, who in reality had done very little training, so they learned as they went along.

One such officer comes to mind, who was conspicuous in his brand new, immaculate uniform, complete with Sam Browne belt. He was out of his depth and relied on senior NCOs to give him guidance. I thought this mixed up jumble of men in Oswestry were a very long way from being a proficient Army.

A Regimental guard mounting was laid on one evening by the Regiment, providing six guards, six fire pickets, from six batteries. The Colonel and all Battery Commanders were on parade. Dress was No. 1 and the trumpeter was in position with RSM Quarterly, complete with sword on parade. The officer in charge of the guard mounting was the one just mentioned and as RSM Quarterly positioned the guards and pickets with trumpeter's calls, he handed over the guard mounting to the officer, who stood like a ramrod, frozen for an uncomfortable time. RSM Quarterly smartly stepped forward, spoke to him and took over the parade, and being the professional soldier that he was, the guard mounting went off to perfection. A large crowd was watching the Regular Army at work and saw the officer's embarrassment. I never saw that officer again, so he must have been moved on.

A company of actors arrived and gave entertainment to the troops by putting on shows and sketches in the marquees. I saw a performance put on by one man which I found very moving, and linked in some measure to Hoxton, but in those days England had thousands of Hoxtons. He gave a wonderful performance of an old man speaking to his imaginary wife and from a box behind him he would occasionally do a quick change, with make-up and wig, ageing himself as he went along. He had a struggle to pay the rent and eventually looking very old and bowed, became destitute, and in a desperate quavery voice, sang to his imaginary wife the old song 'We've been together now for forty years and it don't seem a day too much.' In the dialogue, they were to go into the workhouse, he in the men's side and she in the women's, being allowed to meet for only one hour each week. Then with very moving scenes, the song concluded with a distraught, shaking old man saying a distressing goodbye at the workhouse doors in a sorry voice. The trembling old man walked off to his side of the workhouse, then with a flourish, he whipped off his wig and old coat and the bowed over old man turned into a smiling young man, receiving wonderful applause. It was a moving performance and I had tears in my eyes. I still think, after all these years, that it was the best performance I have ever seen, and I wonder if that young man ever became an actor of great renown.

I'm afraid that the attitude of Sergeant Morgan towards me had not changed. He was very sarcastic and short tempered, making no attempt to offer help and guidance on the workings and mechanics of the gun, which every NCO was supposed to know. The one thing in my favour was that he was unpopular with the rest of the gun team. One thing did worry me was that as No. 1 on the gun, he may be asked for a progress report on me if a vacancy for full bombardier came up, so I knew that with him I wouldn't stand a chance, but as I performed my other duties satisfactorily, I could only hope.

Early in August we moved back to Lichfield, when it was inoculations all round with swollen arms to prove it, and back to barrack room routine. Work concentrated now on painting guns and vehicles from dark green to khaki camouflage, with patches of black. All brasswork was painted, which cut out a lot of polishing, but we certainly took on a warlike appearance, coupled with barrack room rumours that war was imminent.

I was very surprised and pleased to receive a letter from my mother, who informed me that as my father had left the Navy after 23 years' service they were now living in a house in Teddington, the mortgage being paid from his quarterly pension. She had visited Gran and had obtained my address from her, my teenage sister had prompted the letter to be written. I had written often to Gran but I had never received one letter back; Emmy wouldn't bother for me. My mother invited me to come for a weekend any time I could, so I immediately put in for a weekend pass, my first ever. Many were issued every week to reservists, so I was granted a long weekend from midday on Friday to Sunday midnight. I was fortunate in having all the rail fares paid, but not buses. After finding out how to get to Teddington I set off in regimental uniform, riding breeches and spurs, thinking that I might as well look my best on this important visit, and hoping that with luck, I might manage another pass and look up Gran. With her crippled fingers she couldn't answer my frequent letters — Emmy could but didn't.

I eventually arrived at 70, Connaught Road, Teddington, a pleasant tree-lined area, and knocked on the door with mixed feelings, wondering if I should have come after all. My mother opened the door and after making a fuss over me she welcomed me in. My young brother aged 13 and sister aged 7 were home from school but Rosina and my father were not yet home from work. I felt and indeed was, a stranger, finding it awkward to say 'Mum', but Rosina came in first, a very pretty girl of seventeen, and we got along like a house on fire and seemed to be on the same wavelength. There was still the nagging thought of my father when he came in, and I wondered what his attitude would be. He came a bit late, having a job looking after the boiler house in a factory. On seeing me he said, "Hallo mate," then washed and had his meal. I tried to ignore this, lost in Rosina's chatter, and later on he thawed out when we all had some drinks in the local pub. The next day Rosina took me out and about and seemed proud to hold her soldier brother's arm. The day passed all too quickly; what a lovely girl she was, putting me so quickly at ease.

She told me that she and Mother generally had a bad time from my father, and on Friday evenings, my mother would go to a pub near his works and force him to part with her housekeeping money before he spent it with his cronies. He always called Rosina 'Lady Muck' because she liked to dress nicely, and recently gave my young brother two black eyes, narrowly escaping prosecution from the school authorities. My mother had apparently almost lost her life when carrying Joan, the younger sister. Mother was at the front door speaking to a neighbour when my father ran and jammed her in the door, bringing on a premature birth with complications, so putting her life in the balance. However, the Saturday night went off quite well. I didn't want to go out, as I had so little money.

My father, with some glasses of rum and a few pints inside him would be transformed. He could sing and yodel, setting everybody singing in the pub, all the old songs well known in Hoxton — a real Jekyll and Hyde character, with everybody convinced what a good guy he was. I was given a small bedroom during my stay and was made very comfortable, but I still had that uneasy feeling, as my father had hardly spoken to me. Sunday came and I made it clear to Mother that my deadline to leave was no later than 2 p.m., having worked out a timetable to allow me time to spare. Dinner would be at 1.30 p.m. so as not to lose time I would eat my meal fully dressed, protected by a cloth. I was in the garden after a good spit and polish session, with Rosina laughing and teasing when a shout 'dinner', so in we went and sat in the 'best room', dinner being laid out really nice. The two younger children were eating in the kitchen. I heard voices in the doorway and Mother came to me, ashen faced, whispering that the old man had come in with his father and mother from Hoxton, all boozed up, and that now there would be trouble. I felt on edge when in walked my father with the grandparents I had never seen. They sat at the table and Mother spread the dinner to five places, then we were ready to eat.

The grandfather, a tall, weatherbeaten looking man, nasty with drink, started singing and thumping the table. Mother looked terrified when he said to me, "You're the soldier boy I've heard about, well effing-well sing." I told him to be quiet and eat his dinner. My father then shouted at me and Mother screamed as the grandfather tipped the table over, sending the dinners and gravy pot on to Mother's best carpet. My father and grandparents pinned me into a corner and I had to fight like hell to defend myself the Hoxton way, boots and all. My mother was on my father's back and screaming like mad and the grandmother was belting me with a huge handbag, which felt as if it had a paving stone inside. They were used to a rough house, with the grandfather having a really hard dig with his bony hands, a real Hoxtonite. My father got a few in but my blood was up and I held my own. I managed a headlock on the grandfather and forced him to the front door, having considerable trouble holding a madman, trying to open the front door as well with the shrieking old woman bashing the back of my head with that cursed handbag. I got him outside and pasted him good and proper, then threw him on to the pavement. Then I grabbed the grandmother and booted her in the rear, sending her sprawling, when her bag flew open and among many things was half a bottle of whisky smashed. As they made off swearing, my father ran after them.

I went in to survey the damage. I had a large bump coming up on my forehead, a nice black eye in the making, a swollen, cut, top lip with a bloody nose and a thumping headache from that blasted bag. Both hands were painful with skinned knuckles, so I knew that I had held my own and that they had left with a few 'souvenirs'. I was worried about my uniform, as 'Redcaps' were always on the prowl at main line stations, looking for the slightest excuse to pick on a soldier. Mother was distraught, crockery had been thrown underfoot, five dinners trodden into the carpet and furniture damaged. The two youngsters had run into the garden, and I found Rosina on her bed sobbing her heart out. I persuaded her to go downstairs and help to clear up the mess, as I had my own problems, urgent too, so a quick wash and stemming my nose bleed, I undressed quickly and tidied my uniform as best I could. Fortunately there were no rips or tears, but grease and bloodstains to clean off. With my small kit and experienced hands I soon brought my trodden on boots up to standard and with a general clean up and polish I felt passable, but my face looked a mess and was gradually worsening.

Mother made a cup of tea and after taking some aspirins to ease my throbbing head, I had to dash, as I was already getting close to the danger time limit. Before I left, I wrote a note for my father, telling him that if he laid a hand on my mother or Rosina, I would arrived unexpectedly one weekend and give him the hiding of his life. I learned some weeks later that he returned very late that night, read the note and kept quiet. I knew my father was handy with the boxing gloves, but I meant what I said.

The journey back was uneventful, except that on the train I got a few hard stares and a few smiles when I smiled back. I too could see the funny side of it from a stranger's point of view.

On entering the guardroom at the barracks, the Sergeant made no comment, for which I was grateful and in the barrack room I made out that a couple of drunks had set about me, but showed them my skinned knuckles. I could hardly admit that my father and grandfather had done it. During morning parade, my face looking a bit the worse for wear, I was given some hard looks by the officers and Sergeant-Major, it being considered unbecoming for an NCO to get involved in brawls, but thankfully nothing was said.

Sergeant Morgan had a field day, and commented, "Someone did a good job on you eh, cockney bastard." Now I had just about had enough and it took strong self-control to contain myself. I was in a terrible rage, I thought that if I could get him alone in the town, I would make an awful mess of him.

It doesn't make for happy reading, but my young brother had his tonsils removed and stayed in hospital overnight, only to be found dead in the morning, the night nurse stating that she had seen nothing to cause alarm, yet he choked on his own blood.

On a happier note, I mention this purely for its humorous side, from time to time the Army have spot medical inspections and I recall one bordering on near panic during the midday break. The Orderly Sergeant shouted in the barrack room door, "Everybody report to the MI room at 2 o'clock, short arm inspection." There was a resulting mad dash of men with towel and soap to the washhouse to clean their genitals. The picture this conjures up is beyond belief. Another aspect of Army life, be clean or else. . . .

The Artificer decided after checking the guns that one of them needed a new liner in the barrel, so he, a crew of three plus a Scammell driver and myself, towed the gun to an RAOC Depot for the liner change. I wandered around the workshops, very interested, watching a long line of men at benches doing watch repairs. One of them told me that Army watches were of the highest standard, and I certainly would have liked one.

In the barrack room there was an underlying tension, everybody wondering if war would come. Judging by the conversation, most hoped that Neville Chamberlain's piece of paper and peace in our time was reliable. Yet newspapers predicted the opposite, and all the signs pointed to war being imminent, with air raid shelters being put into the parks, reservists coming in train loads, and the TA mustering in thousands. For myself, I had read a lot about Hitler's activities in taking other people's countries and I thought that someone somewhere would have to stop him, if I were to be involved, so be it. I had no one to worry about family-wise, unlike the reservists, who had wives and children.

I had a trip into Lichfield on the Saturday evening, and foolishly missed the last bus back so, cursing myself, I decided there was nothing for it but to walk back, having no money for a taxi. I knew that Sergeant Morgan was Guard Commander, which made me feel like a rat in a trap. Having walked about three miles, the headlights of an open sports car lit up the road. It pulled up and a young officer of the South Staffs smilingly told me to hop in and he would take me back to barracks. I explained about having missed the last bus, so he said he would drop me outside the gates, out of sight, then I must get in as best I could. His car clock showed 1.15 a.m., and I could just see Sergeant Morgan rubbing his hands in anticipation. The officer dropped me off, and I watched from the bushes for the sentry to move off on his beat. I had been on this guard, and gave him ten minutes to return, then the problem of the Orderly Officer, who could turn up at any moment occurred. The sentry went on his rounds so I quickly removed my boots, leaving them out of sight, then looked round the guardroom door and saw Sergeant Morgan sitting behind the table, facing me with his eyes shut. I tiptoed to the table and with my face close to his, my heart banging like a steam engine, I lifted the large heavy signing-in book and straining every nerve, turned it round, laying it on the table without knocking anything or making the slightest noise, and with a scratchy pen, signed myself in 11.59 p.m. Sergeant Morgan sat dozing and I lifted the book and turned it until it lay in its original position. The sentry hadn't returned, so tiptoeing out, I collected my boots and carrying them, slid through the bushes to avoid meeting either sentry or Orderly Officer, and safely made it to my barrack block. There, soaked in perspiration, I got into bed, contented that I had got one over on my enemy.

I knew from the rules that when the Orderly Officer turned out the guard, he would be told by Sergeant Morgan of anyone absent, when the book would be inspected and signed. He would report one man absent and I would be found, signed in, with the Orderly Officer possibly rebuking him, I hoped so. Just before morning parade, Sergeant Morgan approached me with his face aflame, and in a fury shouted at me that I would be reported and placed on defaulters for signing myself in the guardroom. I replied that if he did that, I would report him for sleeping on duty. He stared at me, wild-eyed and said, "You watch out you cockney bastard, because I'm going to get you," then walked off. He never did report me, he dare not, for it was a case of the biter bitten, but I did notice that he was a bit wary of me after that, probably wondering how I signed that book.

I put in for another weekend pass to see Gran, but I was too late, as they ceased to be issued forthwith. It was close to the end of August and we had steadily been building up to a war footing. Eight 3.7 guns, Brens replacing Lewis guns and with the Battery complement of men doubled, with new recruit intakes and reservists, it was a hard slog training them all from morning onwards. I worked hard, hoping for my second stripe but the average wait was two years, and in any case I was junior to other Lance-Bombardiers, so I had to be patient. Most men were busy writing letters to their families and I wrote to Gran, telling her that I wouldn't be able to visit her now, but I wished her well, knowing that I would not hear from her, as I hadn't up till now. That concluded my letter writing, as there was no one else I wanted to write to, particularly at Teddington!

Everything in regard to the Battery and the Regiment was in A1 order, though there was some last minute dashing around on small check-ups, mostly MT. 'Crasher' Carr drove his Scammell too close to a gun barrel, piercing the windscreen, so there were frantic attempts to get a replacement window. An amusing history of Crasher was that when sober, he knocked down road bollards, but slightly inebriated, he was a perfect driver. Sometimes, sitting in the back, there would be 'hairy' rides cutting corners, mounting roundabouts and watching the heavy gun swaying on the back. He was an old soldier and a jolly man, always in high spirits. Gunner Hills was another likeable character, a Londoner who, married with a large family, joined the Army to escape debts. He was an incurable comic, who would never let anything get him down, and was always scheming to find ways to meet his wife. He would say, with a wink, 'To get a bit of how's-yer-Father, in case it healed up." His meaning was clear.

One peculiar chap was one of the officers' batmen, a highly strung, very emotional man, who would easily break into tears. I think he had a problem. We had good officers and respected them. Lieutenant Long, a regular officer and very strict, Lieutenant Lister, who it was assumed to be the son of the small motor engine manufacturer, Lieutenant Barnes, a very down to earth man, who didn't beat about the bush, and Captain Page, a tall handsome man and a gentleman, all regular officers.

As war now seemed imminent, we younger elements were keyed up with the excitement of venturing into the unknown. Nearly everybody had someone in their family who had served in the Great War, so none of us would be going into it with blinkers on, should war come, but the possible consequences, I pushed to the back of my mind. All I wanted was to get overseas, anywhere. I received a postcard from Jack Wright with a photograph of the troop-ship he was on in the Mediterranean, saying it was as blue as it was made out to be. I also received a letter from another pal, Fred Harman, on the same ship, but I never heard from John. Fred added that they all missed me and wished that we were all together. Such is the meaning of comradeship.

CHAPTER TEN

The British Expeditionary Force

On the morning of 3rd September 1939, a parade was called and we were told to assemble close to the NAAFI, when an important announcement would be made by Neville Chamberlain at 11 a.m. on the radio. We all heard that England was now at war with Germany and everybody went mad, with hand shaking and back slapping all round, but some looked worried. There was an instant Confined to Barracks, so in the evening the NAAFI was packed out. We had a good sing-song, spending every penny we had on drink, knowing that being regulars, we would be the first in action. We were never to forget this day, with all exits well guarded. It bothered some of the men who had women in the town, especially Darkie, who said that his girl was 'up the spout'.

The next day on parade, the Colonel gave us a speech in which he exhorted us to remember our training and not to let our Regiment or country down, and that he was sure that every man would do his duty to King and Country, adding that within a few days every man would be issued with brown paper, string, and tie-on labels to parcel up all surplus clothing and personal belongings, addressed to our homes with any attaché cases, all to be sent free of charge. It was stated on Battery orders what we would be allowed to take with us, and this did not include riding dress, puttees and spurs, also peak cap; we wore the side hat instead. I was fortunate in having a large old attaché case, whereas some men were hunting around trying to buy one. I packed everything securely in the case and the parcel, locked and tied, but my problem was where to send them. If I sent them to Emmy she would sell the lot, and if I sent them to my mother, my father would do the same, so in the end I sent them to Rosina, hoping for the best.

I had quite an accumulation of items, many cap badges of other regiments, my book of written ballads and poems, quite a lot of small photographs given by friends, plus personal items like school testimonials and birth certificate, etc. When I returned in 1945, Rosina had the photos, school testimonials and birth certificate, but everything else, with my treasured book, my father had sold in the pubs, which made me very bitter.

We were to wear the service dress buttoned tunic and trousers. No battledress uniforms came our way, so with gas mask tied on the chest and anti-gas capes rolled and tied on to our backs, we looked more like Christmas trees. Our rifles had the sights trued up by the 'tiffies', with kitbags packed, we were issued with

80

haversack rations, a large wound dressing and a tin of emergency rations. We formed up and took a last look at Whittington barracks on the 11th September 1939. We marched off to war. TSM Nichols, who had a fine singing voice soon had the column singing 'Roll out the barrel' and 'We'll hang out the washing on the Siegfried Line', which had us marching in fine fettle on a hot sunny day to Lichfield Station. A whole station had been allocated to us, with Military Police on the platform seeing that every man boarded the train and didn't nip off to the other side. Many tried to get to a telephone, but were prevented from doing so. Once on the train and it moved off, most men went quiet, immersed in their own thoughts, but the inevitable packs of cards began to appear and games of solo soon had the chatter going. I sat idly watching the countryside flashing by, looking forward to whatever was to come. Up till then, it hadn't been announced where our destination was to be but it had to be France. For all the precautions that had been taken, I heard that two men had absconded and I wouldn't like to be in their shoes when they were caught. We were told that we would be known as the British Expeditionary Force, BEF for short, the same as in 1914. Fortunately I saw nothing of Sergeant Morgan, as all senior NCOs were doing other duties on the train, so I was left alone. That night, we arrived at Southampton and it was a new experience, embarking on a ship for the first time in my life and enjoying every minute of it.

With Military Police all over the place, we boarded the Channel ferry SS *Canterbury*. Tea, bully beef and bread was issued and it was pretty crowded below decks, with five units of Scottish regiments, four in kilts, one in trews plus some RAF personnel. Everyone seemed in a cheerful mood and such rivalries as existed between regiments were forgotten, but then, gunners seemed to get on well with everybody in general. As the ship ploughed through the sea, I couldn't resist staying on deck, watching the waves changing colour. The destroyers tearing back and forth had a beauty of their own, and it was comforting to know that we were so well protected. I had never taken much interest in the stars before, but now, in a clear night, I saw the sky filled with so many that I found it awe-inspiring.

On arrival at Cherbourg there was some confusion, as everybody was mixed up, moving to the gangways, bumping into each other, with orders being shouted all over the place whilst trying to sort out the various units. The Scots disembarked first, we followed them, the RAF last. We sorted ourselves out and formed up in columns of three. The Scots led with their pipes and drums and the column marched through the town of Cherbourg with crowds seemingly coming from nowhere, women waving and throwing flowers from windows. I think that my chest must have expanded at least three inches with a great feeling of exhilaration at marching through a town in a foreign country, my first sea trip, strange people and different smells in the air. We must have looked good to them too. One of my first impressions of France was of the dockers, in berets and corduroys, shouting and gesticulating to each other in their own language, which sounded very strange to me.

France — September 12th 1939

Somewhere in the town we broke off from the column and reached our destination, a convent, where the Battery had been allocated an empty wing with adjacent grounds, and before being dismissed, we were ordered to respect the request of the nuns for quiet and seclusion, and on no account to approach or speak to them. The floors handed over for our use were at the top and quite spacious, but thick with dust, accumulated through the years, together with loads of cobwebs. We selected a floor space at random, laying down our groundsheets on the dust, having found our kitbags already waiting for us. After sorting out our immediate necessities, we were issued with two blankets each and I realized how much a bed was missed.

During the several weeks of our stay, we had to clean the place up, and were almost choked to death by the thick fog of dust which we disturbed with the French besom brooms. The cooking staff had their problems too, but did us proud under the circumstances, with immediate bully beef sandwiches and tea until supplies arrived to prepare better meals, when the field kitchens, with stacks bellowing smoke all over the place, produced a hot meal of bully beef stew, and a greater variety was provided as time went by. As we now ate and drank from our own mess tins and mugs, there were no plates to wash, each man being self-contained.

On our first morning parade at the convent, we stood mostly with sore red faces, having washed and shaved in cold water, and some had bloody pieces of paper stuck on their faces, and we realized it was to be the rugged life from now on. We were told by our Battery Commander that he would now be leaving, and that Major Freer-Ash, standing beside him would be taking over command. Some wag immediately christened him 'Fag-ash' and when it was discovered that he was a Territorial officer, reservists were saying, among other things, "That's all we need, a Saturday night soldier!"

He inspected the parade and, with no thought of the filthy rooms which we hadn't had time to clean, would pass through the ranks saying, "Take that man's name and number," thus endearing himself to one and all. We were not allowed out for three days, and in the meantime we rearranged our floor spaces in a better way, with a decent path between to walk through. Trying to be quiet was impossible with our studded boots making a continuous clatter going up and down the flights of narrow wooden stairs, especially to the ancient lavatory. This consisted of a flagstone floor with two foot-shaped indents in it, on which to place one's feet whilst precariously balancing in a bent position with trousers down, trying not to miss the hole in the flagstone behind. This was so awkward for us, and apparently for the officers as well, that subsequently latrines were dug in the grounds for all, with hessian sheeted walls.

We were issued with our first tins of fifty cigarettes or pipe tobacco, which was to be a weekly issue whilst on active service. Foolishly, instead of selling them, I started to smoke for the first time in my life and became hooked, but was only a light smoker. On the third day, we were all getting restless and eager to see the town when a pay parade was called. No records had yet arrived, so a flat grant of 160 francs was given to every man, and this would be sorted out at a later date. We were to be allowed out from 4.30 p.m. until 10 p.m.

I could hardly wait, but once out, I found a different world and whichever café I went into, I found the assistant most helpful and honest, counting out my change and helping me to understand with the aid of many gestures. As I understood it the rate was eight francs to a shilling, which was a large sum when compared with the French soldiers' pittance, so with the cost of living so much lower in France, we were quite well off.

I enjoyed the food in the various cafés though missed the fish and chip shops at home. But the French soon cottoned on and eggs and chips were eventually available everywhere for the British soldiers at any time. I thought the French bread was very tasty. I enjoyed window shopping and noticed how cheap everything was compared with England, so I suppose it was all relative to earnings. As the night approached I found my way back to the convent and found a strong guard in evidence, so the Major meant what he said, all in or else. Men were still coming in at midnight, being let off on their excuse that they had lost their way on their first night out, but it was a different story when between our blankets on the floor, drunken reservists related their exotic experiences in the brothels in great detail. This went on all through the night, and at reveille some of the men were enraged to find their boots full of pee.

On the morning parade we all received a good dressing down from the Major over the noise and singing, which offended the nuns, and he ordered that everybody must now be back at 9 p.m., and anyone returning later would be charged and punished. Also silence and respect must be observed at all times. I agreed with him entirely, as the drunken singing, combined with the clatter of boots on the stairs all night must have been heard by the nuns. Senior NCOs only had torches and were unable to stop it and no officers showed themselves.

The Padre addressed the parade and said a few words on the subject of VD, aimed mainly at us younger soldiers, warning us of going with loose women on the streets and in the brothels, stating that it took the syphilis germs a minute to penetrate the sheath and without one we were doomed anyway, making it all sound rather frightening, though the reservists were muttering in the ranks, "Silly old so-and-so." That night the Padre was seen coming out of a brothel, so he must have put his trust in God too. We were all issued with a tube of cream, to be squeezed into the penis after any intercourse which might take place, for some protection against VD.

That morning, a side of cow was brought in and we thought we were in for a treat, only to have to bury it in the ground later, when it began to stink, so it was back to bully beef stew. I had another enjoyable day out looking round the town, eating and drinking and bumping into mates, eventually finding my way back to the convent in good time. There was a repeat performance of the previous night and as reservists formed the guard, they were letting late comers in so an officer stood by the gate to stop it. I had seen drunken soldiers in the town, some in kilts, but as yet no Military Police. 'South of the Border' and 'Mexicali Rose' had a good airing that night and I found it impossible to sleep. A concerted effort by officers and warrant-officers could have stopped it, but the next morning parade had the Major again in a fury, cutting the return time to 8 p.m.

I found the pavement urinals strange to get used to, with just a waist high trough and front cover. Being British soldiers the French public used to stare at us, which put me off somewhat. I saw things I would never have dreamed of, for instance, in a café a British soldier, served by a pretty girl, made some overtures to her, then holding her hand they disappeared upstairs to have what he asked for — 'jig-a-jig'.

The next morning on parade the Major went into a terrible rage, threatening field punishment to all late comers that night, and return time was reduced to 7 p.m., but being the third day, most men were broke so in the main, it was a quiet night.

Having heard so much about the brothels, I decided to see what they were like, so one afternoon I walked into one, called the 'Airoplane', shown in neon lights, and the place inside was about a quarter full. I bought a beer, and was charged an exorbitant price, when a girl whom I thought looked about sixteen, dressed only in a G-string and shoes, very pretty with long black hair, came over and sat on my lap. In a flash she quickly undid my flies and slipped her hand in, at the same time giving me a passionate kiss, all done with the speed of practice. I couldn't get up the stairs quickly enough, paying a fat 'Madam' at a table 10 francs and the 10 francs in the room on the corridor. It was over too quickly for me, the girl wanted it that way, a fast finish and out, so that day I had my first taste of what France had to offer. The girl was out to get as many clients as possible, and on my way out, I remembered the Padre and searched my pockets frantically, looking for my tiny tube of cream!

On arrival back at the convent I saw a taxi approaching with some reservists inside, standing on the footboards laughing and whooping it up, then they ran into the convent without paying the driver his fare. He was shouting and doing a French version of the Highland Fling, so one of the officers came out and had to pay him off to get rid of him.

As yet, our guns and vehicles had not arrived, so apart from general duties, turns at guard, tidying and cleaning, for which there were ample supplies of 'Janker Wallahs', we could get out after dinner and return for tea if we wished. Along with several others, I went bath hunting, with soap and towel, looking for cafés which obliged for a small payment. I kept thinking of the girl with the long black hair, so one night I returned to the 'Airoplane', but it was different this time. The place was packed solid with soldiers inside, almost to the doors, and the girls, of which there were many, were taking men up the stairs non-stop to the balcony, with 'Madam' collecting a small fortune. Along the balcony men were no sooner in the cubicles than they were out again, and as I did, moved to the end and down a staircase which led to the side alley outside. Then the girls on the balcony would open their legs and wipe themselves with a piece of rag, then throw it down amongst the cheering crowd below, who dived like a Rugby scrum to retrieve it. There was only one way in and it was as hot as an oven inside, and as I struggled and pushed, making my way out, I looked as a great cheer went up, and saw a big RE Sergeant carrying a young girl up the stairs. He had stopped half-way to maul her, much to the amusement of the crowd. I wondered if he had a daughter of that age, he was, I thought about 40. I was relieved to get back into the fresh air, and passing the alley there was a flow of urine running onto the pavement from soldiers who, on leaving the brothel, were peeing on the walls.

Nantes

Our few weeks passed quickly and the time came to leave the convent. We entrained to Nantes, a town I had never heard of and at the railway station, formed up in threes, the Major addressed us, saying that every man must fill his water-bottle, and that any man using his Emergency Rations could face possible court martial, as it was considered a serious crime. Once on our way, in wooden seated carriages, the talking point was about the great times we had had in Cherbourg. During a stop at a station, we found ourselves alongside a French troop train, and during the few minutes' halt there was much handshaking through the windows. Wine and cigarettes were exchanged and the weather being hot, the wine created a thirst, resulting in many empty water-bottles. I thought the French cigarettes were foul.

A whole day went by without any sign of food turning up, and as it only takes one to set the ball rolling, one man opened his Emergency Rations and ate it and soon it spread to others. I didn't touch mine and kept it safe on my person, as now some men were finding theirs stolen, presumably by those who had now eaten their own.

At the end of our journey, on arrival at Nantes, we were ordered by the Major to produce our Emergency Rations. He was furious to find that about 40 men had none, so later on some punishment was given, but not court martial. The Major had withheld food issue on purpose, as a test under possible future hard times to come.

My first impression of Nantes was of a town with cobble-stoned roads and streets, very old pretty style buildings, a tramway system and very attractive looking shops, so I instantly took a liking to it, and decided that my stay here was going to be an enjoyable one.

We were allocated a field on the edge of town, conveniently close to enjoy its amenities. I was also to find the people of Nantes very friendly indeed. Our guns and transport were waiting for us, but we were all ravenously hungry and thirsty and it took some time for the cooking staff to make enough bully beef sandwiches and tea, but fortunately an advance party had fixed up a lot of things, including tents, in preparation for our arrival. It was early

October, with the weather hot and dry so at daybreak, after makeshift washing with a cupful of water and a rough and ready breakfast, we all started to work, first marking out gun positions and Command Post, then getting the guns in their right places. Circular walls had to be built around each gun, with two entrances, plus a stepped wall lower down inside, on which to place the ammunition. There was a good supply of sandbags, timber and corrugated iron sheeting. Some of the men would be digging out a large dug-out by each gun, or would fill sandbags, whilst others would build the walls with them. Any hopes of being given quarters in the town were dashed, the dug-outs, 6 feet deep, were to be our sleeping area.

The hot weather and hard work soon had us stripped to the waist, eventually becoming well sun-tanned, with hardened muscles. The dug-outs, when completed, had sandbagged floors, roofs made from timber and iron sheeting, covered over with a layer of sandbags, and steps leading down, constructed with wood risers. It all looked rugged, but good, and we all felt that our hard work had been worth while. Many thousands of sandbags had been used and in the course of construction, we sang all the songs of the day. The officers had an extra large Command Post dug-out, also ammunition arrived in truck loads. This was placed in small dumps, protected with sandbagged walls around the gun position, with a hundred rounds laid on the stepped walls in the gun pits. All-important latrines were dug and made with warnings that any man caught urinating against the gun pit walls would be severely punished. So we were ready and with Predictor and Height and Range Finder ready, we had 'Take Posts' and everything was tried out and eventually made ready for action. Bren-guns on anti-aircraft mountings were set up in strategic places, so now it was the continuous gun drill each day and back to discipline, parades and strict guards.

The cook staff were by now well used to the field kitchens, and there was continuous smoke drifting over the gun positions. Lining up for our main meal, we always enjoyed the 'variety' of the food, such as bully beef stew, bully beef fritters and chips, bully beef salad, bully beef sandwiches and boiled eggs. The good strong tea was there and always welcome at any time. As all the cooking was done in the open, the area eventually became a greasy quagmire when it rained. Pilchards were plentiful, mostly for tea, but were not very popular owing to a 'tinny' taste, and we were having them far too often. We were all glad when we could go into the town for two eggs, chips, bread and butter, which every café supplied instantly. We certainly kept the chickens busy.

Our problem was water, which was brought in twice daily in towed trucks. Our ablutions, and trying to do some laundry was very restricted, causing grumbling amongst the men, when in the hot weather, a change of clothing was needed every other day. Bath squads took turns to the municipal baths, but not too frequently and no laundry arrangements were yet forthcoming.

The word Reservist was fading out now, with everybody being so used to each other as we all mucked in. For me, being an NCO became natural, but it wasn't my nature to toady up to anybody. I worked conscientiously and was prepared to be judged on that, but I found promotion slow in the Regular Army. This also applied to senior NCOs and warrant-officers, who had stayed as they were in Lichfield, yet wartime conditions had doubled the number of personnel in the Battery. The atmosphere between Sergeant Morgan and myself had not changed, he not wanting it to, so we said as little as possible and avoided each other as much as we could, but he did stop calling me names now. I guessed he would tire of it eventually. I noticed that he had few friends and whenever I saw him out, he was always alone.

A hurricane lamp was issued to each dug-out and for sleeping, each man laid his ground sheet down, but when it rained, we wore them to keep dry. It was a rugged life, and Lichfield was already just a memory.

I did write a letter to a pal, Fred Harman in Singapore. He had written to me saying what a wonderful place it was, but still wished he was with me in France. He included John Knott and Jack Wright. Just to tease him, I mentioned how becoming the French Mesdemoiselles were! I wrote nothing home and received nothing.

CHAPTER ELEVEN

A new home

I was relaxing in the hot sunshine on the gun position one day when a schoolboy came up to me and introduced himself as Emile, aged eleven; very polite, the French. With the help of my French-English dictionary I discovered that his mother was wanting to do the soldiers' laundry and would I let her do mine. I jumped at the chance and gave him a pile, so smiling happily he went off, saying two days. Some of the blokes watching said that's the last you'll see of them, which did give me a nagging doubt. In two days however, Emile returned with my clothes, beautifully washed and ironed, so I changed quickly and gave him another lot. He said the charge would be 10 francs, and when I shook my head, indicating no, he thought I wouldn't pay and became very excited. I calmed him down and painstakingly explained that so much laundry was worth more, harking back to the way my gran had slaved for pennies, so I gave him 20 francs, which I could well afford as I was hardly spending anything. I also found him some more customers, when he would bring a small cart. He rushed off with the 20 francs, and as I always had a slab of Cadbury's chocolate, obtained from the NAAFI, I gave him a large piece. He always called on his way home from school and we sat 'talking', via the dictionary, and at times he would become angry when I couldn't get some word right. Then I would laugh and soothe him down, yet he picked up English more easily than I did French. I found out that his papa had left home, that he also had some younger brothers and sisters, also an older sister.

One day be brought an invitation from his mother to pay a visit any evening that I could manage, so I told him to come each day until I could let him know, as I was a soldier 24 hours a day. He was a bright lad and quickly understood. The free evening arrived, so I spruced myself up and went with him. We had now been issued with battledress and gaiters so I looked quite smart. I had money in my pocket, some bars of chocolate and I asked Emile what wine his mother liked, and so armed with that we reached his front door. On the way Emile had pointed out some landmarks, so that I could find my way back.

On arriving at his home, a handsome woman of about 35, with a nice figure and an open smile welcomed me in and overwhelmed me somewhat by giving me a big hug and the best chair. I had made a good impression, but the barrier was the language. However, with my little dictionary I got by, causing lots of laughter. She fussed over me and when I gave the children the chocolate and her the wine, I almost became one of the family. She kept mentioning Annique, and it dawned on me that it was her daughter, expected home at any minute. The front door opened and my heart missed a beat when standing before me was a beautiful girl of 17 or 18. She had naturally rosy cheeks and lovely expressive eyes, jet black hair and was about five feet four inches tall. When her mother introduced us she was very shy, which made two of us, and I knew now why that little monkey Emile had asked me if I was married.

The evening went like a dream, and I could see that Annique liked me too, especially with the laughing that went on, trying to make each other understood. It was great fun and a real treat to be in a homely house again. I was hoping that this wasn't a one-off thing and that I would be invited again, as I had to come back to be with this lovely little family again, and also, 'Cupid' had struck me well and truly with his dart! I could think of nothing else but Annique's lovely face, with her enchanting ways and I relished every moment I was with her.

I was told to come whenever I had a free evening, and this caused my mates to ask me why I wasn't going out with them, but I kept quiet until one night Annique and I were in a café, when some of the lads walked in and stared at us. The next day I had to put up with a lot of ragging, and was told that I was a dark horse, and how did I find such a nice looking girl as that. It went the rounds and I was given many winks and nods, accompanied by such remarks as "You lucky bastard" among other things, all said with rough good humour. I would now go to the house, pull the door string and go straight in, and usually found Annique there.

One evening Emile came to the gun position saying that his papa was home, and told me not to come. Foolishly, hoping to make a good impression on my possible future father-in-law, I went and knocked on the door. A short tubby middle-aged man with a pointed beard opened the door and in broken English, gave me a torrent of abuse, saying that his children had told him about me and that if I didn't go away, he would send for the police and if I returned, he would report me to my Colonel. I tried to reason with him but he went into a frenzy, so I cursed myself for having inadvertently made things worse for Madame Le Budec, the children and Annique, so in frustration and anger I walked away, worried as to what might happen to them.

I made my way to a known café and squeezed in with two mates near the door, as the place was packed out. I had some drinks to relieve my feelings when in came Sergeant Morgan, swaying a bit with his usual nasty expression. Looking around the café he spotted me and coming over he snarled at me, "Get off that seat, you cockney bastard."

I replied, "Bugger off," when he made a grab at me. He shouldn't have done that because quick as a flash, I snatched a thumb and wrenched it right back. I had learned a thing or two in Hoxton. In a second he was flat on his back, looking up at me.

Jumping up and holding his hand he said, "I'll now have that stripe off you in the morning."

Not taking my eyes off him I said, "I have two witnesses here, and if I lose one stripe I'll make sure you lose three." He stared wildly at me and left, but never again did he insult me or try to provoke trouble. His thumb was bandaged for a week and I'm convinced that he thought I knew Judo, which I didn't.

Two days passed, which dragged for me, then Emile appeared, saying that papa had gone and that Annique had been locked in her bedroom for two days, could I come round tonight, which fortunately I was able to do. The mother, poor woman, was in a terrible state, covered in bruises where she had been knocked about, and with tears running down her face and with no thought of modesty she lifted her dress, showing me the insides of her thighs, where she was black and blue with bruises. I comforted her as best I could and she put her arms round my neck, very upset. I was thinking, give me five minutes with that coward and I would injure him for life. I sent Emile to buy a bottle of cognac and persuaded her to have a good drink to try to bring back that lovely smile she had. It didn't, but it did stop the tears.

Annique had been refused food and drink for two days, locked in her bedroom, which also meant the loss of two days' wages, bringing more hardship on the family, as the father had never sent a penny, although he worked at the Renault factory, near Paris. I knew that Annique was earning 70 francs in wages, so I gave the mother some money to bridge her loss, and I noticed the look of relief on her face. Annique came in from work, looking very pale, with dark shadows under her eyes, so I decided that a night out with a meal would buck her up. I conserved all my pay solely to be with Annique and her family, and as everything was so cheap, I didn't do too badly. In the café, the sparkle came back into her eyes, helped by some glasses of wine, then on the radio in the café there was played that popular beautiful song *J'attendrai* and holding my hand, she softly sang it.

The war situation being very quiet made no difference to the Battery, as it was all go, with continuous training and extra guards placed on vulnerable spots around the gun position so as to keep out civilians, also meaning Emile, but I always had an eye open for him. All of this meant less time to see Annique. Contractors now did the men's laundry, but Mme Le Budec still did mine and that of some friends. A lot of the men's laundry was being returned mixed up, although every item was numbered. As I was taking charge of guard duties three times a week, with no time off for sleep, it reduced my visiting Annique to once and sometimes twice a week, so we made the most of our time together. Although I was foreign, Annique's mother couldn't have treated her own son better than she treated me, and there was affection both ways. I had never known a loving family before, and had it been in my power, I would have done anything for them, in return for the kindness they showed me. I never went there empty handed, and the children looked for it.

We now had a new CO, an India time-served soldier, and he arranged a courtesy visit on an exchange basis with a French AA battery. We were warmly welcomed and they put up a good show, with guns on high mountings, using live ammunition, but it seemed to me that once started, with cries of 'allez-oop' the guns fired fast as they could, reminding me of the First World War. When the French battery visited us, we had a biplane towing a sleeve and our guests saw some good shooting, bracketing the sleeve with four exploding rounds in a small square. Four guns were on view, and four used in action, so our French comrades had a good day. As the French were renowned for being artillery experts, I felt sure that closer to the front, they had more modern guns.

To break the monotonous routine, route marches were organized, passing beautiful vineyards and countryside, with an occasional rest at a café, enjoying a cool beer, done at the discretion of Lieutenant Long, who was a good officer and liked by all. Those were happy days, with thoughts of war a long way off, and on bath days, in shirt sleeve order, towel and soap at the ready, we would march through the town, trying hard not to slide over on the cobbled roads in our studded boots.

One day, with no warning whatever, typical of the Army, we had to pack up and move, limber up the guns, and load thousands of rounds. We were told that a TA Battery from England was taking over. This information stirred it up amongst some of the men, grousing, "Why can't the bloody TA build their own gun positions?" Fortunately we didn't move too far, only to the other side of Nantes, nearer to the sea, but in order to let Annique know where we were and to see her whenever I could meant crossing the whole town. No one was allowed out until the new gun position was made operational, with the same hard graft as before, but our hearts weren't in it, thinking that we were just sweating our guts out for softees coming from England to take over ready made. I was aching with frustration and desire to see Annique. I also missed seeing Emile, always hoping to see his face pop up unexpectedly with a message.

One morning a Sergeant came around the guns shouting, "Who is Guillaume and Annique?" I called out and he told me that there was a woman crying at the entrance and asking for me. Of course this attracted attention and when I saw that it was Annique's mother, she ran and flung her arms around me, saying that Annique was crying herself to sleep every night for 'her William'. I had an unwanted audience watching this. I made her understand that I had no control over Army moves, so I couldn't let her know, and that I was upset too. She explained as best she could the tram routes and I told her that as soon as I was able, I would come along, then looking happier, she smothered me in kisses and went, waving goodbye. By now everyone had gathered round, watching this, resulting in many ribald comments such as, "You're not satisfied with stuffing the daughter, you're doing the mother as well!" And, "What have you got that I haven't got?" and many more unprintable from rough soldiery, but really harmless, so I took it all in good part, I had to, with quite an unsavoury reputation.

Seeing that Mum had now stirred up the fire inside me, I had to see

Annique, so I made a duty swop to get out earlier — some pals had sympathy with my situation, having seen Annique and myself together, and so, as the time arrived, I wished that I had wings, but the journey was easy enough but time consuming. At the door, I knocked in case the father was back, but what a welcome I got from Mum, she certainly liked me, but I couldn't see that I was anybody special. The reception I received brought tears to my eyes; anyone would have thought that I was a long lost son returning. I had brought some bottles with me to celebrate, so we all stayed at home and when the family went to bed, Annique and myself forgot time, until I realized that I had a long journey. After leaving, I found that the trams had stopped running so I made a fast walk, following the tram lines, and not knowing the name of the gun position, couldn't get a taxi. Resigned to it, I just plodded on, when along the deserted road a 15 cwt. truck roared up to a halt, and what a relief it was to see a mate of mine, Driver Ted Malham. He said, "Hop in Bill, I've been looking for you everywhere," then he drove off at top speed. He knew about Annique and myself, also about Sergeant Morgan, so on a flimsy excuse, he drove the truck out and found me. This is the true meaning of comradeship. On arriving back, I hid down, and when Ted signed himself in on the clipboard, he ticked me off as well. I thanked him for being such a pal when I needed one most, but he said to keep my mind on the time, as well as other things. Instead of dug-outs, we had tents, so I went to sleep contented, feeling that all's well that ends well.

One morning Captain Page came and asked me if I could use a typewriter. I told him that I had never touched one, but that I would give it a try. He said that BEF leave had started, and he needed an extra hand in the battery office and stores, so he would give me a day in which to learn to type. I was given a room in the stores house with a table, chair, typewriter and a stack of paper. I tried the whole day, using up masses of paper and ending up with eye strain and a splitting headache. I felt that given time, I could master it, but not in one day. The Captain was clearly disappointed but he was asking too much, so I was put into the stores, which I was not happy about at the time. But it turned out to be advantageous, in as much as I could see Annique every night, being free of other duties. But how stupid and unthinking it was of me not to have written down her address! My mind was so totally on her that it never occurred to me to write the address down, which was to bring so much heartache later on. Love is truly blind, I'm afraid.

I soon got into the routine of stores work, most of it handling dockets and indents for feeding and clothing a battery of roughly 350 men, and also keeping a stock of replacement issue, for nothing new was issued without first receiving the old worn article. I soon found out why the meat issue on the gun positions was so small. Every night we were cooking the best cuts for ourselves, pork chops with kidneys, lamb chops and steaks, then the officers and their portions, with the remainder distributed to the gun position. We ate any amount of tinned fruit and puddings laced with tinned milk. We were living like fighting cocks but I was a 'new boy' and the old hands would not let me touch anything, so it wasn't possible to muscle in, but just share the good living. Our beds were piles of spare blankets.

It was the good life, but I put a spanner in the works later on, because I forgot the old adage, 'if you can't beat them, join them.' An invitation arrived from Battery HQ for us to attend a party given in the town. The Stores Sergeant said, "I've put your name down, Annique." He would persist in calling me that. However, in order to 'muck in' I said I would go. The function was in a small dance hall, so a good evening was had until, whilst dancing with a French girl, I saw the floor come up and hit me. When I came round on my pile of blankets next morning, I felt ill and faced an irate BQMS and Sergeant, who had carried me back. The drinks had been lavish at the dance but I only ever drank beer and I was convinced that someone had laced my drink with a delayed action 'time bomb'. When Annique saw me that night, she remarked how pale I looked, so I told her that I had a cold.

Now for my 'spanner in the works'. I was shifting a pile of blankets when, underneath, I came across a mail bag half full of issue tins of cigarettes and tobacco, which looked suspicious, as all tobacco issue was kept under strict lock and key, under the control of an officer. I knew that this was a fiddle, a private hoard, and instead of leaving well alone, I thought that although two wrongs don't make a right, what's wrong in relieving the thief of some of his ill-gotten gains. In the course of time, in taking tins for my pals, whom I met in the cafés and smoking myself, the contents of the bag dwindled to about half, when one day the Battery Quartermaster Sergeant came to me and said, "A bag of cigarettes are underneath those blankets, have you taken any?"

"Just a few," I replied.

Then angrily he said, "Half the bloody tins have gone, on my BEF leave I could have made a packet selling them," so he went and the next day so did I — back to the guns! I found out the fiddle before I left. With a constant coming and going of men, if one left, he would be told, "Get your cigarette issue at your next unit," and then they would keep his tin. When a new man arrived he would be told, "You should have been issued with your cigarettes before you left," then keep his issue also, so the mail bag was slowly filling up, and I was glad that I did what I did. He must have told Captain Page that I wasn't required any more, rather than risk complaining about me, because Captain Page, being a fair man, would ask me questions and he couldn't risk being shopped and court-martialled. I lost out on my frequent trips to Annique, that was the bit that hurt. However, I had made a mistake and had punished myself by it. Anyway, I really enjoyed the rugged life outdoors on the guns.

A short time after my return to the guns, a rota had been worked out whereby a day off was granted, but it worked differently with NCOs, much depending on requirements. A chap with whom I was friendly, a Militiaman, 6 months married before leaving England and a Salvationist, who was a country chap of 21 years of age and very likeable asked me if I had ever been duck shooting. I told him the only ducks I saw in Hoxton were in the butchers' shop windows. However, he was to borrow a sports rifle from a farmer and having a day off next day, his plan was to go out onto the breakwater and shoot ducks. I already knew that my day off coincided, so I agreed to join him on his shoot. At the last moment, TSM Crotty came to me and told me to forego my day off, as I was needed for duty, so my friend went alone to the duck shoot. It turned out that he was at the far end of the breakwater and a sudden squall blew up and washed him into the sea, where he drowned. His body was found on the beach, where with myself as one of the party, we collected him on a handcart. He was covered with a ground sheet, and an ambulance took him away. He looked pretty grim, with staring eyes and his fingers dug into his throat. It was an upsetting sight and I realized that by a stroke of fate, I missed being with him in the tragedy.

The Major came to the gun position, bringing with him drums of khaki paint to repaint the guns, as the Brigadier of Ack-Ack would be paying us a visit the next day. With paint brushes working overtime, the job was completed, not without some competitive spirit amongst us all, so hunting around I came across a can of black paint and did my gun in camouflage, making it smarter than the others, my 'artistic talent' coming to the fore. The next day, with everybody on their toes, Brigadier's inspection took place, also a demonstration, which satisfied him and his staff.

He then gave the usual complimentary speech, with the Colonel present, crowding round my gun and having a discussion. As they moved off a long streak of black paint showed across the back of the Brigadier's service jacket, and on being told of it, he became angry and went off in a huff. The Colonel ticked off the Major, who angrily tried to find out who used the black paint. Everybody stayed silent, including Sergeant Morgan. If he had shopped me, I would have sworn blind that he had ordered me to do it. The paint, I found out, was bitumastic, which stayed tacky and was used in sealing leaks.

The weather was turning to rain now, being late autumn, but it was still warm enough to enjoy, and as pressures built up, on top of three night guards, I found that I had to do a turn on sentry as well. At this time there appeared to be lots of men coming and going. Robinson, who had broken his leg returned to the Battery. It was slightly bowed and he had a slight limp, as it was a bit short, but he was glad to be back and I was glad to see him, he was a nice bloke.

An incident happened one night, which could have been serious. Orders were that when on guard duty at night and anything suspicious was seen, a challenge of 'Halt, who goes there' was to be made three times. Now of late there had been in the early hours incidents of odd officers springing out of bushes at the sentry, who would then be ticked off for not being alert enough. This caused some anger amongst the men, some saying much more of this and they would fire into the bushes to 'Put the shits up them'. Well it almost happened. A Scot on sentry heard a noise in a bush and he fired a round into it, whereby an officer jumped up complaining that the round had missed his head by an inch. When Jock was being told off he warned the officer that anybody who deliberately crept around in the bushes at night deserved to be shot, thus getting himself into hot water. The night I was doing sentry I saw a shadow flit by the officers' area, so I challenged and fired high, whereupon an officer appeared in his pyjamas, asking very curtly, "Did you challenge three times Bombardier?"

I replied that I had, even though I hadn't, adding, "With respect sir, I suggest that next time, you show yourself clearly." He glared and walked away. It had made everyone nervous, this leaping out from behind a gun or a bush and me firing a round caused a turn out. Captain Barnes congratulated me on my alertness, not knowing that a brother officer was involved. It was obvious that someone sooner or later would be hurt, so the night-time leaping about tapered off.

I had a narrow escape one night, when returning from an evening out I heard the sentry's challenge and a round whizzed over my head, and on another occasion one of the cook staff was shot in the thigh.

I was detailed to take charge of two Vickers pom-poms, situated on a cliff top overlooking the harbour in Nantes. It showed the very strongly built breakwater, where my friend had been swept from and drowned. I was given three men, making two per gun for a temporary period only, to protect a flight of three French seaplanes anchored in the harbour below, should they come under attack. Each of us was to take a turn at sentry duty. When we arrived a gale force wind was blowing and the two tents already there looked like being blown away, so we immediately tightened the ropes and banked up the earth on the pegs to weight them down. We had brought hurricane lamps, containers of water, bully beef and bread with a small stove to make tea, to last us two days. TSM Nicholls, who took us there (and it was a very steep stumbling climb to the top) asked if I knew anything about the guns, and when I said that I did not, he replied, "That makes two of us." Together we examined one, found the safety catch and the working of the gun, with us going through a silent action and the other men looking on. When he was satisfied, TSM Nicholls on leaving told us to look out for the visiting Orderly Officer that night. Refixing the gun cover, we sorted ourselves out, and for warmth, stayed in one tent. But the wind howled its way through every crevice and by nightfall torrential rain fell, so after making sure that the guns were securely covered, we sorted out sentry rota. In this vile weather, it was as well that we all did a spell. I marvelled at the effort taken to bring guns fixed to a heavy naval mounting and the railway sleepers they rested on, up the steep slope, a superhuman effort.

The wind became ferocious, doing its utmost to sweep guns and tents over the cliff, which meant banking great piles of earth on the pegs and round the bottom of the tents, trying to keep the wind out. On sentry duty, it was best to crouch in whatever space one could by the guns, for fear of being lifted over the cliff edge. In the early hours I told the sentry that he must be alert in case of an Orderly Officer visit, he no doubt thinking that on a night like this, we would be tucked up in our tent.

I had a call from the sentry saying that he felt certain he could hear stones falling down the slope, but could see nothing. I took his rifle and half cocked the bolt, so no round could enter the chamber. I told him where to stand, obscured by a gun, and if the officer appeared, to jump out, banging the bolt and shouting, "Halt, who goes there?" I would be close by. We looked like two ghosts in steel helmets and dripping ground sheets. Then I heard, "Halt, who goes there?" and the rifle bolt banged home. Standing with the sentry, I saw a young 2nd Lieutenant with his own torch shining on his face, round eyed and shouting, "Don't shoot, Orderly Officer." This is what I wanted; if they liked playing silly buggers, so did we.

He looked quite shaken when he took the sentry's rifle and slowly drew the bolt, but no round came out. He remarked, "Strange, Bombardier, the rifle wasn't loaded!" then after a brief formality, he returned down, using his torch. By morning the weather improved, with the rain easing off, so we knew that the guns would need a going over, then I heard a plane's engines revving up. Looking down at the three seaplanes, I noticed a large bomb slung beneath each one as they taxied forward at speed to clear the water, going flat out towards the curved breakwater. The two outside planes cleared it but the middle one hit it with a terrific explosion, showering wreckage everywhere on the water. The other two planes flew on their mission and in my mind's eye I could picture the pilot desperately trying to lift that plane over the wall.

The day passed by and was very boring, being isolated up there and thinking of Annique waiting for the knock on the door that never came. It seemed to me that women had a permanent cross to bear, they always seemed to be waiting for someone. Evening came, a dry one although still windy, and I warned the sentries to be vigilant during the night, with no touching the rifle bolts this time. It turned out that there was no need, as around midnight, a car pulled up noisily on the road below, headlights full on and after loud door slamming, the Orderly Officer climbed the slope with torch on and whistling loudly. He paid his visit and left as breezily as he had arrived. When morning came, I handed over to the new unit and when our truck came, we thankfully returned to the Battery, feeling the need for some sleep, which wasn't forthcoming.

Getting to see Annique was becoming more difficult, with pressure of duties such as Battery Orderly, taking charge of fatigue parties, gun drill and guard duties, plus the extras thrust upon me, such as the harbour one. But any hopes I did have of seeing Annique were soon dashed, when RSM Quarterly sent for me. He had another job for me, in his words, "It's a job I didn't want, as I've enough on my plate, but it has got to be done," adding that he wanted a no-nonsense NCO. The BEF leave depleted units of roughly 10% of their strength, creating the situation of all units sharing duties such as the harbour pom-poms. This one was no different in that respect, but there were other reasons, as I was to find out. He told me that a 15 cwt. truck would take me, a three man guard, armed with ten rounds per man and rations for one night only. We were to follow his car to an RASC vehicle park, where we would do a night guard, which was being supplied by all the surrounding units within a ten mile radius, and it was now our turn. After a run of about 8 miles, we arrived at the vehicle park, where about 200 vehicles of every description were assembled, having its own petrol supply pumps.

It was a Northern Ireland RASC unit, billeted in a converted factory, with rows of roughly constructed bunks inside, for sleeping. The RSM took me into a room and commented that this 'shower' had been causing a lot of trouble and they couldn't be trusted to guard their own vehicles. I was given my orders, to have one man patrolling, albeit there were comings and goings all the time, but I was to keep a sharp look-out for drunken behaviour and where possible, to contain it as reports had been coming in of drunken driving. There would be two men resting, one on sentry spread through the night. I had a makeshift guardroom, sited in a corner close to the entrance, and I was to take orders from no one, and that he was Orderly Officer until the next day. He would look in during the night, and I was to take no nonsense from anyone, and if I found myself in a tight corner, I knew what to do. After handing me some charge sheets his last comment was, "Is that clear Bombardier?" Then he left. His orders, attitude and the charge sheets made it sound a bit ominous, but he was such a strict man, I wondered if I was in for a hard night.

We settled down in our allotted corner, with a small table and two makeshift beds and at about 6 p.m. I posted one sentry outside for his two hour stint, with orders to report any signs of serious disturbance. Tired as I was, there would be no sleep for me this night. It was now about 8 p.m., so with sandwiches and hot tea, it was time for the sentry to have his when I warned the three men to be alert in case of trouble, to carry out orders and to sign charge sheets, should it be found necessary.

Nothing out of the ordinary was happening, except there was quite a lot of rowdiness, which I thought would quieten down later as the men slept it off. There also appeared to be between two to three hundred drivers there and I hoped for a trouble free night. I made notes of each sentry's comments in the book, also that men were coming in shouting, rolling drunk and making quite a racket. I felt vulnerable, but they ignored us, so until fighting actually took place, or damage was done, I left well alone. The ones who were trying to sleep were shouting and swearing as well, so I saw why the RSM called them a 'shower'; with nobody to enforce discipline, they were just a rabble.

In the early hours there was a roar of rage in the doorway, and in came RSM Quarterly, brushing himself down. He had tripped over an unconscious drunken driver in the pitch darkness outside. Two of the guard carried him in, with the RSM looking around in a temper at the racket going on. He told me that on no account was I to let the prisoner go, to take his pay book and fill in a charge sheet, concluding that he would return at 6 a.m.

Just after he left, a Lance-Corporal came over to me and said that he and his friends would carry the prisoner to his bunk. I told him to go away, as the driver was under arrest and that he stayed where he was, on the orders of the Orderly Officer. He became very abusive and threatening, so I warned him to go away, which he refused to do, so I relieved him of his pay book and told him that he was now under open arrest, then away he went. I then filled in the second charge sheet, stating all that he had said, plus his abusive manner, unbecoming to an NCO, challenging the authority of the Guard Commander (myself), signed by myself and two members of the guard. I now knew that I was in for a rough night when the Lance-Corporal returned with a Corporal, and there was a repeat performance. I stood my ground, warning him of his responsibilities and told him to go away, but when he resorted to threats of violence, I ordered one of my guard to load his rifle and stand in the 'on guard' position. Then I placed him under arrest, charging him for using abusive language with threats of violence, and demanding that I hand over my prisoner, who thankfully was snoring away. I took the Corporal's pay book (AB64) and with a lot of mouth from the pair of them, filled in the charge sheet meticulously, recording all that was said and done, and placed the three pay books securely in my pocket. I also told the two relief guards to keep their rifles loaded, just in case. I took it for granted that the RASC would be armed, being soldiers first and drivers second, the same as anyone else in the British Army.

It was not over, for the two NCOs returned with a Sergeant, who ranted and shouted, using his rank to bully me into releasing my prisoner. I ordered my two men to hold rifles at the port, safety catches off, because now the rabble turned their attention on me, shouting abuse, and various things were thrown in my direction. I then told the Sergeant that I was only answerable to the Orderly Officer, that I now placed him under open arrest and charged him with conspiracy with two other NCOs, already under arrest, to incite trouble and relieved him of his pay book. Ashen faced, he gave it up meekly, the steam having gone out of him. I then warned him to go away, as he was in enough trouble already. Filling in his charge sheet looked frightening, and I wouldn't have been in his shoes for anything. So there it was, four AB64s and four charge sheets filled in with all details of names, ranks and numbers recorded on each, duly witnessed and signed by myself and two men.

I saw many faces staring in my direction, with no let up of the shouting and abuse, so I told my two men no sleep, keep rifles loaded, safety catches on, my own as well, all written down in the guard incident book, as I had to be accountable for my actions too. I personally thought that it wouldn't take much for some of the drunks to storm us, but time was passing quickly and when sentries changed, I told the one going out to stay close to the entrance, in case I needed him.

Promptly at 6 a.m. in came the RSM, who received shouts and catcalls, which infuriated him. We moved our gear outside then in the small room, he said to me, "What have you got to report, Bombardier?" I gave him the four pay books and charge sheets. Quietly he read them through, also the incident book, then looking up he said, "You've had a busy night, did you place them under arrest, as stated in the charge sheets?" I replied that I had and that the guard could verify it. He said, "Very well done Bombardier, very well done, now I will sort this shower out. It won't be necessary for you to appear at the Court Martial, as all charges have been witnessed and signed satisfactorily." Then the bombshell dropped, when he told me that during the night the Battery had packed up and moved, but mine and the guard's kit was packed in the rear party truck and he had left instructions that food and tea would be waiting for us on our arrival back.

I went outside to see the four men under arrest. They were looking very forlorn, not like the mouthy cocky lot they were in the night. They were waiting for the Military Police van for which the RSM had sent, to take them into custody. My head ached, crying out for sleep, this being the third sleepless night, and the worry of having no way of contacting Annique made it seem worse. I cursed myself continuously for my stupidity in not writing down her address, and I guessed she would be worried too, as well as her mum. There seemed no way that I could let her know and some wild thoughts were racing through my head like dodging the rear party and going to the house. I knew the consequences if I did, whatever the reason, desertion on active service, no, I couldn't do that, and I sank into a mood of deep despair. The faintest hope I might have was if the rear party drove through Nantes, giving me a chance perhaps to go to the house and write down the address.

On arrival at the now deserted gun position, the RSM was as good as his word. Boiled eggs, sandwiches and hot tea awaited us, and the rear party consisted of two lorries, a three-tonner, 30 cwt. and a 15 cwt. truck. The BQMS was in charge, and my heart sank, knowing that I would get no help from him. I was surely reaping my 'reward' now and he was in the 15 cwt., which might have nipped off with me in it. Charlesworth, a mate of mine was the despatch rider (Don-R) but he was to lead the way, with his maps, and I also learned that we were to go on our journey away from the town anyway, a driver saying that our destination was Arras, he thought about 300 miles away. We all have to pay for our mistakes and this was one of them, and because of it, a girl's heart would be breaking, a girl who, as it turned out, I was never to see again, but could never forget.

We set off immediately, with two drivers to each lorry, with the four of us squeezing in where we could. I thought that the 30 cwt. was overloaded, but curled up I was soon asleep, our first stop being Abbeville, then by dark, after the Don-R making an error, we passed through Amiens to make a detour and stop for the night at Rouen, where we parked at a transit camp controlled by Military Police. I wandered around and saw the cathedral and had a few drinks, feeling terribly sorry for myself, lonely and missing Annique so much that it hurt. I had some much needed sleep in the billet and in the morning luckily having my small kit from the guard duty, had a wash and shave. A meal was obtainable there, and we went on our way again, but after an hour's travelling, the 30 cwt. lost power, with the engine knocking and it was thought that the big end had gone. With much rearrangement, we crammed as much as we could into the three-tonner, which then went on its way to Arras with the 15 cwt. The Don-R would stay with us whilst we moved along at 15 m.p.h. and he scoured around, looking for an Army Depot to get the 30 cwt. in for repair. He found a vehicle depot where on arrival we spent some hours while mechanics worked on the engine, the verdict being that the small end had gone. Somehow it was made sufficiently able to get us to Arras and no faster than 25 m.p.h. so, well stocked with fuel, off we went, with instructions to hand in the lorry for major overhaul. On arrival we were situated at Tilloy, a village south of Arras. The Battery split into two troops, one going to another spot a few miles away and my troop of 4 guns sited at Tilloy, with Lieutenants Barnes, Long and Lister, and TSM Crotty in charge.

The average British soldier as I saw it, had adjusted well to the French people, and they had accepted us with good humour and kindness. They got on well because of their happy faces and willingness to join in anything going on, such as learning to sing songs in French in the cafés, with the locals ending up rolling with laughter at our terrible efforts. We always enjoyed drinking with them. One thing that caught on was the French custom of café-rhum, and from our first trips into the cafés, we soon got hooked on it, and it became standard practice on entering a café to order café-rhum, then beer and a meal. Coffee with sugar would be simmered in a tiny pan, then the rum tipped in and poured into a glass. It was delicious.

CHAPTER TWELVE

Tilloy — Arras, 1939

It was now November and although the nights were cold, the days tended to be warmer when the sun shone. Our gun position, situated south-east of Arras, turned out to be very interesting. We lay just off a road in a large field, where at a prominent corner was a Scottish cairn stone memorial, about 10 feet high. It was fenced in, with a bronze plaque on the face of the stonework, bearing the words (as far as I can remember) 'This ?th Battalion of the Black Watch had held the line, repelling repeated attacks at great sacrifice in 1916, thereby preventing a breakthrough by the German Army.'

The guns were placed in front of a copse of dead trees which were bare skeletons with long slithers of rusting steel from exploded shells protruding from the boughs and trunks. Looking at these, I thought what a dreadful time the soldiers must have had then, yet they stuck it out to hold the line. Bravery seems such an inadequate word to describe such action.

No time was lost, and with urgency, as winter was not far off, we all worked with a will, setting the guns and Command Post in position. As in Nantes, dug-outs and sandbag walls were built, and with timber, and corrugated sheeting we were pushed to the limit. In digging, almost every spadeful of earth revealed something, rifle rounds by the dozen, buckles from equipment, a well-preserved Army boot, many bones and a jaw bone. A hole was dug a distance away for bones to be dropped in, and when our work was completed, the hole was filled in. Many dud shells were dug up, and this was a hazard because of the risk of a spade hitting one on the nose cap and exploding it. So many were recovered that a dump of them was laid well away from the gun position and eventually an RAOC lorry took them away under an escort, showing red flags.

Some idiot lit a fire and placed a dud shell on it, which exploded, sending shrapnel whizzing all over the place. Fortunately no injury or damage was done, but with 4,500 shells on the site, it might have been a different story. The officers were very angry, and couldn't find the culprit, but it was made clear that anyone trying to do the same thing again would certainly be court-martialled. In a spare moment I wandered over to the copse for a closer look, when my toe struck a protruding iron box, so returning later with a spade I dug the box out, to find it half full of Mills bombs. I looked at one, seeing it stamped 1916 and primed. I thought that if I showed this lot I would be in trouble for

101

digging it up anyway, and there were some fools who would take one home on their BEF leave as a souvenir. The brass parts on the grenades were green, otherwise they were in perfect condition, so to speed up deterioration, I dug a deep hole and filled the box with earth, then buried it with the lid half open. After what had been dug up I realized that we had disturbed a field of the fallen, hallowed ground in fact, and the memorial had said it all.

With all construction work completed, we settled down to routine gun drill, guard duties and some Bren-gun practice. We also had one Boyes anti-tank rifle, reckoned to pierce with its solid round 1½ inches of armour at 350 yards and 1 inch of armour at 500 yards. On entering the tank, the round would spin inside, killing the occupants.

The field kitchens relied on wood for fuel, so parties were sent out forever foraging for wood, chopping down some dead trees, etc. The smoke given off by the field kitchens sometimes became a fog over the guns, but complaining couldn't change the direction of the wind. We always had a wood smoke taste in our tea, and an oily flavour in the stew.

Just off the gun position were the remains of a small house. Three brand new Humber staff cars had just been delivered. I happened to be passing at the time and I saw TSM Crotty with Lieutenant Long standing by the cars, admiring them, when Crotty asked the Lieutenant if he might try one out. With the officer's consent he got behind the wheel, but on pressing the starter, the car shot forward and smashed into the wall, folding the front of the car in. The Sergeant-Major jumped out, red faced, so I shot off quickly, hoping that he hadn't noticed me. Another surprise regarding TSM Crotty was that one morning he sported a black eye and naturally everyone was bursting to find out how it happened. The story came out via the Mess steward, that an argument had broken out when Crotty made the remark that all married women were legalized prostitutes. A Staff Sergeant thumped him, saying, "My wife is no prostitute." So for all his years in the Army, Crotty could still put his foot in it.

The weather now broke, with rain teeming down, nobody escaping the discomfort, but I think the cook staff really had the worst of it in the open, cooking on the smelly field kitchens, especially trying to burn wet wood, resulting in the clinging smell of smoke everywhere. I began to have a taste of conditions of the First World War; mud everywhere, getting worse by the hour, cold and wet at night, we daren't take our clothes off, so we kipped down on the dug-out floors, carrying mud with us, lying in our greatcoats and using our kitbags as pillows. A lot of repair work was needed, cutting water drainage in the areas of the dug-outs, reinforcing the clay steps with wood, which had begun to deteriorate. Our boots were almost double their size, with gooey sticky mud, that looked like black porridge as we squelched about.

Our regular diet now was bully beef stew, tinned fruit or prunes laced with evaporated milk, bread and cheese, jam and pilchards, but the mainstay was always the scalding hot tea. Life had to go on in the Battery, whatever the conditions, which meant slipping and sliding on the metalwork on the guns, reminding me of Robinson. The increased weight on one dug-out roof caused a collapse, resulting in one man receiving a broken pelvis. Men were getting fed up with the miserable life on the gun site, forever cleaning and oiling the guns, protecting ammunition from wet and damp; it was a never-ending job, with everyone grousing all the time, the main topic being when would their turn come for BEF leave and hoping it would be Christmas.

One night there was a set to with Gunner Turner who was on sentry in the early hours shouting like a madman, causing everyone to turn out, wondering what was up. It turned out that Turner swore that he saw a group of kilted soldiers coming out of the mist, muddy and bloody, with bandages on them and led by a piper who passed him then disappeared into the mist again. He seemed very shaken and nothing would induce him to do a guard at night again. I must admit that I felt a sense of foreboding about the place and at night I felt ill at ease.

Washing oneself was a problem because of water rationing. An allowance was issued in gun buckets, metal and canvas, to every five men. Lots were drawn for first wash on to the fifth and so as to have a warm shave, we all developed the habit of using the last of our tea. The water was brought up twice a day in towed carriers and hot baths were laid on at the municipal baths in Arras, but owing to the large number of troops in and around Arras, it was a case of waiting for our turn to come up. One could obtain, on payment, a bath in the village if and when one could get time off, and then only in the evenings. We carried out our gun drill mechanically now, and the guns seemed to become part of us. The bully beef stews, fritters and pilchards were very monotonous, with a break now and again of fresh meat and vegetables. The cooks did their best, but in time, the pilchards became hated and I saw boxes of them buried because they weren't getting eaten and stocks piled up. The food issued was sufficient, but appetites were sharpened by being constantly in the fresh air, so friends who did get to the village would bring back food with them. We must have consumed thousands of eggs, as the cooks were constantly dishing out hard boiled ones at tea-time. Like the rest, I really looked forward to a visit to the village, where we were always welcome to have a good meal with our café-rhums. I wonder if the French people remember us, if only for that? I know that once we went off the rails a bit in one café, which had a piano. One chap could play, so there was a good old sing-song with everybody getting drunk by starting at the top shelf and sampling drinks of every colour, with the café Madam shouting, "No bon, zig-zag," tapping her head. We returned to the gun position gloriously drunk, and I had a fat head in the morning to prove it.

Because of the incessant rain, we had to keep the guns well greased and keep their covers on. All ammunition had to be kept dry in the gun pits by using tarpaulin sheets over the sodden sandbagged walls. Then water started to find its way into the dug-outs, no matter how we tried to stop it. It was now December and very cold, also there were looks of envy as names were regularly notified to prepare for BEF leave. We were issued with dubbin to rub into our boots, a little too late, as they were already sodden, but it helped. The latrines were most uncomfortable to use, just a hole in the ground, with hessian walls which tended to blow over in the wind. The cold crept into our bodies so much that there was a rum issue at night, which was strong, and I felt a warm glow when I drank mine.

My friend, Driver Malham saw the visiting MO and had a nasty looking whitlow lanced with a razor blade, upon which he nearly passed out. Life was rugged and we had seen no war yet, but we had our problems when a dug-out roof collapsed and the heavy incessant rain soon had it filling with water, soaking kit when it was fished out.

Two weeks before Christmas, the Brigadier of Ack-Ack paid us a visit, when he must have considered the site untenable, as we had orders to move, which we couldn't do fast enough to get out of that mud hole. Soon on the road it was destination Boulogne, to a large empty hotel on the sea front. It was heaven to have beds and wash places where we could clean off the Arras mud. Our spirits rose accordingly and we settled into a kind of barrack room order, with the cooks now having a first rate kitchen in which to show us their skills with fresh meat and vegetables. The hot showers were very relaxing after the Arras experience and I washed everything I could lay hands on and sponged what I couldn't, but my battledress looked a stained creased up mess. Fortunately, I had in my kitbag my service tunic and trousers plus a spare pair of boots, so when I went out with buttons shining, I looked quite tidy. A long queue formed when the storeman opened shop for kit replacement, only to run out of most items quickly. Socks were in greatest demand, and the weather had taken toll of boots, with no means of getting them repaired. I noticed that all the stores staff wore new uniforms and boots, etc., which fact did not go unnoticed by the men, who gave them plenty of 'stick'.

Christmas arrived and we had a good dinner, traditionally served to us by the officers and warrant officers, with an issue of a bottle of beer per man. The cooks had excelled themselves, and in addition to some carol singing, the cook sergeant, bombardier and a cook formed a trio and sang in perfect harmony a selection of popular songs from the 'Mills Brothers' and very good they were too. This went down well with everybody.

Being free to go out Christmas night I wandered around Boulogne, thinking of the pleasant time I might have been having with Annique, looking at the gaily lit shops. After settling in a café, I soon had one drink too many and on leaving, lost my way and was wandering around looking for some familiar sight and finding myself in almost complete darkness. Then I heard a shout and saw a French dock worker running towards me. He held my arm and edged forward a couple of yards and stopped, pointing out to me an edge where there was a sudden drop into the sea. I couldn't thank that good man enough for preventing my early demise, and he said he knew my hotel and guided me in the right direction, so that I arrived back in good time. I was never a person to dwell on what might have been, but I was indeed grateful to that Frenchman for being in the right place at the right time.

Referring back to the journey from Arras to Boulogne, as we had a few problems *en route*, plus a late start, it resulted in us having to park somewhere for the night and conclude the journey to Boulogne the next day. Lieutenant Long had left earlier and arranged everything, assisted by the fact that he could speak French. Our rendezvous was a large farmhouse, where the guns and vehicles were parked, and we were shown our billets for the night. We then assembled in a huge recreation hall, where rows of tables were nicely laid out, with tablecloths and plates, cutlery, etc. We were given a first class meal, starting with that French speciality, soup, plus wine. The French certainly knew how to cater for large numbers, especially at such short notice. I saw Lieutenant Long in discussion with the farmer and his wife, and he handed over a large wad of bank notes.

Everyone was made aware of where the toilets were for use during the night, with a warning of severe punishment if anyone was caught relieving themselves elsewhere, and abusing the hospitality of the farmer and his wife. Smoking was strictly forbidden as we had straw to lie on and guards patrolled all night, with senior NCOs to see that the orders were carried out. The guards were very vigilant by the guns and ammunition, though fortunately I was not called upon for duty, so I bedded down in the empty cow sheds with the rest. It was very comfortable and warm, though there were a few silly arguments when someone would grab some of his neighbour's straw for himself.

During the night, a pal woke me up and whispered that a girl refugee was in the adjacent large barn, in need of some comforting, so we crept off and on our hands and knees in the barn, searched for the supposed spot where she was. Then torches started shining in odd places, and it turned out that quite a few men were on the same mission as ourselves, so back to my bed spot I went, hoping that if the poor girl existed at all, she made good her escape.

At the hotel a letter arrived from Annique and judging by the rubber stamps all over the envelope, it had travelled backwards and forwards across France, but on the address side, all it had was William Harding, 6th Battery in the French style. I thought all credit to the Army Postal Service to persevere until it reached me. When I saw it my heart lurched with a bump and on opening it, I found one sheet of paper, half writing and half tear-stained kisses. I became very worried, knowing that my heart ached too, but how could I ever see her again? I was in an impossible situation, tied to the Battery and duty. It is said that love will find a way, but the only way I could think of was desertion, I shook that out of my mind, knowing that it wouldn't work anyway. Leave was non-existent and I pondered long and hard as to what was best to do in the circumstances. Hurtful as it was, I felt that if I didn't answer the letter, Annique would assume that I had never received it, and I would soon become just a memory, but if I did write back she would be hoping to see her William coming through the door. Even if it was possible, what if her father was there? So I decided to leave it, with the faint hope that as this peculiar war progressed,

I might somehow work a surprise visit in the future.

I badly wanted to know the contents of the letter, and the only person who I knew could read it for me was Lieutenant Long. In order to ask him, I would have to approach TSM Crotty, who being of a sarcastic nature might refuse, so I took the bull by the horns and asked Lieutenant Long direct. I could see he didn't like it, but read the letter to himself first, then very sharply said to me, "What the devil have you done to this poor girl?" I protested, saying that I had been honourable to her and that I loved her. He then read to me the English version of it, the gist of it being why didn't I let her know I was leaving, and how she missed me terribly, that her heart was breaking and she cried herself to sleep every night thinking of her William. She sent me a thousand kisses and told me that Mama and the children missed me terribly. She sent me her undying love, and saw me in her dreams.

Lieutenant Long very coldly thrust the letter into my hand and walked off, making me feel that I was the king of rats, but it wasn't the way he thought of me at all. I wondered later on if this affected my promotion prospects, as he was my Section Officer. This threw my mind into a turmoil and it affected me like a sickness for several days, but painful as it was, I knew that if I wrote, I might lose self-control and land in the deep end. How my heart ached for Annique, as in my mind I kept seeing her face and the family. If I ever visited her, I was sure that I would never leave her, and I looked at her tiny photograph often.

I found myself hardening in my attitude to others and not suffering fools gladly, especially the ones who thought I was easy. One man in particular who thought so was Gunner Smith, who was cocky, lazy and insolent. When on a punishment fatigue party, snow shifting, when I was in charge, he virtually refused to start work until I threatened to place him on a charge. He made a movement as if to work and as I walked away, a snowball hit me on the head and a stone fell down. It hurt, so I went back in a blazing temper and told him that he would be reported. I fetched the Orderly Sergeant, who formally charged him, keeping the stone as evidence, and he also noted the bruise on my head. He received 5 days loss of pay and had seven release days off (one day a week) confiscated. He always resented authority and invariably brought trouble on himself.

A friend of mine, Charlesworth, a despatch rider, came to me one day and told me he had been on a mission in Nantes with the RSM concerning four men on a field court martial, in which I had been involved. He told me that the outcome was that the three NCOs were stripped of their rank and were given long spells in a military prison, and the driver was given 28 days field punishment, also meaning loss of pay. He told me to count myself lucky to be here, as gangs of Irishmen were searching the cafés for me to beat me up and hang me from the nearest lamppost. I thought that it served them all right, they got what they deserved. I asked whether he might be returning to Nantes, but he said there was no need as the business was concluded.

He said, "You certainly put it in for those four blokes Bill."

I said, "I didn't, they put it in for themselves and I'm glad they got whacked."

Gunner Turner was still in and out of trouble of a minor nature, and in between breaks he would seem like a reformed character, which never lasted, because he was one of those men who could never bend to discipline. Yet for all that, he was likeable and a bit of a comic, but having no pay, he was always scrounging cigarettes.

We received newspapers from England on a sharing basis and prominent in the news was the poor state of men's clothing and boots in the BEF, there being small stocks of replacements available. On one front page, a soldier was depicted wearing socks with large holes in them, holding up his 'housewife', showing needles but no wool for darning.

A visit was laid on to see George Formby and his troupe performing at a theatre in Boulogne. I was one of the lucky ones drawn and was seated in the gallery, whilst VIPs and General Staff Officers were down in the front. The show was great fun, with plenty of girls and George Formby singing his best known songs with his little ukelele. 'Sitting on a mine in the Maginot Line' went down well.

A comic came on stage with the newspaper showing a large foot with no heel or toe on the sock, shouting, "Has anybody here got bigger holes in their socks than these?" When a soldier shouted, "I have," he was brought on stage. Sitting on a chair, he took his boots off, showing socks in exactly the same condition as those in the newspaper, with nothing covering his toes at all. This set everyone off rocking with laughter, which was ammunition for the comic, who challenged several front rank officers to come up on stage and remove their shoes. They declined, with faces as red as their staff tabs.

A couple of days later, we read in the newspaper that the state of the socks in the BEF had now reached Parliament, and within two weeks, new kit arrived and everyone was issued with two pairs of socks, plus exchange of clothing. But I still couldn't get a new battledress in exchange for my worn, stained shabby one, as there were not enough to go round. I had my BEF leave in mind, but then, many others were in the same position.

I was asked discreetly by a sergeant if I would like to see a cock-fight, and as I only had a vague idea what it was all about, I said that I would, but received a warning that no officers must hear of it. The sergeants, with the exception of Morgan had become more talkative of late, ever since the RASC episode became known, spread around by Charlesworth and the men who were on the guard that night. The trip to the cock-fight arrived and took place in a barn on the outskirts of the town, where a small ring was fixed up and quite a large gathering of people turned up. There was considerable excitement, with money changing hands and bets being made as two men in the ring showed off their cockerels by thrusting them at each other and getting them worked up to fighting pitch. I settled down and watched long spurs being attached to each bird, and when thrown into the ring, they fought to the death, the winner standing on his dying opponent with the long spur stuck into its body and giving a crow of victory. I obtained very little pleasure from this spectacle, as all I saw was two creatures fighting to kill each other merely to satisfy man's lust and greed, and when I was invited again, I declined.

It was the end of January when my turn for BEF leave came round, ten days, including a day's travelling each way to the UK. I was not asked where I wanted to go, it was automatically laid on to home and back, covering all travelling expenses, including buses. I did think about going to Nantes, but I knew that Gran couldn't live much longer, so at least I could go and see her, if only for the last time, not being aware of my own fate if and when this war hotted up. There were only a few hours' warning of departure, so in some haste, I found an iron in the hotel and pressed my service tunic and trousers, which had been crunched up in the bottom of my kitbag, cleaned buttons and brasses, shone my boots and there I was, fit for a parade once again.

My brown belt had always looked good and it did now, and when I dressed I looked more soldierly than I did wearing battledress. So, with kitbag, gas mask and armed with my travel documents and pay allowances I left on a truck with my mates shouting, "Good luck Bill, have a good time, etc." I crossed the Channel from Calais, wearing a life-jacket, and on arriving at Dover with the excited crowds, I noticed the glum looking faces of the men waiting to board the boat for the trip back. I arrived at Liverpool Street Station, glad to be on leave, but not really feeling exhilarated at the prospects of home. Still, it would be great to see Gran, as I had heard nothing since my depot leave. I boarded a bus and had my BEF pass punched and on arriving at Redvers Street I stood on the platform as the bus slowed down, ready to alight when, without any warning, I was booted in the rear, and I and my kitbag landed in a heap on the pavement. I saw the conductor grinning as the bus sped away, and had I got hold of him, with the rage I was in, I would have battered his face. I knew there was a strong blackshirt Mosley element in the area, and guessed that seeing 'BEF' prompted him to do what he did.

What a way to start my leave, covered in dust and a few bruises! So I dusted myself down and went over to the Star and Woolpack to have a pint and calm myself down, as I was so angry. No one knew I was coming, so I had a meal in a café afterwards. Everywhere looked so dull and dreary, but on entering Redvers Street I had a few friendly waves of the hand from familiar faces. I knocked on No.9 and a surprised Emmy said, "Hallo Billy, like a bad penny eh!" I spoke a bit, and asked her how Gran was and was told she was very poorly. I went upstairs to see her, now a very frail old lady, hardly able to move her joints and on seeing me she started to cry as I embraced her, so I gave her a small amount of the cognac I had brought with me and after a long talk, she cheered up.

My room was the same as I had left it, dusty and untouched, so I searched around for some sheets and bedding. Gran said, "You know Walter is on leave but he's down at the pub till closing time." It appeared that he was given leave while his ship was having an overhaul. She said that the house was quieter since he had been recalled back to the Navy and Emmy was better off with some GPO pay and the Navy marriage allowance, but she was still hard on the two boys.

When Walter came in, we got on well together, him telling me where his ship HMS *Witch*, a destroyer had been, and me talking about my cave-like existence in France. He was as happy as a king, loaded with drink and suggested that we go out later for a pint, so I agreed, but knowing that I couldn't and didn't intend trying to match him drink for drink. My ration allowance wasn't much, so it was a good job I had saved up for my leave. After the tiring day travelling, I dusted the room, made my bed, searched for bugs and then had a couple of hours' welcome sleep. On waking, I washed from the old jug and bowl. Nothing had changed but I was glad that I had come home, as I could see that Gran probably would not last much longer and I guessed that I was seeing her for the last time. After her, there was no one else. She told me that her old age pension and my seven shillings allotment was drawn by Emmy and covered her rent and few needs, as she couldn't eat solid food now and drank very little because of incontinence. I stocked up with tea, sugar and tinned milk, with eggs and bread handy in the mornings, as I bought dinners in cafés. I had to eke my money out carefully and worked out what I needed for each day. Gran had no news of my mother or her other daughters, so it was very sad for her to lie in bed without a visit from her family. No one visited Albert, so he was like an outcast, but I couldn't use my travel warrant to look him up. I was all right for cigarettes, having acquired extras from non-smokers.

Evening came, and Walter asked me to go with him to the Basing House pub in Kingsland Road, and we were made welcome by the brothers who ran it. They looked like actors, with bleached hair and lipstick, with some make-up. Walter started giggling after a drink and said, "Wait here, I won't be long." About fifteen minutes later he returned and we went to the bar where Walter had free drinks all evening and anything I wanted was 'on the house', with the two brothers fussing over me and taking my name and address in France, promising me some parcels, etc. I asked Walter where he had been and giggling, he said he had looked over the brothers' flat upstairs, so I thought that what he does is his business and said no more. We were both in uniform, and I saw quite a few people in uniform now.

Walter was tipsy on the way home after seeing him drink pints of Watney's Stingo, and near closing time was tipping rum into it. The next day we went elsewhere for a drink and on the way home had a photo taken, which turned out very good, a nice memento of 1940. The market hadn't changed, and each day I had a dinner in Fortune's pie shop, this time two pies and mash.

A lot of young men had been called up and during a visit to the shop, Jim told me that trade had fallen off and the young chap who had taken my place had been called up, causing Mr Reid a few headaches, also giving Jim some worries over his own job. He very warmly shook me by the hand, wishing me good luck and saying that when the weather broke, the 'Balloon would go up in France if he judged the Germans rightly.' In the Hackney Road shop Len said that he also had a fall off in trade, but that he wasn't worried as he could turn his hand to anything, and that lots of people were leaving the area. He gave me his address and insisted that I write to him, but I never did.

I had two days left, and Walter went back, so we had a farewell drink, him telling me that his ship, the *Witch*, was a 1918 destroyer which was always wet inside with condensation, resulting in their clothing always being damp. Emmy hardly spoke, so I spent a lot of time with Gran and she was very happy to have me there. Frances next door spoke to me quite a bit over the garden fence, and I could see that she was happy to do so, but her mother kept coming out and although polite to me, would get the girl in. How I craved for a girl-friend, but with the mother around, it wasn't to be. The time came for me to leave, so with a few farewells with neighbours and a tearful farewell with Gran, I went, never dreaming that Redvers Street, my old school and the Band of Hope would disappear under Hitler's bombs in the near future.

The journey back was uneventful, and on the train many of the men had their wives and girl-friends with them to see them off at Dover and I witnessed many distressing goodbye scenes.

Back at the Battery, life was going on much the same, with men going on leave as others returned. The roads were still icy and I was given one detail to collect lorry loads of coal briquets for the hotel, the quantity now only enough for cooking and washing purposes. For baths, we went to Boulogne, where cafés supplied a good service with tickets in their windows announcing 'British soldiers bath 7 francs', so that solved a problem, with the cafés gaining trade as, once inside, a drink or two was always consumed. I became bored stiff with the usual round of gun drill, attending to fatigue parties in and out of the hotel, with guard duties thrown in. I took my turn as Battery Orderly, attended to mail and became an officer's general run-about.

A visit was laid on to the British Military Cemetery at Etaples not far away. The lay-out and the grounds were so beautifully kept that I was very impressed with it all. I came across one grave bearing my full name, same regiment, aged 18, died 1918, and I became very thoughtful as I looked at it.

With the weather on the break, in late February orders came to move, so leaving the hotel spic and span, we went on to Amiens and settled near by into an existing gun position, so it was back to the rough again, a gunner's lot. We were situated close to a farmhouse, so life wasn't so bad, with a plentiful supply of fresh water, vegetables and eggs, with the field kitchens back in operation, giving off the usual clouds of smoke. The farm girls appeared to be very provocative and men had, whenever possible, lots of fun in the village cafés with them, resulting in a few 'buns in the oven' when we moved off!

On the 6th of March a telegram arrived to say that Gran had died, and could I attend the funeral. I felt quite upset inside, but it was not entirely unexpected. I showed it to my Section Officer, who said that only the death of one's natural mother could qualify for a compassionate leave. A letter quickly followed saying that Gran had died in St Leonard's hospital, leaving a pound note under her pillow 'For Billy'. My mother had written it, saying that she would buy a few flowers for Gran on my behalf. Emmy had never written once, not even to tell me Gran was in hospital, but it didn't matter, now that she had gone. I knew one thing though, and that was that I would never go back to Redvers Street again. So Emmy had her wish, the whole house was now hers, so there was no place for me there in the future. If I ever did have another leave, I would stay at the Union Jack Club, Waterloo. I heard no more from my mother, except for a funeral card saying that Gran had been buried at Manor Park Cemetery. I felt that I had done my duty to Gran.

I now received my full pay, the extra seven shillings making quite a difference, doubling what I had been used to. April arrived and with it, orders to move back to Tilloy. On arrival, the gun position looked devastated and badly in need of repair and in parts, rebuilding. The dug-outs were almost full of water, which took some bailing out, then the worst job of all, lifting out the sandbagged floors, covered in mud, and recovering them with freshly filled new ones. The roofs needed strengthening and the gun pit walls had to be rebuilt in parts, so there was plenty to do, and little time in which to do it, which meant working hard and fast to make it tenable. The food situation was not good and it was back to bully beef stew and its various other disguises. The cooks made it up with treacle and suet puddings or tinned fruit and the inevitable pilchards. Nobody went hungry, but the diet was rather monotonous.

The cold and damp rewarded us with a rum issue each night. With rain on and off, we all started wearing our anti-gas capes when on guard duty, with the officers turning a blind eye to it. The capes were weatherproof and covered us fully, making us look weird on a misty night. An example of this was when Charlesworth, on a trip to Regimental HQ in the early hours parked his motor bike out of sight at a World War I cemetery and sat in the visitors' room, having a smoke, when he heard loud footsteps coming down the road. Not wanting to get caught, he looked out of the entrance in the mist, making no noise in his rubber soled boots and wearing his steel helmet and gas cape. He came face to face with a French civilian in clogs, who on seeing Charlesworth, screamed and ran like mad down the road. This unnerved Charlesworth, who mounting his motor bike, roared off in the opposite direction. I wonder if that Frenchman tells his grandchildren about the ghost he saw coming out of a British war cemetery, with the added embellishments of time!

CHAPTER THIRTEEN

What a mess!

Warning was given of a visit by the Brigadier of Ack-Ack, and we were told to prepare the gun position for inspection. Major Freer-Ash came along in his Austin Seven (a mechanized mess tin a reservist called it) and following him were lorries loaded with duck-boards and buckets. He supervised the laying of the duck-boards around the gun pits and Command Post with buckets of water placed here and there, so that if the boards became muddy, they were to be washed clean, and if any sank in the mud, they were to be repositioned and washed. He gave strict orders that no one was to walk on them, so everybody squelched along the sides of them in the mud. On the day of the inspection, we cleaned our boots with dubbin or gun grease, and wore them instead of wellington boots.

The Brigadier came with his staff and ignoring the duck-boards went stomping about all over the place, very business like, being more concerned about the guns and ammunition and the effects of the weather on them. We gave a demonstration drill, as he wanted to see that the electronics were functioning OK. Then off he went, thus giving us the privilege of walking on the duck-boards. Everybody was on edge, waiting for the sun to come out and bring us some relief, but before that happened, a lorry was allocated to the units around, including us. This would collect 50 men and take them to the municipal baths in Arras.

I was one of the fifteen who went, armed with clean underwear, towel and soap. On reaching the edge of town, the driver stopped, saying that as he was being pushed to the limit, searching for units dotted about to bring in his next batch, we would have to make our own way to the baths. We should hurry as several lorries were bringing men in, arriving non-stop, and we were only allowed fifteen minutes bathing time, our first in three weeks. I was thinking that the baths were only a short way off, and it didn't occur to me to do anything other than make our way there, which we were doing, when out of the blue came an immaculately dressed Staff Captain, in gleaming riding boots. He brought us to attention and in a state of rage, shouted and raved at us to such an extent that his voice went high pitched. He looked younger than me, and kept calling us filthy pigs, a disgrace to the British Army and so on. Being the only NCO present I had to bear the brunt of it, especially when I tried to explain the appalling conditions which we had to endure all the time. We stood there lined up, dirty, muddy, unshaven, with uniforms all creased up, for we hadn't taken off our clothes for three weeks. As he gradually worked himself up to a state of hysteria, his voice almost going, I thought to myself what a stupid bloody idiot, what a way to run an army. I would just like to see those fancy boots on the gun position. An RSM and staff of the Military Police arrived and with a large gathering of civilians now collected, we were brought to a smart left turn and doubled away to a garage, converted into prison cells, the Staff Officer promising us that he personally would see that we received maximum punishment. Seeing the state we were in, and knowing that we were going to the baths, I explained about the mud and the dug-outs. The RSM said he had a certain sympathy with us, but we were relieved of our pay books and formally charged with being in public in a dirty slovenly manner, failing to uphold the high standards of the British Army. The truck driver would also be charged for not taking us to the baths as ordered, and when he turned up an hour later, he was relieved of his pay book and formally charged, after which he took us to the baths, the RSM saying that our pay books would be returned to the Battery in due course. I thought that will please the Major, fifteen of his men being charged with being filthy.

The baths were working flat out, with steam everywhere, the converted showers taking 30 men at a time, with long queues, timed to 15 minutes each. No wonder the driver could hardly cope with his trips. It was sheer luxury to stand under the hot water and become clean again, but we were constantly being admonished to hurry up, as others were waiting.

On our return to the Battery, I reported to Captain Barnes, officer of the day, and told him what had taken place in Arras. His reaction was to say, "Blast it, as if I hadn't enough to think about." He added that being a Staff Officer, this could turn out more serious than it appeared, and he would have to 'take the can back'. He told me to stay there while he tried to find out if the Colonel was available. He rang through on the field telephone to find, fortunately, that he was. I noted that he went over the Major, explaining what had happened, stating how bad the conditions were here and that the men involved were having their first bath in three weeks. I heard the Colonel's voice clearly saying that he wasn't having some damned Staff Officer picking on his men and that he would contact the Brigadier immediately. I hoped it was the same one who had been stomping around in the mud earlier. Captain Barnes looked relieved, saying keep your fingers crossed, the Colonel's on our side.

Later that day, an immaculate 15 cwt. truck turned up with two equally immaculate Military Police, who were stepping gingerly across thick mud, trying not to spoil shining boots, and handed in fifteen pay books. Captain Barnes handed them back to their owners, saying all charges dropped. To me, he said that on no account were we to leave the bath detail truck until it arrived at the baths in future, as we may not be so lucky next time getting involved with the Staff Officers. I thought good luck to the Colonel for sticking up for his men.

We were given a break to visit Vimy Ridge, a First World War battle ground, where I believe 60,000 Canadians died fighting. I found it very interesting, the huge mine craters and shell holes, so numerous that most overlapped each other. Nothing had been disturbed, and there were many rusting relics of the war lying around. My group went into the 22 miles of chalk tunnels which in themselves, were a masterpiece and in one, we saw a British officer's quarters, with just a bed and the barest necessities. Next door, where the chalk partition had been pierced after the war was a German tunnel with officer's quarters, a good bed with many extras and a carpet, and the difference in the degree of comfort was very obvious.

Being adventurous to the point of stupidity, I saw a side tunnel, so I went in to find the hole decreased to a size where it was hands and knees to crawl through, and in pitch dark one of my hands went into emptiness, indicating a drop, so I quickly crawled back and found myself covered from head to foot in white chalk dust. Fortunately my group had stopped farther down, listening to the guide, or I could quite easily have been lost in that maze of tunnelling.

We had all been warned about fifth columnists and told to be extra vigilant at night, and this evoked the odd rifle shot from nervous sentries. The weather turned hot and dry, which uplifted everybody's spirits, the ground drying hard, enabling us to lay out clothing and kit to dry and air. The guns were cleaned, ready for action, walls were repaired and laundry arrangements made, making us feel like human beings again.

At night we could see flashing lights in a triangle around our position, so Lieutenant Long climbed a tree and pin-pointed the estimated spots, and sent out patrols to try and catch whoever it was. The idea of the triangle was for enemy bombers to unload their bombs in the centre, hoping to hit us or other units. The searchlight units would direct their beams into the sky and on finding an enemy plane, would hold it while we would try to blast it out of the sky, and many had an uncomfortable time as we saw our shell bursts flashing quite close to them. As this was now becoming a regular nightly event, it was practice for real. One night Lieutenant Long ordered me to take a patrol, following his instructions sent via a field telephone from the top of a tree, to try to catch a fifth columnist flashing a light.

Six men and I went as quickly and quietly as possible to a clump of trees, when in the darkness I saw a dim figure, so I spread my patrol out, with orders not to shoot in case someone got hurt, then we charged forward to catch the culprit and our capture turned out to be a full sized marble statue of a nude woman. I was amazed to see this, in a wood of all places, why it was there I couldn't imagine. When I reported this to Lieutenant Long he drily remarked, "Lucky for her that she was marble." Despite all the patrols that went out, no fifth columnist was ever caught, as this was their back yard.

An RAOC officer called and inspected the ammunition and we loaded most of it on to the large trucks which had arrived with him, but leaving us enough to carry on with until a new batch arrived. I was detailed by the Major to take two men and enough rations to last until the next day and guard a small dump of 5,000 shells destined for the Battery. He was explicit about looking out for possible fifth columnists and to be extra vigilant. Our light truck followed his car for a few miles to the dump, where he left us to it. We made a hollow in among the ammunition boxes for one man to rest in and I planned a continuous guard of two throughout the night. I was taking no chances on this lot going up. The two men were Welsh, one tall and thin, the other short and stocky. The time was 5 p.m., so after a meal, I gave my instructions, which didn't go down very well with the short one, who looked to me a nasty type of man.

He stood up and said to his mate, "Coming?" so the pair of them went to make off. I asked them where they thought they were going and the short one, a typical old sweat said, "To the nearest village." I told them to do as they were ordered, and that if they disobeyed, I would place them under open arrest. They talked it over, muttering to each other, when the short one said, "We're going, no matter what you say."

So I said, "I'm ordering you to stay, but if you go, you will find the Field Security Police waiting for you and a Field Court Martial to follow." The tall one looked worried and some more muttering took place.

Then the short one said, "OK, we'll stay." I used my authority to the full from then on, keeping them on edge. The night passed off OK, the three of us doing our share of sentry so that I could watch them, with two men on, one off — a long tiring night.

In the morning, the Major turned up, with trucks and men to load the ammunition. I ordered the two Welshmen to help with the loading and made them sweat it out, and I took great pleasure in standing by and keeping them at it. They knew I could have reported them to the Major, and I didn't have a clue where to find Field Security Police miles from anywhere.

Life wasn't all that dull on the gun position. The cook sergeant had just returned from hospital, and had a large scab on his arm. He was an excellent cook, and for a treat, he made some long 'spotted dicks'. He was busy, with his arms deep in the dough, mixing and then kneading it, with us looking forward to the end result. Eventually it was cooked and a good helping was had by all, including custard, which was very much appreciated. Suddenly someone noticed that the scab was missing from the cook's arm, and word went round quickly that it had come off in the dough. This almost caused a revolt, and some men were pushing their fingers down their throats, trying to be sick. The cook sergeant told us we had nothing to worry about as there was none so pure as the purified. What a character he was. Sometimes a taxi would come to the gun position and a young woman dressed in the height of fashion would 'collect' him, then arm in arm, walking to the taxi, they would face good humoured whistling and shouts of approval from the men, then drive off.

One day he came to me and said that there was nothing for dinner and little time left to provide anything, would I join him on a foraging party, but no one must know. I agreed, and with six others, armed with spades, we set off in a

30 cwt. truck. I had already asked someone to cover for me on the gun, then we drove around remote farms, pulling as many cabbages as we could, and dug up anything going until we had a good load on the truck. We were so engrossed in our illegal business that no one saw a farmer, who ran towards us shouting, then let fly at us with his double barrelled shot-gun. With pellets whizzing around us we were quickly on the truck and away back to the gun position, where unseen, we unloaded the truck and I was back with my gun. A little late, but we had a good dinner with freshly cooked vegetables. Then a Frenchman arrived creating a fuss about soldiers plundering his field, but our officers denied that it was us, so all's well that ends well.

About mid-April four guns pulled out to another position elsewhere, forming two Troops. I stayed with my Troop, having Captain Barnes in command, with Lieutenants Long and Lister and some new young officers who had just arrived. Lieutenant Lister enjoyed using a dispatch rider's motor bike, tearing up a nearby hill, and one day he did a somersault, which gave him a nasty tumble but it didn't stop him, he still enjoyed rough riding.

Just as we were settled into our daily routine, the Major came along with a three-ton lorry, carrying red brick rubble, some drums of oil and a large amount of cotton waste. His orders were to pound the rubble to dust, mix it with oil and with the cotton waste to clean off the paint from the bronze trunnions, plus all the brass parts of the guns. All the brass cases of the shells were to be cleaned in the gun pits, and in doing so, we removed all ordnance numbers and other stencilled markings. I thought this was wrong, as an abrasive such as brick dust could take away the cushion fit when loaded into the breech of the guns, risking a blow back on firing.

We stank with the oil and looked like Red Indians, the slightest breeze caused grit to blow into the eyes, and we detested what we were doing. It was warm weather, and having little water to clean ourselves with properly meant the smell of the oil clinging to us a long time. This business didn't last long however, as an RAOC officer appeared on the gun position and started checking the shell cases with instruments and calipers, resulting in hundreds of cleaned rounds being taken away. This tale came from one of the RAOC drivers, that a report had come through via a Spitfire pilot, who had seen the guns gleaming in the sunshine; also I saw in the distance the Major and the RAOC officer having words. The guns were repainted and anything bright was covered up, the warm days a promising sign of a good summer to come.

My birthday came and went, just like any other day, with no mail, and I thought that if I received none, I would not have to reply to them.

Gunner Kent almost got both of us into trouble one day, when we were discussing something in the gun pit, looking outwards over the top. He shouted, "Yoo-hoo Lister!" and ducked down, but I was not prepared and was almost seen by Lieutenant Lister as he looked back, only to trip over on some timber on the ground, giving himself a shiner of a black eye. I gave Kent a ticking off and made a mental note never to get involved with him alone again.

German air activity was on the increase now day and night, at which time we would have to go into action, but during the day the planes were very high and hard to see, probably taking photographs. With all BEF leave now completed, we had a full complement, and with night activity causing us to be in action most nights, time off was very restricted. One afternoon, being allowed a few hours off duty, I went for a walk down some country lanes and came across what could be the smallest British war graves plot in France. It brought home to me the meaning of the poem which says 'There is some corner of a foreign field which is forever England,' for I found in the corner of a field, fenced off and quite small, five headstones of men of the Royal Artillery who were buried there — an officer, a gunner, and three drivers. I stood and pondered on how it could have happened, they looked so lonely there.

CHAPTER FOURTEEN

10th May 1940 — war at last!

The Colonel paid us a visit with the Major and told us that the balloon had gone up, that the Hun had attacked neutral Belgium and from now on everyone must be on their toes at all times. Our persistent training would now pay off, and prove its worth, and I guessed we would be seeing plenty of action now. All visits to the village were stopped and we were told to stay by the guns at all times.

Activity by the Germans increased sharply and when in action, night or day, we could see our exploding shells bracketing the planes, making them dive about, which showed how accurate we were getting, some at a great height too. One morning we were caught off guard when seemingly from nowhere, with a roar of engines, a flight of seven Dornier bombers came over the woods at tree top height, with our guns pointing in the direction to which they were going. This all happened in seconds, when Captain Barnes shouted at us to take cover, as planes were overhead raking our positions with machine-gun fire from the tail gunners. Captain Barnes, standing on a gun pit wall was shouting, "Independent fire," whilst he fired a Bren-gun up at the planes from the hip. Our four guns loaded and fired as fast as we could over open sights, and as the bombers became dots in the distance, smoke was seen among them. A French call stated that an enemy bomber had been hit and had crashed. We all liked to think that we were responsible for that. If so, I hope it was the one where I saw the German tail gunner grinning down as he fired his machine-gun. Most uncanny, seeing my first German of the war in such circumstances. Fortunately no one had been hit and no damage was done, but a few German bullets were retrieved from the sandbagged walls as souvenirs.

On the night action, Sergeant Morgan missed one of the members of the gun crew, who was found hiding in the dug-out with his fingers in his ears and refused to come out. He was placed under arrest and was taken away the next day. At this period a reinforcement arrived and came down into my dug-out. He was a sergeant and introduced himself, asking me if I was on No. 1 gun, and I replied that I was. He said he was worried that TSM Crotty had told him to take over the gun the next day. He seemed a polite, quiet type of man, and I asked him what the trouble was. He replied that he had done no training on any gun at all, so could I explain to him what to do in the morning. I asked him what he did do and he replied, "Not much, just keep the men doing something." I then asked how he became a sergeant and his reply angered me. He said he was TA, and in England, promotion came easily. I then asked him if he had been in a gun battery and he said that he had, but they had no guns. I told him that in no way could I help him to take charge of a gun, too much was involved, and what if at a moment's notice we went into action? No, the best thing to do was to go to the Sergeant-Major and explain his predicament, and he would, I was sure, take an understanding view of the matter and fit him in somewhere else.

The next morning at 'Take Posts' the sergeant was there, not having heeded my advice, and as the gun drill took place, he stood there unmoving, with we, the gun team, receiving no commands. The conclusion was that he left soon after. I felt annoyed that I was struggling hard to get promotion, whilst these chaps seemed to get it for next to nothing in England.

There was little rest now, with the guns firing on and off day and night, with the *Luftwaffe* flying around in all directions, plus the hard work afterwards, cleaning up, swabbing out and oiling the gun barrels, checking hydraulic systems, etc., and replenishing ammunition.

On 18th May the situation began to look serious, when refugees appeared on the road leading from Arras, and Captain Barnes ordered me to take six men, three Bren-guns, two boxes of ball ammunition per gun, to be taken by 15 cwt. truck to the river Scarpe to guard and if necessary, defend three bridges on the river, one Bren and two men per bridge. Driver Malham took us up the road, then stopped, saying that he was breaking the governor on the engine to gain more speed when patrolling from bridge to bridge. On reaching the Scarpe river, I sited the first two men and a Bren-gun with firm orders that should the need arise, as a result of Germans appearing, they must stop them, telling them also to find what cover they could with maximum vision, and that as I was patrolling between the three bridges, I would see them from time to time, until we were relieved.

I posted the other men with Brens on the other two bridges, then Malham drove flat out patrolling along the river. On the third run, at the farthest bridge, some British Infantry came running over, led by an officer who snarled at me, "Get the hell out of here." So with the two men, Bren and ammunition, we went, and I found the next bridge already occupied by British Infantry, with my chaps sitting on the roadside, waiting for us, so with them in the back, we sped to the last bridge, not knowing what to expect. On arriving, I saw British Infantry running across, taking over the bridge, and their officer said to me, "Leave the Bren, Corporal, I can do with that."

I replied, "Sorry sir, Battery property," and on to the truck it went, with ammo and men. I saw in the distance Arras and Douai receiving a hammering, judging by the crump of bombs in the distance, and the thick pall of black smoke rising from both towns. I thought to myself 'Poor devils', with the women and children in mind, and in the bright sunlight I caught the glint of silver from the wings of the planes.

On our return, we exceeded speeds of 75 m.p.h. and on arrival at the

Battery, our guns were in action, firing flat out and I saw flights of German planes at different levels, with our shells bursting among them. I ordered the six men to look for Bren-gun AA mountings and set the Brens up to take on any dive-bombers. I then ran to my own gun, acting as ammunition number. Our fire kept the German planes high, but a few hundred yards further along the road, some were diving down and machine-gunning refugees, who packed the road solid. There was nothing we could do, as every man had his hands full to keep the German planes up and hit them if we could, but Brens and the cooks with rifles were having a go at them. A runner came and told me to report to Captain Barnes immediately. On leaving the gun pit there was a loud bang in my right ear, and turning quickly I found myself looking at a smoking revolver, very close to my head and held by a young 2nd Lieutenant, a new officer. I said, "Sir, you nearly blew my bloody ear off," but making no reply, he rather sheepishly put his revolver away and walked off.

It began to quieten down now, with the planes moving on, but everyone had black streaked faces from sweat and cordite, and there were gun fire fumes and smoke hanging about everywhere. There was no respite, but a frantic dash to renew depleted ammunition stocks in the pits, and clear away the empties, so as to be ready for them again. I reported to Captain Barnes, who asked for every detail and said, "Well done," when I concluded by informing him that the three bridges had been taken over by British Infantry and our weapons, etc. returned and placed on ack-ack mountings.

The cooks were fantastic, and they soon had plenty of strong sweet tea issued, with a bully beef sandwich per man until a hot meal could be organized. The time was about 1 p.m., and I then took notice of the refugees trudging slowly along the hot dusty road, with women pushing prams and handcarts piled up with the few belongings they had snatched, and children holding on to their mothers' skirts. I think what surprised me most was to see quite old women walking along, bowed over from the weight of enormous bundles on their backs. In the distance there was some screaming, which I assumed was the result of the dive bombing and machine-gun fire. I was disgusted to see all kinds of motor vehicles, military and civilian crawling along with lots of horn blowing and hooting, and several taxis crammed with French and Belgian soldiers. With no room inside, there were men hanging on the sides, clinging to the tops, forcing the refugees to move over so that they could get by, and passing us with much gesticulation, pointing to Arras and shouting "Les Boches." In return, they received very uncomplimentary shouts back, with whistles and cat-calls. Forgetting the rule of not speaking to an officer first I said to Lieutenant Long, who was close by, "Look at them sir, it's their country and they are running away, why are we here?"

Angrily he turned to me and curtly said, "Mind your own damned business Bombardier, and do as you're told." Well, I got my answer, and apart from speaking without permission, about which he was very strict, I thought my question a fair one, forgetting that 'Ours not to reason why, ours but to do or die'.

Children passing by were given swigs of tea, as were the grateful mothers, and some of the men gave their sandwiches. Most of us rested around the guns, quite exhausted, having had only snatches of sleep during the last few nights, coupled with the busy days, and the weather bordering on a heat wave. It was now late afternoon when the Brigadier made a sudden visit with the Major and ordered the guns to horizontal position, and a good number of shells to be set at fuse 1.5 and we were to adopt an anti-tank role, but I didn't think that our ammunition would be much use against tanks.

The young officer who had fired his revolver at German planes, narrowly missing my ear, came up to me and told me to take the Boyes anti-tank rifle and two men with a substantial quantity of ammunition 100 yards down the road to a fork, where he said that tanks would probably appear. We made our way to the designated spot with the Boyes rifle and waved to the officer, who waved back, satisfied with our position. His instructions were that if tanks appeared within range, to fire at them, the Battery alerted, would open fire also. I was in the road, so I said to my two men, "We'll set up behind that hedge over there, out of sight, or our own guns will blow us away like chaff." I set the range setting at 350 yards and waited.

We had also brought our rifles, so I arranged a guard duty, at darkness three of us would share, as it turned chilly and there was nowhere to sleep, so we sat around on the alert, keeping our eyes open. I gave orders to report any suspicious noise, but no shooting, because of refugees, but a loud challenge must be given, if needed. I was feeling very tired after the events of the past week, and tension built up as in the breeze, we all heard the clanking of tank tracks, which meant eyes straining to see in pitch darkness.

In the early hours, the sentry gave a loud challenge, which was promptly answered and the Brigadier appeared with the Major and TSM Crotty. The Brigadier complimented us on our alertness, saying that he had a job to find us, very good concealment with good frontal vision. In the beam of his torch he glanced around and asked, "When did you last have a hot meal Bombardier?" I replied that we had a sandwich and tea yesterday midday. Very sharply he asked, "Have you not had a hot drink since?" I replied that we had had nothing. Very curt and with a cutting edge to his voice, he told the Major to see that we had a hot meal as soon as possible. He then said, "Carry on Bombardier."

The grass was soaking wet with dew, so weary as we were, we moved about to keep warm, when there was another loud challenge, and to our delight, two cooks brought a container of hot sweet tea and some food. I thought God bless the Brigadier. But the biggest surprise was the reservist who served as NAAFI representative for the battery. He came with the cooks and gave us each a tin of fifty cigarettes and a half pound slab of Cadbury's chocolate, saying, "On the house lads," giving us a warm handshake and wishing us good luck. I thanked him for his generosity to us, knowing that he gave nothing on tick and his manner seemed to me a goodbye, as if he never expected to see us again.

19th May

Daylight came and looking round at each others' bloodshot eyes, we hoped we would be relieved, but thankful that no tanks had arrived, on which to try this new anti-tank rifle. A runner arrived with a message to report back with men, weapons and ammunition immediately, as the Battery was moving out. On our return I handed in the Boyes rifle and was just in time to get some tea and a sandwich. Orders were to leave everything bar essentials, all weapons, ammunition and tools, etc. It was a rush job, with everybody on the go, loading up thousands of rounds for the guns on to large trucks, getting the guns ready for the road and limbered up. Worst of all, we were ordered to leave personal kit, and protests made no difference, we were to travel light, so everybody made a mad dash to retrieve personal and sentimental items. Field kitchens were left and some tents used by the officers. Everyone was pushed and driven to the utmost speed to get away as quickly as possible, giving me a nasty feeling that the Germans must be fairly near.

When ready and pulling out on to the road, it was a problem moving the endless stream of refugees as humanely as possible, feeling pity for them, but we did manage the large Scammells and guns with quite a convoy of trucks and lorries. I thought that if the German planes had come over, they would have had a field day, our only protection being Brens mounted on 15 cwt. trucks. The Major was up the front doing his best, getting the convoy lined up ready to move, and when completed, the officers studied maps, a decision was made and Charlesworth, the dispatch rider went on ahead. We moved off slowly, still having the refugee problem, but other dispatch riders were busy clearing the road, then Charlesworth came roaring back, stopping with a screech of rubber on the tarmac and shouted to the Major that two miles ahead were Jerries, who had fired at him. Well, Piccadilly Circus wasn't in it, the Scammells pulling the guns needed space to turn and with the convoy turning, it was chaos. We had obviously started off in the wrong direction to Arras. When we did eventually line up to move off again, the officers realized that the dense crush of refugees made movement hopeless, so out came the maps again and some secondary roads were found, and once on them, we picked up speed, moving quite fast, with an almost clear road ahead.

Our fast speed brought us to our destination, a place called Sangatte, near Calais by evening, and we found ourselves close to the sea. I had a doze on the journey, but sleep was out of the question this night, as the ammunition had to be unloaded and stacked in small dumps, as well as everything else. Our site was sandy, set in a clearing of some trees. When the Scammells had set our guns in position they prepared to move off so I ran over to Crasher Carr and asked him where he was going, his reply being, "To pull some other guns out from somewhere." I never saw him or the Scammells again, so we lost our vital transport. Also, I didn't know that our other Troop had been placed at the other side of Calais, at Fort Vert, with three guns, the fourth being out of action.

Our guns were set up with Command Post, everything open, with no protective sandbag walls, and action stations was given for a test drill, to see that everything functioned correctly. I then saw how cleverly our position was sited in the clearing, with surrounding trees sufficient distance away to give good observation from the guns. Somehow, and I don't know how, the cooks provided hot sweet tea, but this time a tin of bully beef to share between several men, and Army issue biscuits which looked like large dog biscuits, very hard to break when eating. Searchlights now lit up, raking the skies at the sound of engines, bringing us into action until they found and held a target in their powerful beams, when we would open fire, causing the plane to dive and weave in an effort to escape into the darkness. In the distance I occasionally heard bombs exploding, and it was now 20th May.

During the night, whilst the guns were firing as fast as they could be loaded, my left ear drum went, a stab of pain as I lifted a shell, then in the darkness my gun changed direction of fire, so that I stood underneath the barrel as it fired. This was an added aggravation to my already splitting headache. When daylight came, I didn't report it, I was only too thankful to lie down by the gun and rest my head, also I remained totally deaf in that ear for years after.

Fresh boxes of ammunition were brought up ready for the next action. We were given permission to open our emergency rations, which consisted of a cubed block of chocolate containing all the vitamins, etc., to take the place of proper meals for 24 hours, so I was told, but most of us ate it straight away. Later that day the cooks found a nearby farm and managed to come back with hot tea and plenty of boiled eggs, with bread and butter, which was very welcome in restoring energy, and seemed to put a new man inside me. But most of all I needed sleep, which was not forthcoming. It was good that the cooks had brought the stocks of tea, sugar and milk, which was quite bulky but typical of the thinking of the British soldier, whatever happens, tea takes priority. The day passed fairly quietly, apart from the odd small actions at enemy planes passing over at great heights.

The guns being in order and well stocked with ammunition, the men were allowed to get what sleep they could lying around the guns with the sun burning down on them. When night came, it was action again, in co-operation with the searchlights. It was now 21st May, and events were hotting up, when around midday two Royal Navy destroyers came in quite close to the cliff, not far from us and opened fire on the long winding ribbon of the road leading from Boulogne to Calais. I had very keen eyesight then, and could see the small puffs of exploding shells among small dots moving along the white ribbon of the road. This went on for a couple of hours, then the ships sailed away, with me thinking what good shooting I had been watching, confirming that the Germans were close to the Channel ports. The day passed lazily, catching up on some sleep, with another night in our draughty position, once again working with the searchlights on targets as they came along.

May 22nd broke into a very hot bright day. We had tea and bully beef sandwiches again, which was very sustaining to a hungry stomach. I think it should be said that Army cooks deserve the highest praise, as under the most trying conditions, they never failed to produce a meal of some sort, as shown in this account. Some time before eleven, Lieutenant Long, with his binoculars and field telephone, climbed a tree. The telephone was linked on the ground to TSM Crotty and we were soon receiving orders on fusing shells and laying the guns. When we opened fire in a ground role and on his directions, shell fuses would change accordingly, plus changing direction of fire as ordered. The firing was fairly constant but slowed down a bit. It was very hot and thirsty work but occasionally we would break off to fire on some enemy planes passing overhead, then carry on under Lieutenant Long again. During this time, a flight of RAF bombers flew over in the direction in which we were firing, then the sound of bombs exploding could be heard, but the planes never came back our way. I knew now that something must have gone terribly wrong for the Germans to be so close, as I had gone on leave from Calais. Also at this time, a car arrived at our position and an Army officer from it conferred a while with Captain Barnes, then drove off. Word went round that he was a tank officer, and I thought that I saw some tanks in the distance later on.

. Some enemy shells were now coming our way, but landing amongst the trees, well away from us, but it showed that they had our direction. In the distance their guns could be heard firing, followed by the whistle of their shells arriving. Our four guns were firing fast now, making a deafening racket, which affected my left ear rather painfully. Then without warning a French coastal battery, with guns turned inland, opened fire with a terrific bang and their projectiles passed over. There was a flurry of German shells, which hit one of the three turrets, which looked to me substantially built, and I had a glimpse of soldiers or possibly marines running from the guns. The German shellfire was building up, with more coming our way, but well off target. It was obvious that the Germans couldn't see us, but they saw the French guns.

A message from Lieutenant Long was relayed via another officer who came and said, "Bombardier, you and two men will go two hundred yards forward of the gun position and set up a Bren-gun. You will take a spade and dig a slit trench. You will also take two boxes of ball ammunition, eight magazines in all, a spare barrel for the Bren, with your personal rifles. You will on sight and within range open fire to hold back any Germans to prevent penetration of the Battery." I saluted, thinking to myself I don't think I'm very popular around here, but I accepted the orders with good heart, and intended to carry them out. The officer returned with two men carrying spade, Bren and boxes of ammunition, with the seven spare magazines, so we left the battery with our own shells going over our heads, as well as those of the Germans.

I chose my position as ordered, 200 yards forward, and ordered the two men — whose names I cannot mention for obvious reasons, so I will refer to them as Smith and Jones — to dig the slit trench knee deep, with the excavated earth banked up in front. On completion I set up the Bren to range 100 yards, then cocked ready we filled the seven spare magazines and waited. Roughly 15 minutes later, the Germans sent over a terrific barrage and the Battery was firing at a cheeky German spotter plane when the barrage intensified, plastering shells all over the place, having now found their target. I knew our guns had been hit, when they stopped firing, and the Germans also shortened their range, resulting in our area becoming a mass of exploding shells, with deafening explosions and flying shrapnel. I shouted to Smith and Jones, "Keep your eyes open," when Jones, with no warning leapt out of the trench and ran like a hare, dropping down as shells exploded near him, then he was gone. I shouted to him to come back, but I doubt if he heard or cared amid the shrieking and exploding shells.

Jones had no sooner disappeared when I was unnerved by a high pitched scream from Smith as he tried to climb out of the trench. I grabbed his collar and dragged him back, where we struggled. He screamed again, so I laid on him, when he quietened down, but was in a bad state of hysteria. I had been shouting at him all this time, flaming mad at Jones's desertion, with Smith trying to do the same. The barrage was as intense as ever and I thought that with Jones gone and a raving lunatic left with me, the Battery hit, I had no chance in this situation so as I could see no Germans in the distance, I thought the best thing to do under the circumstances would be to make it back and make a report to Captain Barnes on this very serious turn of events.

This was my intention when the barrage eased off, so as Smith lay whimpering, I put two Bren magazines in my thigh pocket and the other five in my battledress blouse around my chest. Smith screamed again and jumped up, so I made him carry the Bren, my idea being to weight him down with a couple of rifles as well, to prevent him doing what Jones had done, but I was too late, fear gave him wings and he was out of the trench, Bren as well, and ran blindly through the barrage screaming like a madman. Something inside me snapped and in a raging temper, now having two run off and no Bren, I went after him and as the shells came close I threw myself down, then up after him. I now had murder in my heart, a blind rage to kill him if I got my hands on him. I reached the edge of a ten foot drop to the beach, but I was puffed out, the weight of the magazines had told on me. I saw Smith on his knees, whimpering and with his hands had scooped a hollow in the sand and had placed the Bren in it, intending to bury it.

I roared at him and made a dive to grab him, and on seeing me he screamed and ran off down the beach, being very lucky that my hands just missed him. Shells were dropping close to where I was on the beach, some landing in the sea with a hissing noise of hot metal hitting cold water. I retrieved the Bren but it was in a bad state, where fine sand had stuck to the oily surface, especially in the working parts. As my rage abated, I became aware of a long line of French soldiers standing pressed up tight against the face of the low cliff. I was in a state of tension, half expecting to see jackboots come flying over the cliff edge, so with urgency I had a try at cleaning the Bren with my handkerchief. It needed stripping down, so I thought that I would fire it to perhaps clear it, so I cocked it and pulled the trigger, only to hear a click, and also a loud gasp.

On looking up, I saw in front of me a young French soldier, white as a sheet, his eyes staring. My Bren was pointing at his belly and I believe he had come over to speak to me, but I was so engrossed in what I was doing, I didn't notice him there and I felt that judging by the hard looks of his comrades, that had my Bren fired, they would have soon polished me off. They must have all witnessed the behaviour of Smith and Jones, so I muttered to him, "Pardon M'sieur" and walked off with enemy shells still coming over, the barrage not yet abating. I had a useless Bren, three rifles in the slit trench with ammunition and spare barrel. If I ran the gauntlet of shellfire back I couldn't do what I had been ordered to do. I was sure in my mind that the Battery had been hit, so I felt that there was a chance of meeting up with some of them farther along the beach, and reporting the two cowards to one of my officers, Smith being the snowball trouble-maker.

I felt so hot and soaked in sweat under the hot sun, carrying the Bren and magazines, that the thought of looking for the Battery farther down didn't seem worth while, and the last two hours had taken their toll. So I wearily trudged along the beach, following the footprints of Smith and Jones in the sand on the way to Calais, which turned out to be a very long walk indeed, about 5 miles, without seeing a soul on the way. I felt really fed up at the way things had gone and was thinking 'to hell with it all' when I heard a strange whooshing sound and looking back, I saw a dot coming fast towards me so I threw myself sideways as a spent shell hit the sand, standing on its nose, smoking, with the centre part blown away, right where I had been standing. Looking at it for a moment, I thought what a grand souvenir it would make, then carried on with my trek to Calais.

Quite close to Calais I saw a section of beach littered with what I thought to be sticks, but on reaching them, I found that a considerable number of French rifles and bayonets had been discarded. This gave me an uneasy feeling, and didn't look at all encouraging, as it seemed that a large number of French soldiers were giving up before the Germans even got there. It made me feel like a rat in a trap. Then I arrived at the harbour, the Bren and magazines feeling like a hundredweight. There were quite a number of men of various units milling around, looking lost in a disorderly fashion, when Military Police started to round them up. I noticed a ship leaving the harbour with, I thought, vehicles on its decks and soldiers lining the rails.

The Military Police lined everybody up into two lines, myself in the front row, situated near a group of Army officers, who were having a discussion. At the harbour entrance two Royal Navy MTBs appeared, entering at high speed, with shells hitting the water all around them. One went to the shelter of the harbour wall, while the other sped to the jetty where we were. A bearded naval officer jumped ashore and spoke to the senior British officer. I just managed to catch the words 'two hundred' when at that moment a dispatch rider rushed up and handed the Army officer a piece of paper. After reading it, he spoke to the naval officer, who boarded his craft, which roared off at high speed, stern well down and bows lifted, followed by the second one. As they left the harbour, again some artillery shells straddled them, but thankfully missed, and I realized that the Germans must be close to do that.

The senior British officer addressed us quite loudly saying, "Men, I have just received this message via the radio from Dover from Mr Winston Churchill, stating that no man must leave who can fight and the town must be held at all costs, to the last man." With that, the lines of men were taken in groups to the town and placed with infantry, whom I found were the Queen Victoria's Rifles, 'C' Company. Evening was upon us and weary as I was, I felt very thirsty and hungry. Fortunately it was just at that moment that I was handed a ration of bread and bully beef, and was also able to drink my fill from containers of water which were brought up. An officer came to me and said he would take the Bren, as it could be put to good use, and he was delighted when I handed over the seven full magazines. What a relief it was to be rid of them from where they had been rubbing against my ribs. He then said, "Royal Artillery, I see." He took a Boyes rifle and clips of rounds from a man and handed them to me, saying, "You will probably make good use of that," handing my Bren to the soldier. It was an exchange, so I was lumbered just the same.

I tied my handkerchief around the breech and bolt to keep the sand out which, as it was very fine, seemed to get everywhere, then feeling very tired and the light failing, I slipped away to a hollow in the sand and slept soundly until the sunshine aroused me. My feet felt tight in my boots, and when I removed them I found them packed with sand inside. Luckily I was again in time for some welcome hot tea and a sandwich, but would have liked a lot more.

May 23rd and I saw that we were in a line situated between the sea and the inland lighthouse. Water containers were brought round for us to replenish our water-bottles, and as mine had been empty since early yesterday, I was glad to do so. Some hard biscuits were also handed to everyone to eat later. The day soon built up into a scorcher and there wasn't much doing, except to lie around on the sand, which became an aggravation, being very hot and reflecting heat all the time, and the discomfort was wellnigh unbearable. The riflemen were doing their own thing, tending to leave me and others like me alone. My feet became tight in my boots from the heat, but I wouldn't take them off, in case I couldn't get them back on again.

Boxes of .303 ammunition with loose tops were placed at intervals, as supplies to the riflemen when required. I was constantly looking around for a familiar face from the Battery or any of my officers, but I never saw one, and wandering around was not encouraged, although farther back, I did notice men among the sand-dunes. For myself, I had been ordered to be where I was and had no thought of moving elsewhere. I noticed that the NCOs and officers of the rifle regiments were very alert and fresh, having arrived on the ship which I had seen leaving. With smart clean uniforms, I felt quite shabby beside them, not having had a change of clothes for two weeks now, and with some Jerry sorting out my kitbag at Arras, there was nothing I could do about it. I missed having my rifle and kept my eyes open to see if a spare one would become available, as I suspected there would be soon. Most of the time people cleaned their weapons because of the fine sand sticking to them, also being no shade, the torment of the burning sun had to be tolerated by us all. I estimated that I was about 300 yards from the lighthouse and 50 yards from the beach.

Sounds of rifle fire, shell fire and mortar bombs didn't seem that far off and small sections of riflemen would move off into the town. I watched an aerial battle taking place overhead between a lone RAF fighter and his German opponent. The Messerschmitt won, with the Spitfire coming down on fire, the pilot parachuted out, swinging from side to side, and the German fighter flew around, firing bursts at him. The German flew off as the parachute and the pilot settled into the sea a good way out. Keeping my eyes on the spot, it seemed to me ages before the pilot reached the shore. The tide being right in, I saw him stagger out of the sea completely naked and with a big grin he shouted, "Got any trousers chaps?"

Royal Navy destroyers arrived on the scene, with four of them steaming in line, firing broadsides into the town, which they kept up all day. Artillery shells started coming our way, but I was in the riflemen's second line of defence, with the first line in front of the houses, etc., patrolling the streets. All this activity kept everyone very alert, not knowing what to expect, but I was not asked to do anything, so I just sat about on call, if needed. The odd meals were scrappy and not much of them, and when night came, fingers of searchlights probed the skies on the English side of the Channel, but sleep was to be denied me, as I was detailed to take over a Bren-gun guard from a rifleman in a position adjacent to two hospital trains recently arrived from Belgium. My orders were to stop infiltration of any enemy patrols or fifth column, and to take no one on chance. Before the other man left I said, "Wait a moment, there may be some grub inside," but the trains stank so badly with the heat of the day and bins filled with used dressings, etc., that I quickly came out, leaving the flies behind.

The night was pitch dark, so I settled down behind the Bren, reflecting on the events of the last few days and wondering how Annique was faring. How I needed her company right now, it was so lonely there in the dark and I couldn't get the picture of the French at Tilloy out of my mind. Deep in thought, I heard the sound of marching boots, so quick as a flash, safety catch off and bolt drawn, finger on the trigger, I shouted, "Halt, who goes there?" thinking if they're Jerries they are going to get it.

There was silence, then a reply came, "Royal Navy demolition party."

I then shouted, "Advance slowly to be recognized."

In the darkness an officer or a petty officer showed himself and said, "Demolition party come ashore to destroy cranes and other installations." All seemed to be OK, so I said, "Pass" and remembering my orders, I crouched over the Bren as they passed by, about 20 naval ratings some of them giving me side looks carrying between them by rope handles boxes of explosives. Then, with safety catch on, I couldn't settle down and felt restless at the slightest noise. At daybreak I was relieved and on my return, an NCO of the QVR handed me back my Boyes rifle and ammunition.

It was 24th May, and the weather was hotter than ever, and apart from being in one place all the time, I felt as if I was being roasted, and had a raging thirst to go with it. I relied on my water-bottle for sips and hard biscuits to chew. My eyes felt strained with the reflection of the sun on the sand.

The warships were back in line, steaming up and down, still firing broadsides into the German positions; they were our artillery and I was proud of them. A lot was going on somewhere in front of us and we moved forward as a line closer to the lighthouse. It was around here that German artillery fire was landing all over the place, in no set pattern, and small arms fire sounded much closer with officers more frequently taking small groups of men from the line into the town. I don't know the range of mortars, but the bombs from them were landing in and around our position, so it seemed to me that the Germans must be in the town. Their mortar bombs made a loud noise, resembling a car putting its brakes on at high speed before they landed with loud explosions and it was somewhat unnerving. The racket had built up into an inferno of noise now that Stuka dive-bombers were wheeling over, then shrieking down to drop their bombs all around us. Again, the noise was deafening, just like a lot of old women screaming as they fell through the air.

Orders were passed along to stand by ready to move at a moment's notice, with weapons. I felt encumbered with the anti-tank rifle, and was hoping to find a rifle from a casualty. This was the pattern in general for the day, but we never moved. There were many fires from houses and buildings around the lighthouse, also many casualties, which the riflemen seemed quite capable of dealing with. Biscuits and some water arrived, the one meal of the day, and I started thinking about the bully beef stew we used to complain about, and wishing I had some now. I felt sweat dried and among other things, a bath and change of clothes, especially socks, would have been a godsend, as my feet felt as though they were on fire and very sore. I was glad of the cool evening breezes and we were told to sleep where we were and again, the thin pencils of light darted about the sky over England as I slid into an exhausted sleep.

May 25th arrived, with much intensified fire, the Germans throwing everything at us, but our ships were still firing broadsides, steaming in line and occasionally artillery shells would hit the sea in the direction of the ships, but the range was too great. Sudden bursts of machine-gun fire came our way from infiltrating Germans, also the odd shot could be heard to whizz by from side angles, suggesting the presence of the fifth column, which together with the shrieking of the mortars and the dive-bombers was enough to shake the stoutest hearts. The continuous heat was getting to me, as to everybody else, and I found that my eyes began to hurt and my damaged ear was discharging, and with my water all gone, I didn't feel all that good. I asked around for water, but the answer was no, as the water works had been bombed, so I took six water-bottles from the nearest men, plus my own strung around my neck, and glad of a chance to stretch my legs, set forth to find water, I knew not where. I walked along the beach, not risking the town, to where our defence line thinned out. I was surprised not to be stopped, as it was well guarded but I expect the seven water-bottles spoke for themselves. I saw a small fort situated on the cliff, so very warily I made my way towards it and very cautiously entered a courtyard. The place appeared deserted when on a far wall I saw a water tap and reaching it, I found on turning it on, water gushed out. I went mad, greedily drinking my fill then I held my head under it and felt the luxury of water running over my face. With a finger I tried to clean my mouth and teeth. I was sorely tempted to strip off and have a splash down but the quietness of the place seemed uncanny so I decided now, with all the bottles filled, and a last drink, to buzz off. On leaving the courtyard I was startled when an officer and a small patrol appeared from nowhere. Confronting me the officer very sharply said, "What are you doing here?" I showed him the filled bottles, explaining why. Looking at my dripping hair he said, "You are a very lucky man, we've been trying to catch a sniper in here, go on your way."

When I returned to my position in the line I handed the water-bottles back to their owners, who shared them around, so that as many men had a drink as possible until it was all gone. I was asked if I would go back again and fill them, but I told them that I couldn't, as Jerries were about there, having the sniper in mind.

TSM Crotty, whom I was pleased to see, came along, shouting out, "Is there anyone here with coastal gun experience?" in case there may be an odd gunner about. I made to stand up, but he said, "Not you," knowing that I hadn't the experience he wanted. In reality, I wanted to go with him and report Smith and Jones, but he quickly moved on. Some time later I heard a terrific bang and word went round that the barrel had been blown off a French coastal gun. I guessed that Crotty had a hand in that. Suddenly there were several shouts of "Gas", and I saw a yellowish wall of gas creeping along the ground in my direction. Instantly the riflemen had masks on and I looked in desperation for one but there was not one in sight, then with relief the shout went up "Smoke", not gas and I wiped my brow in relief.

On settling down, a Rifles officer came to me and told me to go to the railway station to search for a fellow officer with a message to return to the line. Off I went, finding the station, with plenty of bullets whizzing about among the other stuff the Germans seemed to have in plentiful supply. There were wounded on stretchers laid across the railway lines and on the platforms close to the hospital trains, I enquired around, but the officer in question was not there. So I made my way back, as with nerve-shattering screams, dive-bombers came down, unloading their bombs and I saw a tank cocked over at an angle, so I dived underneath it, just as the bombs exploded. I saw a blinding red flash of flame and explosions so close that I thought my head had burst. Afterwards, on crawling out, I leaned on the tank, which I had felt lift, and rested a bit, feeling dazed and light-headed. Then I wondered if the bombs had hit the station, but I didn't go back to find out, as my head was throbbing badly and I felt as if I was walking on air. Whilst leaning on the tank, I noticed a two-inch hole in the front, it having been hit by an anti-tank shell. It was only later that I learned that the tank had been self-destroyed. On returning to my place in the line, I couldn't see the officer to report to him.

Not far from me, by some burned out trucks near the ruins of a house, a middle-aged heavily built Frenchwoman was sobbing bitterly, standing with blood running down her legs. Several men offered their assistance, but she pushed them away until a medical orderly, carrying his haversack marked with a red cross came along and they went behind a truck and her wound was attended to. She wasn't going to let any Tom, Dick or Harry touch her, because it looked to me as if she had been wounded in the buttocks.

The heat of the day, the smoke accumulating from the battle, the irregular noise all gave a kind of unreality to the scene, with small groups of riflemen dashing here and there with the combined educated voices of officers shouting orders, then the throbbing of engines above all the other noise. I stared up at the sky and a man close by echoed my thoughts, saying, "Good God, look at that lot!" I personally counted waves of up to eighty aircraft overhead, then I gave up counting. Above the dive-bombers were Dorniers droning along, then down came the Stukas. I felt totally disorientated, lying there with my hands over my ears, praying silently, and it went on for hours, the planes seeming to be running a mass taxi service. How I wished we had our 3.7 guns there, we would have blown many of those murdering bastards out of the sky. Now I could see the folly of taking away our transport at Sangatte. The ground fire never ceased either, so we were going to be bombed into submission, resulting in Calais itself being destroyed. A Vickers pom-pom mounted on railway sleepers close by added to the racket as well.

The rifle regiments in and around the town must have been giving the Germans a hard time, to make them go to this length to try and bomb us out of existence, but fortunately the sand helped absorb the force of some explosions. I know that I was 'bomb happy' and felt that I would go raving mad at any minute, but like the rest, we held on to our tattered nerves. Then over everything I heard a sound that struck a chord of memory, a high pitched screaming, then the steady fire of a Bren opening up. Then from the front a Rifles officer ran into the line of fire with revolver drawn shouting, "Stop it, I'll kill the bastard who's shooting my men in the back." The Bren ceased firing and from about fifteen yards away I saw Smith run off, screaming like a man completely off his rocker, so God knows what he had been up to since he ran off from me.

Just then a Rifles officer came up and told me that five of his men had been shot by a sniper from the top of the lighthouse. He ordered me to get the anti-tank rifle working on the top slits. He was a brave officer — bareheaded and still clutching his cane — ignoring fire, and directing men all over the place where to fire. I quickly borrowed a pile of haversacks and propped up the Boyes at the high angle needed to hit the top of the lighthouse. So with maximum range, I fired at the slits with care, using all the ammunition I had. If one entered a slit, it would be nasty for anyone inside on the receiving end of a solid armour piercing round whizzing inside. There was concentrated fire also from Brens and rifles but most couldn't reach the slits. The rifle gave a good kick back and my collar bone felt bruised. Afterwards I saw a spare rifle lying near by, probably belonging to a casualty, so I grabbed it quickly and stuffed my pockets with .303 rounds from the boxes which were being brought up non-stop. Now I felt at home and useful for the first time since leaving Sangatte and joined in with the riflemen on equal terms.

Casualties were being taken away, as this was war with a vengeance, and we did not have the heavy stuff with which to hit back. I heard a sobbing behind me and on looking round I saw a soldier dragging himself along by his elbows, leaving a trail of two red lines behind him. I saw that both his feet were missing, then at that moment, help arrived and he was taken away. The mortar fire became very heavy, with bombs dropping all over the place and I saw the Vickers pom-pom get a direct hit, with a blinding flash. I jumped up instinctively, and ran over to the gun, but it was shattered, with its ammunition belts lying twisted over, its three gunners lying looking up out of dead eyes, with only their uniforms holding them together. I returned to my position feeling very saddened, only to see another casualty from a mortar bomb, unbelievably even to imagine. I had just laid down in my spot, the line being hit with everything, including machine-gun fire, when some riflemen with bayonets fixed ran across our front. A tail end chap was hit by a mortar bomb, which resulted in a low wall looking as if buckets of red paint had been thrown over it. The man completely disintegrated, with his head resting on his neck, his arms and legs close by. His face had a slight smile on it. I ran over without thinking, and saw that his torso was stripped of clothing, including the flesh on his abdomen, revealing undisturbed intestines, such as is seen in a photograph in a medical book, one foot had no boot and one leg was lying bare. How, in a split second, could a man, fully clothed, wearing boots with leather thong laces, an equipment belt round the waist, be stripped in this manner? I have wondered about this ever since.

I then became aware of shouts coming towards me, so I ran back, and was called all the bloody fools imaginable. It was a sickening sight and it seemed so unfair for a man to end up like that. The fire became so intense that we all did the sensible thing and moved over to bomb and shell holes for cover. The one I found was a bomb crater and as I was sliding in, I saw an officer, a Lieutenant RA, crouching down there. I didn't know him, as he was not from my Battery, but after a short time he said, "Bombardier, tell me if you can see what's going on will you?" I hesitated, as I could hear the whine of bullets passing overhead, but I did look over and ducked down quickly.

I said to the officer, "I nearly got killed doing that, you look next time." After about five minutes, as the heavy fire eased, we scrambled back to our previous positions, but as soon as we settled down, another mass of Stukas appeared overhead. I saw nine of them veer off towards the sea and attack a destroyer, the last one of the line of four still broadsiding. It put up a cloud of thick smoke, through which I saw flashes of anti-aircraft fire. The leading dive-bomber went into the smoke, then there was an enormous explosion, with sheets of red flame showing through the smoke. The dive-bomber disappeared, as did the one following up, but the other seven wheeled round and released their bombs on the town and as was their custom, strafed positions with machine-guns. The destroyer, HMS *Wessex*, was crippled and sank later.

Word went round that it was official, no evacuation and Calais was to be held to the last man. There was some talk of a relief column getting through to us from a place called Dunkirk, which cheered me up somewhat. I lost count of time, with bells ringing in my ears, yet everything was carrying on, officers shouting orders and small bunches of men going into the town, leaving our line very thinned.

Someone brought water from somewhere, which slid down parched throats, but there was nothing to eat. The sun was literally burning me up and as evening approached, I made my way to the sand-dunes, which were used for toilet purposes, then on to the beach to splash some cool water on my head and face, when I saw dotted along the beach small piles of clothing. A man staggered out of the sea, and I thought he had just been for a swim to cool off, but as he dressed he told me, "I'm a strong swimmer, and I made it to one of the warships, but an officer shouted from the ship, 'Go back, you are deserting, I can't pick you up.'" He added that he had seen other swimmers who couldn't make it back. I noticed that the ships had now gone, as they had been doing each night during the battle. It looked grim and hopeless now, with men swimming out to warships. I had the feeling that the end wasn't far off, whatever that might be.

After the war, I wrote to the Naval Histology Department about the swimmers, and their reply was as follows: 'That men had swum out to the warships to be picked up. No RN ship would refuse to pick up a man from the sea, and if that man was a deserter, he would be handed over to the military on returning to land to be dealt with.' This is in my own words, but the meaning is clear. However, I could only confirm what the swimmer had said to me. I had a cooling wash on my face and went back straight away, the word 'desertion' in my mind, but I wanted no part of that. On returning, I noticed a feeling of resignation as the night drew nigh, the general conversation being what would it be like tomorrow, the Germans had already thrown everything at us, and what about some bloody grub; what I would have given for a nice cool pint just then. Before trying to get some sleep in a hole, I was hoping that I wouldn't be picked for guard duty. I wasn't, but a lot were, and before I closed my eyes I once again saw the tantalizing fingers of searchlights over England, only this time there were twice as many.

May 26th dawned and I felt trapped, with the battle creeping up to us and the sea behind, and no sign of the warships. There was still a line of sorts, under control of officers, when the firing against us opened up with a greater intensity, it was now like Dante's Inferno. A rifleman next to me stood up and shot a fair distance away, an old woman scuttling across a street fell without moving, such was the high standard of marksmanship. I said to him, "What the hell did you do that for?"

He replied, "Orders mate, we are to shoot anybody dressed in cloaks, etc., looking like priests, as many are infiltrating fifth columnists carrying tommy-guns and some of our blokes have been killed."

We were all sent forward really close to the lighthouse, which now stood as a beacon to devastation, with smashed and shattered buildings all around on fire, the air filled with smoke and burning oil. Columns of black smoke were rising high into the sky, dive-bombers seemed to be coming over in larger numbers than ever, with ground fire against us as fierce as ever. Continuous fire was taking place all along the line, and several times the order 'rapid fire' was given, myself complying with the rest, sending forward a wall of steel, deterring any German attempt to overrun us. There was a grim defiance about it all. Orders were to be very alert and to shoot any Germans we saw. I kept using up my ammunition but making sure that my pockets were filled from the boxes.

All around were scattered army packs, their contents emptied all over the place and I remember seeing a Rolls Razor, but nobody seemed bothered about picking anything up, feeling that the end was not far off, which gave me a sinking feeling in my stomach, the fear of the unknown. NCOs were extremely busy, dashing about under fire, directing fire into certain areas, we ourselves receiving concentrated small arms fire amid the explosions of artillery and mortar fire. There was the slower tat-tat-tat of the Brens, combined with the fast scream of the Spandaus, German machine-guns. Every movement I thought I saw in houses and windows at which I fired I hoped it was a German, but most fire was concentrated in front. This was the infantry doing it their way.

A small explosion with a whiplike crack occurred about six feet above me, leaving a round ball of smoke the size of a football. I asked a Rifles sergeant what it was and he replied, "It was an explosive bullet, if one of them hits you, then God help you." The tension and strained nerves and dulled senses took my mind off the fact that I couldn't remember when I last had a proper meal, certainly nothing since yesterday. The hot sun shining on to the heavily smoke-laden air made it like a hothouse, but I was now sweat dried. A general order was given for 'rapid fire' and the whole line responded with an eruption of deadly fire, a sound that I shall never forget, just like masses of Chinese crackers all going off at once. Then came the order 'cease fire'. I glanced around but saw no warships, missing the steady distant boom of their guns, yet from somewhere shells were going over, or so I thought.

It looked as though Churchill's order 'No evacuation and fight to the last man' was going to be it, but strangely, I never gave any thought to the possibility of losing, as there was still hope of that relief column. A soldier has always looked upon the Navy as comrades in arms and if the worst happened, they would never let us down, there was that faith. I had a shock of all shocks when a rifleman stood up, taking aim at some target, when the back of his head was sliced off and his brains fell out. Then he staggered forward and fell. I was suddenly roused from my feelings by shouts, and groups of men were running forward and behind me an officer shouted, "Twenty men follow me at the double." We stood up with twenty counted off, myself looking at some men who hadn't moved, then realized that they couldn't.

We were doubled somewhere through the town, which was on fire, when I caught sight of a few riflemen running who were levelled in a blinding flash of a mortar bomb. Running through shattered streets of smoke and fire, in oppressive heat, we came to a cobbled road with light railway lines. The officer stopped us at the corner of a building and we could all hear the bullets whizzing down this road, and ricochets bounced off the cobble-stones. The officer said, "When I say go, run over one at a time." This was done, with men bent double dashing across and when my turn came, with a thumping heart I took a deep breath and dashed over. Miraculously we all made it unharmed. We reached a high walled fort and ran over a bridge to a heavily guarded entrance, then up some stairs to a long corridor. Parts of the building were on fire, with smoke and dust everywhere. We were placed immediately at apertures, holes and narrow windows and told to shoot anything out there that moved. Two men at one window looking and firing, one saying to the other, "Over there, see him!" and so on, firing all the time. It made me think of a fairground when one said, "One over there, wait till he pops up again!" Then, "Got him!" At my aperture, I forced my eyes to focus and spotted plenty of movement in windows and figures dodging about so I fired at as many as I could. The cries of the riflemen calling for ammunition resulted in a clatter of boxes being brought up the stairs, with me keeping my pockets filled, as the rate of fire was high. I heard Brens firing somewhere, also thuds and explosions going on all over the place. Along the wall, not far from me, were wounded men, either lying down or propped up and being attended to by an RAMC doctor.

I saw several men stagger back from the windows, where they had been hit, and other men spread over to keep up the rate of fire. My rifle was hot to hold and now and again I would glance round to see if there was any water but there was none, and I began to feel ravenously hungry. Kicking away spent cartridge cases, I saw a clip of rounds, so I picked them up to use when I saw that they were mauve coloured wood bullets in brass cases, so, puzzled about it I showed them to the doctor, who told me they were impregnated with poison and if the wood hit a bone, the minute splinters would create a wound that would never heal. I thought what a diabolical thing to do and threw them into a corner. Some years after the war I checked this with the Imperial War Museum, who said wooden bullets did exist in continental armies but the doctor's explanation was an old RAMC legend and not true, as the wooden bullets were used to cock machine-guns, the wood disintegrating in the barrel.

It was afternoon now and I felt the smoke and dust affecting my eyes, making it harder to focus on targets. There now seemed a madness everywhere, with men cursing and swearing, calling the Germans everything and still keeping up a steady rate of fire. But it was coming back too, with dive-bombers pounding the fort, mortars and artillery fire included.

Some time early in the afternoon a rifleman came running along the corridor shouting at the top of his voice that someone had been waving a white flag from a window, when a rifleman shot him. He went past me and was gone, shouting like a man who had gone off his head. This was certainly a place of madmen and cries for more ammunition were left unanswered, there was no more. It was now necessary to pick targets with greater care to conserve what ammunition we had. I had roughly enough for two magazines left, and a glance at my watch showed 3.30 p.m. Then an officer ran up the stairs and shouted, "You six follow me and bring your weapons." We ran down the stairs with him, with heavy fire both ways, but partly obscured by smoke we ran from the burning Citadel to a building on a corner of the road. Just before reaching it, two German tommy-gunners came round the corner and straddled low, screaming, with their guns pointing at us. This all happened in seconds, they had the drop on us when our officer shouted, "Drop your weapons men," which we had to do or die on the spot. We were then doubled, with hands on heads to a cobbled square where other British soldiers were sitting on the ground. From that moment on, I was a prisoner of war, but it didn't sink in, and I sat down, feeling pretty weary and dejected. There had been an unreality about it all, but now reaction was setting in. One of the men close by said that he had also been in the Citadel but had come out earlier to help an outpost. This sounded like what we were trying to do and as other prisoners joined us, we knew that the Citadel had fallen. This was my fatal day, 26th May, but Lady Luck had stood by me all through, so I counted my blessings, to be all in one piece. Until the day I die I shall never forget those brave magnificent riflemen who did their duty to the bitter end.

Close by was a kilted soldier of the Argylls sitting awkwardly, white as a sheet, and a rifleman being propped up by his mates with a neck wound and blood seeping through the bandage. I laid back, my eyes burning like hot cinders and with a badly throbbing head. I don't think I could have gone on much longer, and I'm sure everyone around me must have felt the same. I was craving for water, but any attempt to move brought a quick response from the German guards, who looked as if they wouldn't need much encouragement to shoot us. A steady trickle of British soldiers joined us, many with wounds, and a Captain among them told us that on being taken prisoner, a high ranking German officer asked him where the heavy machine-guns were. When he replied that there were none the German officer said, "I cannot believe that men with only rifles held up my army."

Taken in the Strand, London in 1938, left to right John Knott, Jack Wright and the author, Bill Harding.

Training camp at Oswestry, Shropshire in 1939. Above, mobile battery food kitchens and below, gun breech inspection.

Kit inspection at camp Manobier firing ranges, Wales, early 1939.

L/Bdr. Bill Harding, top right, with reservists on a 3-inch quick-firing mobile gun.

The author with Walter of HMS Witch while on ten days BEF leave from France, 1940.

Calais in May 1940 showing a section of the town around the lighthouse where units held grimly to the end under intense fire.

Rue Royale, Calais, 1940.

The Citadel, scene of the last stand in the battle for Calais, 1940.

Datum *20. JUNE 1940*

Stalag VIII B

(Keine Ortsangabe, sondern Feldpostnummer
oder sonstige befohlene Bezeichnung)

Ich bin gesund — ~~verwundet~~ — in deutsche Kriegsgefangenschaft geraten und befinde mich wohl.

~~Von hier aus werde ich in das ...~~
~~...schreiben werde. Erst dort habe ich Post von Euch erhalten.~~
~~...Euch schreiben?~~

Herzliche Grüße

Vor- und Zuname: *WILLIAM   ALBERT   HARDING*

Dienstgrad: *LANCE   BOMBARDIER*

Truppenteil: **Stalag VIII B**

(Nichtzutreffendes ist zu durchstreichen.)   *KRGF. Nr. 9785*
Außer Namen, Dienstgrad, Truppenteil nichts hinzufügen. — Deutliche Schrift und Unterschrift.

GERMANY

Officially a prisoner of war.

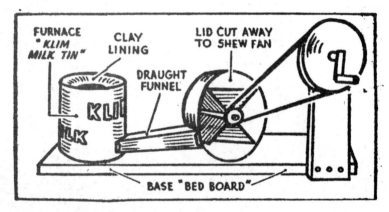

Sketch of a blower used to boil water in the camp.

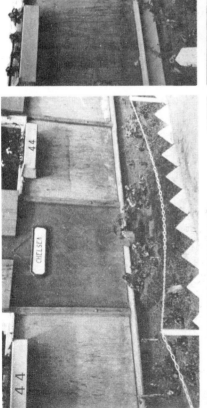

Some huts were named after favourite football teams.

1942 at Laband — army pal in camp concert. Dress made of paper.

1942 at Laband — a stage sketch. Dai Jones, Welsh Guards, on left. Note shabby uniform trousers, and the dress made of paper.

Army pals in a camp concert at Laband in 1943.

POW band in 1943 at Laband, Stalag VIIIB.

The camp workshop in Laband, Stalag VIIIB, 1944.

My French Foreign Legionnaire friend.

The author, 2nd from left, recovering from ear operation in February 1945 in hospital at Stalag IIIA, Luckenwalde, Germany.

John Butler, King's Royal Rifle Corps (left) and the author at the Royal Military School of Music in 1946, waiting for demob.

Graves of British POWs at Cracow military cemetery, Poland.

The grave of Gunner Cook in Cracow military cemetery.

PART III

CHAPTER FIFTEEN

Vor you ze var iss over (or is it?)

As the numbers of men on the cobbled square had grown considerably, a German officer appeared and ordered the guards to get us moving. So tired, worn and weary, though still defiant, we stood up and with a lot of shouting and some pushing, were herded to a line of guards. The German officer, in broken English informed us that, "Vor you ze var iss over, and any man not obeying an order will be shot instantly." We were told to empty our pockets, place everything on the ground, then go to the line of guards, where each man was thoroughly searched. I saw a few men in front of me being punched in the face when something was found on them. This made other men discard things like watches and rings which they tried to keep. All I had left was my identity disc hanging round my neck. The guards were rough and intended showing no mercy to the vanquished. The loss of my water-bottle was a blow, as I knew that when water was obtainable I wouldn't be able to carry any. I also knew what it was like to be thirsty in a desert. I had been on the go almost non-stop since 17th May and felt the need of a bath, a good meal and most of all, a twenty-four hour sleep without being woken up, but this was all wishful thinking, we had seen nothing yet.

As we were marched out of Calais through a town of rubble, fire and smoke, I saw civilians standing in groups staring sullenly at us as we passed by, giving me the impression that they blamed us for having their town smashed up. Suddenly there was a roar of an engine and rattle of tracks on the cobble-stones, so with others, I threw myself sideways for my life as a large German tank thundered through the column. The mental picture I got was of a high turret with two grinning faces wearing black berets looking down at me. We moved along in a straggling column, constantly harassed by the guards, when we were swamped by masses of French soldiers looking fresh and clean shaven, many joking with each other quite happily. Most of them had large packs on their backs, and many had attaché cases or bulky bags hanging from their shoulders, but my eyes fastened longingly on the water-bottles they carried. I asked several for a drink but was refused point blank. It was obvious that they had prepared themselves to become prisoners of war and they had taken no part in the battle. Some even had pots and pans hanging from their packs and many were bowed over with the weight of the huge packs, full of food, no doubt. Obviously the Germans had not searched or taken their possessions, as the French had remained hidden and had done the Germans no harm.

We passed our own casualties, lying as they had fallen, one in particular in the centre of a crossroads, a rifleman still sitting behind his Bren-gun in shirt sleeve order, eyes open, stitched across his chest with bullet holes, and there was a severed hand on the ground by his side. All of this and the attitude of the French made me feel bitter, especially when on reaching the edge of the town I saw German soldiers walking arm in arm with French girls and thought 'so soon'. Our walking wounded were, at this stage, still being helped along by their mates, as yet, no one had been given water and I was beginning to feel desperate.

We were flanked by lines of German soldiers making sure that no one had the chance to escape, and a nasty atmosphere was building up — the French soldiers were being treated quite reasonably, but the slightest excuse was enough for a British soldier to receive a blow of some sort. The town was covered in dense black smoke from burning oil containers, and as dusk fell, a red glow was showing from the many fires burning, making Calais look like a flaming beacon. I felt sure this could be seen from England, as I could now barely see the very faint fingers of searchlights, so near yet so far.

A few miles away from the town was a church, into which as many as possible were crammed, the remainder gathered outside. I was nearly out on my feet, and no food or water was issued. Trouble flared up in several spots when the French brought out loaves of bread from their packs, some with cheese and wine among other things, but when any of our chaps asked for anything, they would be shouted at in an insulting manner, the meaning being quite clear. The French kept together in groups so that they protected each other.

Inside the church, water taps were found and it took time, but I virtually had to fight my way to them to get a drink. When I did, I hung on grimly with the risk of losing my front teeth on the taps whilst I drank as much as I was able to before I was dragged off, unfortunately having no means of carrying water to take with me.

Dawn came, with us being hounded out with curses and blows. There was no way to get another drink and I was now thirsty again. Once on the road, with guards screaming and very free with the rifle butts, the whole rabble of men got moving. I saw that we now had different guards, the ones from Calais must have returned, but the new ones had faces full of hate for us. No food was given and I was ravenous with hunger, still feeling very tired. The night in the church had not allowed much rest, being jammed together and it was so hot. There were the shouts and cries of men having bad dreams, in fact it was a horrible night, and there was always the nagging thought of what the future might hold. I thought constantly of getting away, but the Germans weren't stupid, we were well guarded and driven on by trigger-happy guards, that to take a sudden chance would mean instant death, but like everyone else, I was leg weary.

The day passed in blazing heat, and a lot of men, including myself scratched anything edible from the edges of the fields — swedes, mangolds, potatoes, or whatever, and one had only seconds in which to do this, because bursts of machine-gun fire over our heads would make us move quickly back into the column, running the gauntlet of rifle butts and boots. A half-track at the end of the column fired the machine-gun bursts which just shot over our heads. Evening came and we were all gathered into a large field circled by guards with dire warnings that anyone who stood up would be shot. Still no food was given, or at any rate I never saw or received any if there was some, as the column was very long. Anything I was lucky enough to scavenge from a field edge received a wipe on my sleeve and was eaten straight away. The French lit small fires and proceeded to cook, with virtually no interference from the Germans, but any British trying the same thing soon got a bashing. I saw a Frenchman break a stout stick over the head of an Englishman who was arguing with him about us being Allies, so we had two enemies, the French and the Germans! That night it rained heavily, so I had the discomfort of lying on the grass and getting soaked through.

The morning was heralded with kicks and shouts. I could never understand why the Germans had to scream and shout in order to get their point across. As usual, there was nothing to eat or drink, so I had to forage for what I could find as I went along. With everyone in the same boat, it was a case of the survival of the fittest. The guards would not let anyone answer the call of nature, so it was a case of holding on until nightfall. Endless German military transport was tearing past us non-stop in the opposite direction, adding to our misery with exhaust fumes and dust. The guards were changed every few miles, so always being fresh, they had no feeling for us and kept pushing us to the limit. They took full advantage of the ill feeling between us and the French, as when passing through villages very tight control was kept on us, while the French flocked into shops to buy what they could in a hurry, but woe betide any British soldier who was caught trying to do the same.

As the days passed by with tedious monotony, the forced march was only made endurable because when passing through villages, Frenchwomen would place buckets and bowls of clean water on the edges of the roads. With a rusty food tin, which I picked up in a ditch, I scooped what water I could, but most buckets were kicked over by the enraged guards. These brave women would also stand with aprons held out, filled with pieces of bread for us to take as we passed by, but one sickening incident I shall never forget was when a little grey-haired old lady stood with her apron outstretched, full of bread, when a big brute of a German roared and knocked her to the ground, then kicked her unmercifully. Her screams are still in my memory and this caused many boos and shouts of "Dirty square-headed bastard" with the result that the guards laid into us with rifle butts.

The thirst was wellnigh unbearable and I was forced to cup dirty green water from ditches as I went along and drink it greedily. I also resorted to munching handfuls of grass when nothing was left at the field edges, having been 'cleaned' by the thousands in the column ahead. I bumped into TSM

Crotty and Nicholls, the only ones I ever saw from my Battery. They asked me if I could get them some food at the next village. I looked at them and walked away, never to see them again.

The column was becoming longer with more POWs joining it as we moved from place to place. The Germans got a kick out of our suffering, and I survived like an animal in the field, with eyes constantly on the look-out for any scrap to eat, anywhere. Some nights it rained heavily as we lay in the fields and in the morning, on standing up, every muscle in my body would be seized up and it would take a couple of miles before they loosened up. The hunger pains were indescribable and I was really surviving on my own fat, of which there wasn't much. We approached Cambrai and masses of prisoners were crammed into fields, surrounded by tense looking guards, this being our pitch for the night.

In the distance, I saw some horse drawn tankers and the cry of soup went up, so into long queues we formed. We waited ages, when I passed out and on coming round, everyone was sitting and lying around. I asked where the soup was and received the reply, "None of us had any, the French had it all," so it was another stomach gnawing hungry night. There were various odd shots and shouts during the night, the results of which I never knew and felt too despondent to care. At daylight we were driven on again, I was once more locked in cramp and by now everyone looked a sorry sight. One incident I recall was a big German guard taunting me and a slightly built man of the Royal West Kents with, "Your kink in Canada, Adolf Hitler soon in Buckingham Palace."

The chap next to me replied, "Churchill soon in Berlin," whereupon the German with a roar held him with one hand and smashed a fist into each eye. He had to be helped along with black swollen slits for eyes.

A German staff car, open top, with two officers in the back pulled up suddenly near an elderly Pioneer Corps prisoner. The German officers had noticed his first war medal ribbons and one of them said, in perfect English, "Englishman, you were in the 1914 war."

He replied in a broad Scots accent, "Aye, and I'll fight ye in the next." Without any further comment the car drove off. Starving and exhausted we may have been, but our spirit was unbroken. We had unshakeable faith that England would win, as in all our wars we always lost the first battle, but won the last.

We had now reached Belgium, and were passing through villages devastated with bricks and rubble where houses and buildings had once stood, and in the heat of the day, there was a sickly sweet stench of the buried dead permeating the air. Each day now consisted of mechanically lifting one foot in front of the other, the road just a haze, a seemingly endless one, with the hot sun beating down relentlessly. I managed to scrape by with the odd drop of water, but my mouth was dry inside and there was nothing I could do about it. Every man had his own problems, and if anyone managed to get anything he kept it, it was sink or swim, and every man for himself. All I had left was willpower, and thank God that is one commodity I have never been short of.

We turned back into France, and a sergeant who was keeping a rough check said that the Germans were keeping us on their lines of communication, to protect their transport from possible air attack, hence the twisting and turning. By this time the column had grown into an enormous length, mostly French, and a rumour was passed along that stragglers were being shot. We did hear an occasional shot, which made us think that it was true. We had already seen how brutal the Germans could be, and were capable of anything, being flushed with victory. In addition, no one had as yet been registered as a prisoner of war.

An experience which I had almost confirmed our suspicions, when through sheer weakness and exhaustion I felt my strength ebbing away and I slowed down. In a dream state I saw the end of the column gradually getting further away when a screaming German guard came alongside me and fired his pistol three times at the ground in front of my feet. I stared stupidly at the spurts of the bullets hitting the road. Then he rammed the pistol into my left temple, still shouting, and I felt sold out and resigned to my fate, and wished he would shoot and be done with it. Some of the men at the end of the column came to me and helped me back, and as the end of the marching day was near, I was soon able to lie down and rest.

We reached Doullens and were jammed *en masse* into what looked like a civil prison. My immediate need was water so I joined a queue at a water tap, and had a good drink to satisfy my terrible thirst. I pushed my way to the outside railings, packed inside with mostly French, shouting for food, and British soldiers trying their luck as well. I was one of these. Outside the railings there was a solid crowd of women screaming and shouting names, to which the French soldiers were responding from inside. It was like bedlam, a pandemonium of hysterical voices, with the Germans at that time unable to control the situation. The cries for food were non-stop, with many arms outstretched through the railings, one of which was mine, but with no luck, as anything which was given was to the French — I suppose your own come first.

A French officer close to me, a slim man of about thirty, spotted a woman whom he knew in the crowd, a chance meeting in a million, and he and the girl, in her twenties, were shouting to each other through the railings. The young woman fought her way through to the outstretched arms of the French officer, with tears running down her face, both shouting at each other hysterically. The German guards came along on the outside, and using considerable force, pushed back the crowd of frantic women from the railings. On reaching the girl, who was clinging desperately to the railings and in great distress, the guard gave her a clout, making her let go, whereupon with more shouting, the French officer punched the German through the railings. The German roared out to his comrades within the compound, and they, with rifle butts soon reached the French officer, who protesting violently was dragged away, his resistance proving to no avail. Watching this caused me momentarily to forget my own hunger and shaking legs, I just managed to see the Germans drag him behind a blocked off building and I heard some shots, not knowing whether the French officer had got it or not. Looking back to the girl, I saw her bowed, sobbing and shaking uncontrollably. My heart went out to her, but it all seemed so hopeless, grief and pain had to be accepted as part of the fortunes of war.

The German soldiers arrived in full force, clearing the masses from the courtyard and railings. Men were squatting all over the place in groups, emptying their bowels on the ground, many of whom had diarrhoea. The stench was vile in the hot sun, and I found that I had to tread very carefully where I walked, as there seemed to be excreta everywhere.

We were herded into the prison itself, no niceties, such as being directed where to go, just pushed with blows and curses from cell to cell until each was filled up. I ended up in a tiny cell, a solitary originally, with seven ebony black Senegalese soldiers. Being cramped for space, we all sat with our backs to the wall and our feet to the centre of the concrete floor, which was most uncomfortable. The blacks were chewing betel nuts and had bright red lips and teeth, and their continual spitting looked like blobs of blood on the floor. One of them took from his pocket a cob pipe and placed in it a large pellet which he took from a small box. On lighting it he drew in the smoke with a deep breath but didn't exhale. He closed his eyes, head against the wall, letting the smoke trickle slowly from his nostrils. The pipe was passed round in turn to the other six, who each performed the same ritual. The cell being windowless, it soon filled with smoke and I found myself feeling dizzy. The cell was so small, it could have been a box room. The blacks used a corner for toilet purposes, and I mercifully drifted into an exhausted sleep. It seemed no time at all before the Germans shouting and banging on the doors hounded us out. Aching wearily from head to foot, I moved out into the compound, when I staggered, almost passing out as the fresh air struck me. As we left, Germans from farm carts gave a piece of bread to each man, but there was no chance of seconds as we were being shunted out so fast.

A tank full of water from a running tap enabled men to get a drink without stopping, some using a steel helmet or whatever they happened to have. With my most prized possession, my rusty food tin, I scooped up my water, and those with nothing had to make do with a quick dip in their cupped hands. Then we were hassled back on to the road. My bread and water tasted like manna from heaven, but only served to emphasize the gnawing hunger pains. I was so stiff and aching that painful cramps set in, but I had to grit my teeth and walk stiff legged until it passed. I had lost all count of time, and there was the added burden of loneliness. I just couldn't see a familiar face, whilst everyone else seemed to be with pals, in pairs or groups from their own regiments.

Passing through a village there was the sudden roar of an engine, and an RAF fighter plane flying very low shot by, closely followed by a Messerschmitt. A ragged cheer went up from the column, which enraged the guards. I hope our man got away, although he may have run out of ammunition.

In the open country I saw close to a hedge a small hut, about 50 yards down, so with a quick look round and considerable effort, I ran down. As my hand touched the door handle, I heard shouts of "Halt" in German. On looking round, I saw with a heavy heart two guards with rifles aimed at me, and an officer with revolver in hand, doing all the shouting. With raised hands, I slowly walked back towards the officer. On reaching them, the guards made a grab at me, but quick as a flash, I ducked underneath their arms and darted into the column, then bent double, made as much distance as I could from that officer and the guards. I heard the blokes behind me shouting where they had closed ranks and in turn received the fury of the guards.

When the tension wore off, I felt washed out and exhausted, and realized that the presence of the officer saved me from being a dead man. I felt that if another chance came up I would take it, but weakness was a deterrent, as well as the German bullets.

The feeling between the British and the French was really bad now, and during the night a lot of stealing was going on, with the French making a terrible fuss in the mornings on finding packs and food bags gone or rifled, and by now both factions had moved into groups of their own kind.

Several days later we reached Luxembourg and I had a sinking feeling when I saw the steep hills up which we had to walk. The column had slowed down now, and no amount of bullying to speed us up had any effffect. The fact was that we were virtually worn out, with the blazing sun draining any remaining reserves of strength we had. Some of the men were being helped along by their mates, and were having to hobble on crippled feet, some had no boots at all when after taking them off at night they found either that they couldn't get them back on or they were stolen. My legs felt a bit swollen, and my stomach was beginning to gripe, almost causing me to pass out with the pain, but my feet were OK, and I never had a blister on the whole of the march.

Eventually we made it through Luxembourg, mainly through the kindness of the local people who, when and where they could, helped us with bread and water. Without these kind-hearted people, little though it was, I'm sure many wouldn't have made it. French ladies, I salute you for your bravery in facing brutal guards with your outstretched aprons of bread!

We crossed the border into Germany and reached a town called Trier and as we virtually staggered in, civilians, collected in large groups, jeered, shouted and spat at us. To the victorious German civilians, we must have looked nothing like the smart proud British soldiers they might have expected. Instead, they saw a dirty unshaven starving rabble, mixed up with the French. We were herded into some fields and here the German Army took over from the ever changing guards on the march. Not far from me, a group of French had lit a fire, which they had been allowed to do all along enabling them to cook, but now, on German soil, attitudes changed when a German officer formed a squad into line and with bayonets fixed they marched forward to all the lit fires, causing the French to run like rabbits, cooking pots, etc. were sent flying and their contents spilled, and the fires stomped out. I too made a quick exit, being in their line of march; they meant business.

The Germans were vigorous in implementing their orders, one of which was 'Anyone standing up in the dark will be shot.' On these occasions, there was always the odd shot during the night. I became twisted up in pain as the gripes took hold of me and I had to relieve myself in the awkward position on my side as best I could. This was a messy business, the result of drinking ditch-water, eating grass and anything else from the fields.

When morning came we were separated from the French and personally I was glad to see the back of them. We were then roughly herded to a train of box wagons. As we waited our turn to board a wagon I saw British POWs being forced in by German soldiers, shouting and worked up into a frenzy, using boots, fists and rifle butts until the wagon was crammed full, with men inside shouting and swearing. Some loaves of bread were thrown in and the steel doors closed and bolted when no more men could be forced in.

Then our turn came, with shouts of "Englander swine" and we received the same treatment, being punched and kicked, etc. The Germans were merciless and we were so tightly packed in that when I managed to lift my arms upwards, it was difficult to get them down again. Panic almost took over when the weakest slid to the floor and were trodden on, their standing space immediately gone. The only light and air came from a small grille placed at the top of the wagon.

The heat built up from the sun outside and the packed bodies inside. A stench also filled the wagon as men messed themselves, including myself, the most degrading thing a man can do. It was a living hell, with men trying to get some movement to ease tired limbs, but we were all so weak and all needed to sit down, so as always happens in these circumstances, a person with strong will took over. All those who couldn't stand wriggled to one corner to sit with their legs drawn up to make a little room for us who were standing, but they had to give others a turn as well.

Several times an attempt was made to count how many men were present in the wagon, and it averaged 72. Men tried without success to get to a corner to perform an act of nature, so that combined with the sweat of unwashed bodies and breathing in each other's faces, it all added to the torment.

Obviously the greatest abuse came from those whose bowels were not affected. The train was a long time stationary then when it did move, it was with sudden jerks, upsetting our precarious balance. As time went by, I went into a kind of stupor, dozing and sleeping standing up, then there was uproar and blows struck when blokes slid from the upright position or tried to sit down. My legs and feet went numb and another aggravation was when the train, presumably pulling into sidings whilst *en route*, would keep shunting backwards and forwards very jerkily, making us sway about holding on to each other to prevent collapsing *en masse*.

I have no recollection of having any bread to eat, and certainly nothing to drink. I found very little honesty in that wagon, everybody kept what they got hold of. This was the same on the march and I found that comradeship only applied to personal friends, otherwise it was every man for himself. Those who had fouled themselves managed, with a terrible struggle to remove their underpants, those around pushing back to make room. The pants were thrown out of the wagon through the grille, and I recall one man who managed somehow to reach the grille to look out, his fouled pants in his hand. When the train stopped at a station and in line with the grille stood a German civilian and our bloke threw the soiled pants through the grille into the German's face shouting, "Take that you square-headed bastard." We saw him do it and he shouted, "Bull's-eye blokes!" as the train went on its way.

This situation lasted three days and nights and I stood for three days, when in a dream state during the night I must have slid down with others, with legs criss-crossed over, worn out. The doors opened for the first time in bright daylight on the fourth early morning, with the guards screaming obscenities, dragging men out. I crawled to the opening and fell out, and then I passed out. As I came round I felt a thudding in my back and my eyes focused on a gleaming boot then I saw the owner, a German officer kicking me and shouting, among other things, "Englander swine."

Bent over, with my insides feeling as if they were going through a mincer, on shaking legs I joined a ragged column which was forming up the full length of the train. Someone told me that there were dead in the wagons, there could well have been in mine. I knew of none, but I felt too ill even to care. Refer to Books I and II of *Rough Ride From Trier* by Alwyn Ward, where other men testify that there were dead POWs in their wagons. The train was not at a station, so with much harassment, the column moved forward, passing through a large cemetery where, I learned later, were graves of First World War prisoners. Eventually we came to some large gates, and on entering I found that I had arrived at Lamsdorf — Stalag VIIIB in Upper Silesia.

We formed up into open lines inside the compound, feeling just about ready to drop when immaculately dressed German officers appeared shouting in 'American English' — "Any Jews among you, step forward." I saw a few here and there step forward and they were taken away. One of the officers angrily shouted, "Come, come, England is full of Jews, there must be more of you," then two more stepped forward. They were not satisfied, so a white-coated woman, with two of the officers, ordered us to drop our trousers and lift our shirts, and walking along the ranks, any man to whom she nodded was taken away.

This over, a large number of us were taken to some large stables, with straw-covered cobble-stone floors. I was soon scratching and found that I was alive with fleas. We were all handed three boiled potatoes, with a slice of black bread on this first day, but after a small amount of watery soup was issued with a bowl and spoon, my situation developed into dysentery, so I laid on the straw with trousers down, feeling wretched, with my knees up to my chin and keeping a rough count of passing blood up to thirty times a day. Someone brought an RAMC medical orderly, who brought me water to drink and cleaned me up with some of the straw, and for several days he gave me some small black medicinal squares, which I thought was charcoal. My insides eventually dried up from passing blood, but the dish-water soup always went straight through me. I felt a sick man, very weak and so hungry that I would lie down and attempt to chew some of the straw. The daily food issue was a small amount of soup, a slice of bread and black bitter ersatz coffee, with no milk or sugar. For our enjoyment, loudspeakers all around the large camp gave German marches and martial music most of the day.

The weather was boiling hot, but the only water available was from the two stack pipes in the compound, which were turned on in the evenings only, and to get a drink, everyone had to queue for their turn like long snakes on shaky legs. The Germans certainly turned the screw on us 'Foul, stinking Englander swine.' We stood to the point of collapse listening to some German officer screaming and shouting insults and abuse about England. I thought they were all lunatics.

A lot of building work was going on, erecting huts, and we POWs could get nowhere near them, but one morning, some foreign POW threw some loaves of bread over the wire, one of which landed a few yards from me, but I was too weak to get to it first; two Scots in kilts grabbed it. When I asked for a piece I was told to so-and-so off.

Within a few days, our identity photographs were taken, with boards hanging round our necks with a number chalked on it, mine being 9785. Then came a tiring business of waiting for the number stamped disc and then on to desks, being interviewed by civilians, details taken to forward on to the International Red Cross. I was given a postcard to fill in for sending to my next of kin, on which I wrote my POW number. I now had a problem — should I bother? So thinking of my sister, I put my mother down as next of kin. We were also lined up and shorn like sheep, all baldies. The next day, 700 of us were sorted out for dispatch to a working camp, so the next morning we filed back into the box wagons, but with more room this time. After a day's journey, we arrived at a place called Laband — a small place not far from a large town named Gleiwitz, all within the mining areas in Silesia. At first sight it appeared to be a nicely laid out camp, with rows of wooden huts, latrines, a cookhouse and guards' quarters. There were tall watch towers placed around the camp perimeter at strategic points, with ominous looking machine-guns on view, and shiny steel-helmeted faces behind them. It was to be a camp of mixed memories, some reasonable under the circumstances and some very bad, but it all pointed to one thing, that the hated Englander was not to be trusted.

Our jackets had been stencilled with white paint on the backs 'KGF Kriegsgefangener' (prisoner of war) and a large red diamond on the thigh of the right trouser leg. We were paraded in two lines of a three sided square on a parade ground in the camp, with guards lining the front, looking very businesslike. The centre was the focal point for the Camp Commandant and his staff, an elderly man with First World War ribbons on his chest. He gave a long thundering speech, working himself up until he was purple in the face, and this went on for so long that several men fell down from exhaustion, only to be kicked until they stood up. My own legs felt like buckling, but somehow I stuck it out because there was movement at last as guards were allocated 30 men each as his work squad. But I think the guards were illiterate, the dregs of the army, they kept counting us and marching stiffly to the Commandant, giving different numbers, looking like robots, clicking heels backwards and forwards until the Commandant looked as if he would collapse in a fit. However, we were issued with a towel the size of a tea-cloth, a small piece of clay soap which dissolved in two quick washes, a bowl, spoon and mug.

All of this simple business took hours, with all of us shaking, and in a poor state under the hot sun. When completed, the Commandant had another screaming session when the loudspeakers started to sound very loudly '*Wir gegen faren Engeland*', then a group of British POWs started singing 'There'll always be an England', sending the guards into action to subdue it. The guards then each marched his squad to the allocated hut (or Stube) and there was a rush when we saw two-tiered bunks, made from rough wood, everyone trying to get a bottom bunk. They were so close together that it was necessary to move in sideways to get in your bunk. The bottoms were loosely boarded, with a straw palliasse laid out and one blanket. Then we were hounded out by a puffed up guard, full of pride, leading his captives with bowls and spoons to the cookhouse. It was spacious and new, with large vats of soup giving off an aroma which increased my craving for food, having had nothing since the previous day. The large vats were deceptive, as each man was given only one ladleful in his bowl, a piece of black bread with a small ration of margarine, a spoonful of soft cheese and a mug of ersatz coffee. There was much laughter from the cook and his staff, who had all come out to watch the starving rabble of defeated English swine, with our own guard trying to show his superiority, being of the 'Master Race' by shouting and speeding the queue along, when I for one didn't want to lose one drip of soup from the ladle.

Back in our huts, the meagre food issue disappeared in minutes, and the main topic of conversation was as to when we would get the next issue. The food which we had just eaten only served to increase our hunger pangs. The soup, combined with the ersatz coffee, went straight through me, so I went to the latrines, where I saw a long deep brick-lined pit, with a long front board to sit on, and no privacy, but we were all used to that by now. In order to clean oneself, it was necessary to pull up a handful of grass on the way in. Back in my room and lying on my bottom bunk I took stock of my companions, six Welsh guards taken at Boulogne in the rearguard action, next to me an old sweat from the Gloucesters, the remainder being mostly north country regiments but not another gunner, although there were plenty in the camp. Being in the same boat, we soon became friends, but also soon fell fast asleep.

The next morning was our first working day, and we had no idea what to expect. We all hoped for something to eat, but we soon found out that the previous day's food issue was a debt and we had to give a full day's work before we received the next one. We were suddenly awakened with the door crashing open and the guards running around the bunks shouting "*Raus, arbeit* foul Englander swine," belting us with rifle butts. In a dazed state I stood up to see a German NCO standing by the door with hands on hips, shouting and gloating over every moment. We fell into squads outside, still being pushed around by the guards, and after several counts we marched straight off to work. God, how I hated them. In the whole of my life I could never stand being pushed around, and was always quick to react, but here I could do nothing but take it with gritted teeth. There was a strutting guard in the front leading us 30 men and one in the rear harassing us for the benefit of passing civilians, who shouted and jeered at us, and I saw one spit at us, to whom I glared in defiance.

A voice in the squad shouted, "Heads up lads, keep in step, remember you are British soldiers," which we all did, some in pain, hobbling along in wooden clogs which took the skin off their heels. Our uniforms were looking the worse for wear, and my own was rather smelly as a result of the dysentery, etc., but there was nothing I could do about it. Walking was bad enough, because of weakness, and my stomach felt like a flattened paper bag, gnawing with hunger.

We arrived at the work site, which was situated in marshland, on which was being erected a large factory complex. As yet no roads had been laid out, and a main railway siding was about five hundred yards from the site. I became very despondent on seeing long flat wagons loaded with heavy steel 'H' type girders, painted brick red, which was to be an added curse later on, as the paint never seemed to dry and we became smothered in it. Wet sand had to be used in trying to remove it from our hands, but finger-nails and clothes became clogged with it, and the smell of the paint never left us. One thing that always irritated me was that when the Germans, soldiers and civilians alike wanted anything done, they always had to shout and scream, making it difficult to understand and often causing unnecessary unpleasantness and blows. They could not get it into their thick skulls that we didn't understand their language. We were never ever trusted, and even when obeying a call of nature in the bushes, a guard would be there shouting "*Schnell, schnell, arbeit Schwein.*"

The work was beyond us because of weakness, and this infuriated the Germans, as when trying to manhandle the heavy girders from the wagons, we could hardly move them. Accidents occurred, fortunately none fatal, when girders slipped out of control in the process of being moved. One example was George Maybanks, who had half a finger chopped off when a girder slipped, and when it healed he was back to work. If a guard looked his way he would hold the stump on his nostril, looking as if he had half his finger up his nose, and wiggle it. The Germans had a pet hate, and that was to see anyone picking his nose, which made them fly into a rage. When George got one of them going, he would hold up his finger stump laughing.

A soldier who had served in Egypt told us that the heat there was about the same, so we sweated it out, though water was available from a stack pipe. I did have some kidney trouble soon after, and a very painful experience it was too. As there were several of us, we were taken to the village doctor, who said it was sand in the water and gave us tablets and a glass of water. Then we were taken to a lavatory and I thought I was passing broken glass, after which the pain eased and back to work we went.

We were plagued with giant flies which would settle on our bodies, and we only knew they were there when we were bitten. There were also other varieties, so blokes were soon walking about with lumps and swellings; eyelids when bitten whilst sleeping would swell up, just showing the ends of the eyelashes. Following this was the constant itching and scratching, trying to sleep at night. The guards thought it a big joke, pointing to their own arms, indicating inoculations. We had no such protection or treatment and some men were in a bad way the insect bites bringing on fevers, but the Germans did have a first aid hut, and an aspirin with work was their idea of a cure for all ills, except broken bones. The cry was *"Los, Los, immer arbeit,"* the guard being the boss, and if he said work, even if you tottered there, you had to work. Those darned flies would never leave me alone, forever buzzing around my left ear, attracted by the vile smell of the non-stop discharge from it. It is at such times that everyday things such as handkerchiefs are missed. I ripped the tails off my shirt to use as wash cloths and to swab my ear clean in the mornings, to remove the dry hard crusted discharge. I asked for treatment once, and received only abuse. The German medical orderly would never treat anyone unless he saw blood, and would just turn the POW out.

When the working day ended, we received our daily meal, such as it was. Then came the dreaded *Appell*, when wobbly on our legs and longing to sit or lie down, we would stand for ages in torment, with the ritual of endless counting, the Commandant ranting at the guards who kept bringing back different tallies of their squads. There were also, as usual, small groups of prisoners being reported for petty demeanours at work, such as fainting, which was classed as refusing to work. This was also an opportunity for the guards to show the Commandant how well they were doing their duty in not letting the 'Englander swine' get away with anything. The normal punishment was to run round in a circle, to the point of collapse, which didn't take long. It was a two way thing however, as the British soldier is no fool, no matter what the circumstances, and we were always on the look-out for any advantage, no matter how small. We being the first prisoners in Germany, the guards were too often blinded by their own importance to see the devious tricks we played on them later.

On dismissal, we would wearily go to our huts and bunks, the main topic of conversation being the lack of food and hatred for the Germans and their total lack of fair play. Women were rarely mentioned, as at this time in our young lives there existed no physical sex drive, for as one old sweat put it, "This is more effective than having bromide in your tea." The hard work, the harsh treatment, the semi-starvation and inhuman conditions caused a few quiet sobs during the night, shouts from nightmares and so on. Our one urinal bucket for 30 men always overflowed on to the floor by morning, including the contents of those with loose bowels.

CHAPTER SIXTEEN

Friends among enemies

I now come to the Poles, who lived in dread of the Germans, as their families were held to ransom on their co-operation to work their hearts out for little reward — enough food to live on. British POWs, not Poles, were paid 70 pfennigs a day. So they were slaves and so were we. They must have been warned to ignore us, for if any of them tried to communicate with us, they would first look in all directions, terrified at getting caught. At our half-hour break, occasionally a Pole would, by signs, indicate for us to look at a pile of bricks and then walk away. The nearest POW would find a piece of bread, and in time, they tended to 'adopt' some chaps, leaving something every day and over the years, a strong bond of friendship developed between the Poles and the British prisoners. I never knew of an instance of a Pole being unfriendly, or attempting a dirty trick on a British POW, and I would never hear a word spoken against them.

By contrast, the British POW, wherever I was, never showed any fear of the Germans, an attitude they could not understand. In our own peculiar way, we would resist whenever possible, mostly on little things, and keep acting stupid, getting them into rages, which also had its risks. In their opinion, we were a beaten race, but it never occurred to us that we were and we were quick to learn the things which rubbed them up the wrong way. I recall one day, when a guard swung his rifle across the back of a POW. The stock broke off, and in pain, the POW laughed in the guard's face. It was enjoyable to see the guard carrying his rifle around in two pieces for the rest of the day.

Punishment for petty misdemeanours on parade were handed over to our camp Sergeant-Major to deal with. On principle he should have refused, but did give some token punishments, such as press-ups and doubling on the spot. I thought that it was degrading and he defended his action by saying that his punishment was easy compared with that of the Germans. Maybe so, but in comparison to us, he had a fair sized corporation and always reminded me of 'Bumble' — I cringe before my superiors and oppress my inferiors.

By this time we had sorted ourselves out, and as in all human contacts, men formed small groups as friends, mainly to share the small loaf of bread, which had to be cut into five slices; no easy task, even with a knife, which we didn't have. But most of us found flat pieces of metal on the work site, which we managed to hide when being searched every time we returned from work. When sharpened on a stone, this piece of metal had to do the job, and was

153

passed around. Cutting the loaf was a serious business indeed, the men with hungry suspicious eyes would watch the slices being cut, with arguments and sometimes fights if one slice was thinner than another. There was even a scramble for the crumbs, with a licked finger from table or floor. One day I saw two pals from the same regiment in an argument over the bread, they fought it out toe to toe and when one went down, the other had to be dragged off him. The Scots were the worst. They banded together to cause intimidation, so in the main, they were left to their own devices.

One Sunday afternoon, when parade was over, I was wandering around the compound immersed in thought when I noticed newsreel type cameras being set up near the kitchens. The guard opened the gate leading to the swill bins and pointing to them he shouted, *"Englander hier rein essen hollen."* There was a stampede of POWs on top of each other fighting and clawing in the bins, with only handfuls of potato peelings to show for their trouble. The cameras were recording it all, whilst the Germans roared with laughter. I was as hungry as the rest of them, but I couldn't stoop to that. If the film ever reached the German cinemas I'm sure they would have found it funnier than Laurel and Hardy, due to their warped twisted minds.

Some Sundays later, in the afternoon, roughly in the same place, I saw the German cook place a large cake from the oven on to the window ledge to cool off. It was his loud laugh which attracted my attention, no doubt another torment for hungry eyes to see. The guard was there, but the gate was open, so two POWs went to the guard and tried to engage him in friendly conversation. He responded, and with his back to the gate, another POW darted in and snatched the cake, and was away in seconds. The other two prisoners left the guard, with a wave of the hand, and I shot off quickly too. A roar of rage came from the cook, looking through the window, and within minutes the guards hounded all prisoners out of the huts to form a parade. The guards went berserk, wrecking our bunks because we had nothing else, searching for the missing cake, which was never found. Nobody knew what the fuss was about, only myself, an onlooker, as none of us understood German. But I said nothing in case anyone thought that I had the cake. The Germans were on to a loser with no one knowing what it was all about. Every man was shouted at and looked at closely for signs of crumbs, but nothing was ever found and I was puzzled myself as to where it could have been hidden, for a freshly baked cake can be smelt a good way off. The guard took the blame for not locking the gate, so no mass reprisals took place.

At work, everybody was concentrated on a stretch of ground, road making, to enable railway lines to be laid so that sand filled skips could be pushed along manually by prisoners to the building site, a very tough job. I was one of a small gang laying clinker from boilers and knocking it down into the spongy ground, and although physically weak, I unconsciously started to whistle 'I'm gonna hang out the washing on the Siegfried Line'. The German overseer, a giant of a man who was always showing off a wound scar on his stomach from the Polish campaign, ran over to me and pushed a very large clenched fist under my nose, shouting that he understood the song, so shut up. After a while, my mates whispered, daring me to do it again, so looking warily at him, I started to whistle softly, but stopped as his head moved and he charged over to me shouting and grabbed me by the throat. I was almost choking when a guard rushed over and he released me. I thought that I had had it, and felt shaken up, but several hours later, to annoy him, I whistled so softly that he jerked his head. I stopped, deeply engrossed in my work, so being uncertain he didn't move. I didn't press my luck after that. If we even smiled, it upset the Germans, they were the conquerers. In this period there was almost a bad accident, as Percy Green stepped in front of my descending pickaxe, the point catching him on his forehead and knocking him out. Fortunately he quickly recovered, but with a dent in the bone, a permanent reminder of Laband.

The nights were unpleasant with bugs, the large variety with stripes on their backs. They formed into colonies in the crevices of the rough woodwork of the bunk beds. Our straw palliasses were alive with fleas, they would run up and down my legs and back until in great torment I fell into an exhausted sleep. I have heard it said that fleas and lice are never found together, which is not true — I had the lot!

After evening parades there was a rush to the washhouse where I endeavoured to remove some of the sweat and dirt of the day with cold water and a rub down with my pieces of shirt. My socks disintegrated, so they went, and small pieces of foot cloths were only issued to the people with clogs. I tried to keep my teeth in order by rubbing them with my finger under a running tap. Flies hummed around at night in the darkness and bit us, coming I think from the swampy area.

In our huts at night we would sit naked, with trousers turned inside out, cracking lice between our thumb nails and squashing the layers of white eggs found in the seams. The continuous scratching soon brought sore patches around our genitals, some of which developed into running sores, and the men couldn't work until some medicinal powder dried them up. The bug bites would bring lumps up on our upper arms and it was common, in the mornings, to see each other's faces blood streaked, where we had squashed bugs in our sleep and they stank.

As the latrines filled, so the smell from them permeated all over the camp and beyond. When the pits were full, the surface seemed alive with things like oversized tadpoles. Horse-drawn tankers would come and by hand pump suck them empty, then the raw sewage would be spread over fields on nearby farms. The smell was indescribably vile and the only satisfaction I had was that the German guards had to put up with it as well. I think of all the things which stay in my memory the most, the stink of the Stalags and camps take precedence. This eased somewhat when Red Cross parcels started to arrive, containing bars of scented soap, which I loved to sniff, it was heavenly.

With our evening ration, we sometimes got a spoonful of jam in lieu of cheese. It was suggested that whatever the flavour, it was made from mangolds or swedes and the pips were made of wood splinters. I was inclined to believe this, as they could never be chewed. The soup in the main varied each day from boiled mashy potatoes to boiled cabbage, frog spawn, boiled shredded carrots, onion soup, sometimes barley soup, our favourite, as it filled us up more, not forgetting the hateful sauerkraut. Some men found that, hungry as they were, they had the strength of will to save a piece of their bread for the morning, which brings to mind one man who had somehow obtained a long thin white loaf from a Pole. He must have given a lot for it as the situation was then. Such was his pleasure at having the loaf that he was almost caressing it, enjoying the spectacle of a room full of hungry eyes watching him. Hungry as he was, he was loath to eat it, and for safety he placed it under his head as a pillow that night. When he awoke next morning he found the ends of the loaf missing, cut off close to his ears. He completely lost his reason, shouting hysterically and searching the floor around the bunks for crumbs, but he found nothing and being hounded out to work soon brought him back to reality; but for all the hunger, I felt no pity for him, he could have kept the loaf hidden instead of flashing it about. We never found out who did the cutting.

I had for some time been with a gang moving the steel girders from the railway wagons to the construction area. It was now September 1940 and an awful lot of these heavy girders were needed. I could feel myself flagging and getting weaker every day, so that each girder became a back-breaking ordeal, racking me from head to foot, and at times I blacked out, only to be revived with kicks, as were the others. The gang comprised twenty men, ten pairs positioned along the girder, holding across large heavy pairs of tongs to grip the top of the girder. On command from the German civilian, which was, "*Na alzo, alle man hein rook,*" we would take the strain, lifting together, and swing the girder forward a few inches at a time, with the civilian shouting abuse at us to swing it further. The dead weight, the group being of different heights working on uneven ground was sheer hell, we were truly slaves. The guard too would do his share of pushing and shouting, the commonly used abuse being '*Arbeit*, foul Englander swine', often accompanied with a touch of the jackboot on the rear end. I detested them so much that it burned into me like a hot iron. The guard's name was Schmidt, a beady-eyed evil-looking bastard.

There were days when the rain was torrential, on leaving for work in the morning we would be instantly soaked through. I would feel water running down inside my now torn, ragged clothes. On reaching the work site where the guards were dressed in well protected waterproof clothing, we would be bent over, standing ankle deep in waterlogged ground and continue to move the girders. Sometimes it would rain non-stop and this played havoc with our uniforms. Mine was now shrunken and threadbare, with ragged trouser bottoms, the knees and seat in holes, with tears and rents in my jacket. My boots were literally on their uppers and I hung on, dreading the horrible clogs. The clothes all had a frowsy smell when wet and the search *Appell* still went on in the teeming rain. When back in the hut we would all strip off and hang our clothes on the ends of the bunks in the hope that they would dry by morning. We stayed in our very smelly hut with our blankets wrapped round us, lying on our bunks. The topic of conversation was always home, families, wives and sweethearts. Food was now taboo as some blokes lost their tempers quickly to anyone who spoke of it. One burning theme was the longing to receive mail. Some men found it unbearable not receiving a letter, and this would bring on deep depression to add to the other burdens.

The evening search at the gate was now being done reluctantly by the guards, as they found touching us repulsive, knowing that we were all lousy. We looked a sorry sight, skinny, with hollow cheeks and sunken eyes.

One day on the site a train of box wagons pulled into a siding a few hundred yards away from us, and when the wagon doors were opened, women and girls in summer dresses were hounded out, all in great distress. Gestapo guards, men and women in black uniforms with swastika arm bands, tore into them with short truncheons, making them climb to the top of the heaped coal wagons and start unloading the coal with their bare hands. It was a sickening sight, with the roars and shouts of the Gestapo amid the screams and cries of the women. I hoped the day when these bastards reaped their just rewards would not be far off.

We would, when we were able, with a system of look-outs, fill the large axle grease boxes on the long trains with sand. On the sides of the sealed box wagons were loose drop-in destination boards, and as long as the guards were not looking our way we would swap them about, hoping that somewhere the German army would receive silk stockings and some other place receive army supplies. I well imagined the pandemonium this would cause, and a bullet for certain if we were caught for sabotage. Some months later, with better communication, the Poles informed us that reports came through of trains with red hot axles catching fire, so some of our puny efforts were not in vain. The locomotives were enormous in size and two were used for pulling large numbers of wagons, which seemed endless in passing by, often stopping near us to have girders, etc. unloaded. The many sacks of component parts, nuts and bolts were easy prey to us, as in time, thousands of them were 'lost' or thrown away. Many bags of cement also got 'accidentally' spilled on wet ground!

One day, working on lifting girders, I felt my back go with a stab of pain which increased as I tried to carry on, until I found I couldn't. With signs and expressions I tried to make known my dilemma to the overseer and to Schmidt, the guard, who automatically believed that I tried to dodge work, so they vented their spite on me with relish. I had to go through the motions of lifting in agony until the end of the working day, when I felt completely crippled. That night, I walked up and down the hut, bent over in pain, and when morning came, I felt washed out. Forming up outside, I told Schmidt that I couldn't work so he took me to the first aid hut. It was three steps up into it, when Schmidt had a few words with the fat medical orderly, who with a roar spun me round shouting *"Arbeit Englander Schwein"* and booted me in the rear, sending me sprawling into the dirt, whereupon, with more abuse Schmidt made me join the end of the squad, who then set off for work. My back felt on fire, and I couldn't straighten up properly to keep in step. This infuriated Schmidt, who went off his head, screaming in fury at me, punching and pushing, so in rage, I deliberately kept out of step and walked badly to annoy him more. He pricked me with his bayonet, I believe to give him the chance to shoot me, but by then we had reached the work site, before which I delivered to him a few four-letter Saxon words.

Once on the site with Schmidt busy, some mates quickly took me to a large crane cone mounting, with a narrow opening. I could just squeeze through, and they told me to stay put, they would keep me in touch. I settled down, knees up and dozed off. Occasionally a hand, with a tin of water would appear, with a voice asking me how I was, and, "Schmidt keeps looking for you but we keep saying you've *Shizen gehen."* Then later, an anxious voice said, "Get out now, quick Bill, the squad's fallen in and Schmidt is looking for you." So, rather stiff and painful I made my way to the squad, when Schmidt came at me like a mad bull, but I weathered the storm. Being the cowardly bully that he was, he never reported me on *Appell.* He was, I guessed, afraid of being judged incompetent as the Commandant was really tough on his guards, as well as the prisoners. At the food issue I was stood aside when the laughing 'nice jolly man' cook gave the tiniest tilt of the ladle of soup into my bowl, with a small crust of bread, with Schmidt sneering saying *"Nicht Arbeit, klein essen."*

The following day, I flatly refused to work with the girder gang, steeling myself for the worst, but the overseer, anxious to get his girders on the move waved me away, so Schmidt found someone else to take my place. I was lucky in a sense, as any guard had the right to shoot dead any prisoner for refusing to work, for under German law, it was sabotage against the State. However, Schmidt had plans for me and whilst he was at Laband he hounded me from one filthy job to another, whether it would be ankle deep in mud or smothered in grease. Worst of all, he had me unloading thousands of bricks without gloves, so that with the skin worn off my finger-tips, I would be in sheer agony when I touched water. It was always Schmidt with the beckoning finger saying, "Come, Herr Harding, come." I swore a mental oath that if an opportunity arose I would kill him, but those chances rarely came.

Even one night he wouldn't leave me alone. He came into the room with his jackboots, brushes and polish, with a bowl of boiled potatoes and ordered me to clean the boots, offering the potatoes steaming hot. I looked longingly at them, then told him that I didn't clean German boots, whereupon he gave them to another man, who did them and wolfed down the potatoes. When he did eventually leave Laband, I wished him a horrible lingering death on some future battlefield.

One midday break we were resting on the ground when I saw a brand new locomotive sent to pull long lines of sand-filled skips, and speed up the large factory complex, no doubt to be used for war work. A Royal Engineers prisoner told a group of us that he knew all about railways engines, and he thought the driver looked as if he was asleep. He also spoke of an incline with a bend leading to a swampy pond. He wandered off and as I was idly watching the locomotive, I saw it slowly move along, then it gathered speed, when suddenly the driver jumped up from the ground where he had been dozing and ran after it, shouting his head off. It was now going full speed to the bend, when it toppled over into the pond, and lay there half submerged. The Royal Engineer showed himself, saying that he had released the hand brake. When the Poles found out, they were delighted and the German driver was put on hard labour for not putting the hand brake on. We always acted dumb when it was time to hand in our working tools, as there would always be one or two missing, having been buried, so helping in some small measure to aggravate the German war effort.

One day we were marched from work to a field, in which was a strange contraption, a small tanker with a boiler and fire on one end. We stripped off and rolling our clothes into bundles, threw them inside, leaving boots and clogs outside. The machine was a delouser, the end door was bolted tight and our clothes were steam boiled. We duly retrieved our clothing and dressed, the clothes still hot and steaming, and then returned to work. We looked bad enough before, but now, our clothes being mainly composed of wool, they had shrunk and had hundreds of tiny creases so we did look a pathetic sight. What a pity we couldn't be shown on a British newsreel!

This steaming killed the lice but not the eggs, so within a few days they hatched out and we were crawling again. On return to the camp I saw that something was up, no one was allowed into the huts. A large group of high ranking German officers, the Commandant and uniformed people with large red crosses on their arms were inspecting the huts. One uniformed man with 'Swedish Red Cross' on his armband came over to me and in perfect English said, "British soldier, why are you dressed like that?"

I replied, "Sir, all I have is what I stand in."

Glaring at me he said, "You are a bloody liar." I was wearing worn out boots, trousers almost in rags, a vest, ragged jacket, that's all, my shirt and socks long since gone. He rejoined his group, seeming to me that he only saw what he wanted to see, appearing quite friendly with the Germans. When allowed back into our huts, everywhere looked tidy and spotless, with brooms issued now, all having been done by prisoners kept back from work for the purpose. All this business delayed *Appell* and counting time, but someone stood in for the Commandant, who made a shorter time parade, and our food issue was late too, which hit us in the mind as well as the belly.

Two weeks later we were issued with used Polish army uniforms, cavalry type, many with tears and holes in them, us wondering if they were dead men's clothes. The breeches left part of the calves bare, not too good for winter and rainy weather. When the Poles saw us, some of them cried at the sight of the uniforms and we certainly looked a motley crowd. A small room had been set up as a shop for us to spend our *Lager Geld* (prison camp money), and we were served by a grinning German guard, offering hair nets, lipsticks and face powder, used razor blades and a sharpener, but no razor in which to put the blades. But a couple of men had their own safety razors and passed them around. So much for the good intentions of the Swedish Red Cross and the provision of the shop, but the Germans knew how to turn the screw.

Late October, the weather changed and it started to snow. There was an Oxford don amongst us, who said that he preferred to be a private soldier and had refused a commission with Military Intelligence. In his own words, he wanted to see what it was like serving with the lads, saying that he found it very educational. He spoke seven languages, including German and Russian, but he never let on to the Germans, as by listening, he gained information from time to time. He told us that winter came early in Upper Silesia, and that history records that thousands of Napoleon's soldiers perished here, also many Russians died of swamp fever in the First World War. It was a gloomy outlook listening to him and I thought of the large cemeteries at Lamsdorf. Already a taste of the freezing winds made me shrivel within myself.

One day the don forgot himself when a guard was being particularly nasty to a prisoner, and standing behind the guard he barked out a string of German, when the guard sprang stiffly to attention shouting *"Ja wohl"* with a very surprised look on his face.

One evening, queueing for our evening meal, we were pushed to one side when in ran twelve very fat men, whose clothes were of the expensive type. Gestapo guards in ridiculous winged breeches and swastika arm bands were hitting them on the shoulders with short truncheons. To me, they looked Jewish. The Gestapo in dark blue uniforms kept screaming at them, *"Juden Schwein,"* making them jump up and down when holding out tins for soup. The cook, himself very fat, would purposely wiggle the ladle while the Jews tried, whilst jumping, to get as much as they could. They were made to drink it still jumping up and down, so that the soup dribbled down their chins, still being whacked with the rubber truncheons. They were hustled out, with the Germans screaming at them. The cook laughed enough to split his sides, and for the next three weeks it was to be the highlight of his day, as the Jews came in the same time each day, just tottering skeletons, holding up their now very baggy trousers with one hand, as belts and braces had been taken off them. Now fewer in number, they went, never to be seen again. The guards were very vigilant in making sure that we handed no food to them as they passed. They need not have worried, we never had a crumb between us before food issue. In the time I was at Laband, I heard that there was a concentration camp not far away. Jews were considered to be Public Enemy No.1, as shown on posters on the walls, depicting Jews looking very villainous with large hooked noses, holding young terrified girls in their hands. For all the Jew searching in Lamsdorf, there was one in my hut who was terrified of being found out, and once, when a sergeant went round with a list of names on German orders, to ask each man's religion, the Jew went white, so the sergeant marked him 'Follow the Band', Church of England!

The situation between the guards, civilians and Commandant often became unbearable because of the language problem, and one example, whilst I was in another hut, a small built guard stomped in, shouting something to the nearest man. He looked at him without moving, so he received a vicious punch in the face and the glasses which he wore were shattered. He fell to the floor, holding his eyes, but luckily no fragments of glass had gone into them, but he had to do without his much needed glasses. The follow up by the guard was that he wanted the hut windows opened. I fell foul of him one day, when he screamed at me *"Dragada-dragada."* The don thought it meant sheep shit. On equal terms, I would have rammed that down his throat. This little guard used to count his squad with the flat of his bayonet and was very free with his fist.

There happened to be another Jewish prisoner in the camp, a private who I didn't know, but on account of being able to speak a little German, wheedled his way into acting as an interpreter on the site between civilians, guards and prisoners. This relieved him of having to work and helped in clearing up misunderstandings of language in a small way, and made our burden a little lighter. However, quite a few prisoners, unlike myself, had retained some of their possessions, such as watches, rings and wallets, which they kept hidden and these items became barterable objects. This Jew, with his new found freedom of movement, found a way to do a thriving business between the Poles and the prisoners. Bread and eggs were the usual exchange. It was noticed that the Jew had obtained a locker, complete with lock and key. I only heard of this, although sharp eyes had seen it full of items of clothing and some food, as there are few secrets in a prison camp. To barter at this point in time in Laband was indeed a very hazardous business and he must surely have taken considerable risks in starting it.

In my hut was a cockney from Bethnal Green, East London. He gave the Jew his army pullover for barter and received in return two thin white loaves. The rule was that a piece of a loaf would be given back in payment for doing the deal. Someone had seen the Jew bring in three loaves, keeping one in his locker, and that person informed on him and told the cockney. I was present at the violent bust up which followed, when accused of cheating with a third loaf, he hotly denied it, though on facing his informer, he admitted it but defended his action on account of the risks he was taking. The two men had to be kept apart when the cockney shouted, "I'll get you, you swindling Jew bastard." He meant it, as he was in a terrible temper, muttering all sorts of threats.

The next morning on the work site, the cockney said to us, "There he is, now watch this." The Jew was in conversation with the German overseer, when the cockney shouted, "Hallo, hallo." Both looked round when the cockney, pointing to the Jew shouted, "He's a Jew."

The overseer touched him on the chest, shouting, *"Juden?"*

"Ja," shouted the cockney. A row started between them when the overseer

laid the Jew on his back with an uppercut; he then jumped up and both began exchanging blows. Two guards ran over, with the overseer screaming "*Juden*" when they went to work with their rifle butts. He had to take his boots off, and a guard ran him past us in a pretty bloody state.

I said to the cockney, "You've done a good job, you've given him a death sentence."

Quite unconcerned, he replied, "Serve the thieving bastard right." Our life and experiences had done its job in brutalizing us and nothing seemed to bother us too much except our own personal discomforts.

In another hut there was a reservist from my battery, a Scot, from Edinburgh. We only knew each other slightly, as he was a quiet man who preferred to keep his own company. One morning, when the work squad were forming up, I saw him, Gunner Adam Cook, stooped and holding his head. I took a chance on getting a bashing and went over to him and asked what was the matter. He replied, "I have terrible pains in my head, and when I told the Germans, they beat me up." I told him to try and buck up, and perhaps it would soon pass, then I quickly dodged back to my squad. I heard that evening that an hour after starting work, Jock dropped dead, as a result of a burst mastoid I was told, but it was also said by some of the work squad that for 'refusing' to work he was hit with a rifle butt by a guard. He is buried in the cemetery in Cracow, Poland.

The weather was now bitterly cold, and I wore my old trousers over my Polish breeches. For me the intense cold was painful, with thick snow everywhere. I couldn't feel any life in my feet and hands, my nose and ears hurt to touch, my face made cracking noises when I moved the muscles, and my breath turned white on my mouth. Some of the work involved moving bags of cement, causing pain in my back, but as the work was varied, I managed to cope. It was so cold in the huts that I would huddle on my palliasse with my one blanket wrapped around me, not daring to undress. The food ration stayed the same. Although each hut had a combustion stove, no fuel was issued and in the mornings the urine bucket, plus excreta and overflow on the floor would be frozen solid and would have to be chipped off with a spade.

The Germans were very fond of calling us 'Foul, stinking Englander swine,' but it was they who created the conditions under which we had to exist. Some time later, we were allowed to bring in any scrap wood we could find on the site, and so had the stove going. Wood doesn't last long in burning, but it helped, until the early hours, when it was freezing again inside. When the time came for Red Cross parcels to arrive, it was usual for each man to contribute some wood to make his own tea or meal, as it was while the stove was hot, some of us would sit around it delousing our clothes by dropping the lice on the hot stove and watching them frizzle.

In my hut there was a Lancashire chap who got up to so many tricks he was nicknamed 'Wagger'. He was a born comic and he started getting into conversation with a patrolling guard late at night through the hut window, the doors of which opened inwards from the bars and barbed wire, much to our annoyance, letting in the freezing wind, and we watched in the dark as Wagger, with the help of sign language and poor German, stroked the guard's hand and received two cigarettes. The guard was obviously some kind of pervert.

Also in my hut was a regular soldier of the Lancashire Fusiliers, Jack Pilling, a man I liked very much. He had a top bunk. With a naturally deep voice and in a broad Lancashire accent he would beat the wall with both fists, singing military marches. The pounding which the wall received eventually broke a piece in, but his natural good humour convinced the Germans that he wasn't trying to escape. When he gave a demonstration, they thought he was mad, in a nice kind of way, just another mad Englander. One thing he did, and no one knew how, was to leave a set of footprints in the snow leading from the hut to the wire perimeter, where they stopped, a sure way of getting shot if seen. There was a big set to, with German officers standing around looking puzzled. I guessed that Pilling had walked backwards from the wire in his own footprints, but how he got back into the hut without disturbing the snow, I couldn't imagine. He just said he had done it and no more, smiling all the time. He was quite fearless, capable of anything, and had seen service in India. When we eventually had the combustion stove alight, Jack would heat a piece of rod from the work site until it was red hot and lick it without burning himself once.

Another character was wild man Geordie Dodgin of the Durham Light Infantry. His idea of a big joke was, when having a pee during the night, he would go to anyone on a bottom bunk and shake the drips on to his face whilst he was asleep, with uproar when the recipient opened his eyes. He often spoke of when he went on his BEF leave. He found his wife with a ginger baby, and spent the rest of his leave looking for a ginger milkman! One little chap who feared Geordie was Lionel, an effeminate chap who could often be seen running with Geordie after him. I marvelled how they had the energy, I know I never had.

It was a time when the weakest fell by the wayside. One chap I knew, about 20 years of age, lost most of his teeth and his hair turned grey. He used to walk about staring vacantly at the ground. I saw tall pre-war guardsmen literally fold up; they would walk with a stoop, their big frames couldn't exist on the meagre rations and they would be returned to Stalag VIIIB, where non workers received less.

One day I was approached by a Company Sergeant-Major of the Royal Welch Fusiliers. He was a smart soldier, elderly compared with us, his uniform still looking respectable, as he didn't have to work. He had a lined hollow face with sunken eyes, looking bright and glassy. He was skin and bone, his trousers flapping as he walked. He said he had found the secret of surviving on little food, just keep walking all the time, getting too fit to be ill. I could see that he was on his way out, and whenever I was in camp I would see him marching around the camp with his loose clothes flapping, until one day he went off his head and was taken away.

The winter became very severe with blizzards, and we had to push against the winds at acute angles to move along, with snowflakes as big as milk bottle tops. We covered our legs with cement bags and slid pieces up over our chests to try and keep the cold out. Many men had frostbite, which worried me, as I was certain that my ears, nose and feet would succumb, but with considerable pain, I occasionally massaged them to keep the circulation going. Percy Green had a frostbitten big toe, which didn't smell too good, but it was saved when a guard suggested he kept rubbing it with snow.

In this extreme cold, a young chap from the Hampshire Regiment was punished for refusing to work because he had a fever. He was locked in a small room for three days, after which he was found dead. I never knew his name.

The work went on day and night, with the aid of floodlights. There was continuous snow shifting to be able to get at moveable items for the factory construction, and even with gloves on, the unwary burned their hands on the frozen steelwork. One night an elderly Pole slipped from a height to the frozen ground, looking as though he was badly injured. The guard would not allow anyone to go to him, saying contemptuously 'Polack', so the injured man died alone. I thought to myself how heartless can you get, and decided that the whole German race must be evil.

The guards were so bloated with victory and keeping the cursed Englander hard at it that some even brought in newspapers showing anything with numbers and names, such as RAF 100 planes attack Germany, 90 kaput, *Luftwaffe* 500 planes attack England, 10 missing, along with other items of a similar nature. I used to be amazed to see grown men believing everything, but my comment would be "Propaganda," when the guard would become very nasty and I had to move away. However, this sort of thing went on and the Poles would try to give us bits of news, difficult as it was for them. The situation was such that no matter what was said, I always answered "Propaganda," and one day, just to put one over a German civilian boasting that Italy had bombed England I said, "Italy kaput." I only said it to dig back, but two days later a guard marched me from work back to the camp, then into the Commandant's office and with the Commandant was an officer who spoke perfect English. He questioned me about my comments of 'Italy kaput' and why I was always saying 'Propaganda' to civilians, when I was not allowed to speak to them. I replied that it was they who brought in their newspapers and spoke to me, and as I don't believe a word of it, and my knowledge of the German language being so poor, I said Propaganda. He kept pressing me about 'Italy kaput' and asked if I was getting information from somewhere, was there a radio in the camp? To which I replied that there was not. In various ways he continued to question me about Italy and I had a hard job to convince him that I had made it up on the spur of the moment, and had no access to news whatsoever. He pressed me closely about the Poles, and asked if they were giving us information, but I replied that I had never spoken to a Pole. I began to realize how serious my position was, and that I was a marked man from now on. He spoke at length to the guard, and to me he said I was to keep my comments to myself, as I would find myself in serious trouble and all that concerned me was work. All this to a skinny ragged looking tramp, me, after which I was marched back to work. Thinking hard about this, I realized what a narrow escape I had just had, as the officer could have had me sent to a 'Straf-Lager' (punishment camp), and in my physical condition, I would never have survived. After this, I was branded as a trouble-maker and whenever I was called by a guard or a civilian, I was always addressed as 'Propaganda', so they had all been warned about me. I spoke to no one and ignored all taunts and comments.

By now, everyone in the camp appeared to have sorted themselves out into friendly groups. The Scots, Irish and Welsh kept together, as did the Yorkshire and Lancashire chaps, very clannish, and the rest mingled with each other, but one characteristic I found among the British was that when three or more were together, sooner or later an argument would occur over something, the British being a race apart, quite unpredictable.

Christmas was near and everybody's thoughts were naturally of home and families. We were given a small letter form to send home, which uplifted men's spirits a little. I sent mine to my mother, and later on I received letters from my sister, Rosina, and when Christmas arrived, we were allowed Christmas Day off, the dinner being boiled potatoes instead of soup, with a slice of pork, with no change in the bread issue. The conversation was all about home, with men looking at well-worn photographs, with tears in their eyes, little knowing that another four Christmases were to pass before they saw their loved ones again. I had a feeling of emptiness, not joining in the conversation, but a letter from Annique would have made me punch drunk!

Most of my letter forms in the future I sent to the Nantes police, asking them to trace Annique, but I heard nothing, and guessed that the Germans had torn them up. As the night came and we were barred and bolted in, I sat by the window, watching the falling snow glittering on the ground like silver, and listening to the Germans singing in harmony 'Silent Night' in their compound. Not a word was spoken in the hut, everyone was deep in his own thoughts. As much as I detested the Germans, I thought as they sang 'Silent Night' it was the most beautiful thing I had ever heard, and every Christmas since, when I hear it sung, my thoughts return to Laband.

When that was over, it was work as usual, clearing snow, which in places was up to four feet deep. It was miserable work, with wet cold feet and numbed fingers. Another problem was trying to find wood for fuel for our stoves, as if there was no wood, there was no heat, so in desperation we searched until we found enough, and that was soaking wet.

1941 arrived, with half-hearted greetings of 'Happy New Year' being passed around, coupled with the old cry of 'Roll on the Boat'. One day, on returning from work, we saw a squad coming our way, looking quite smart in new British battledress uniforms and boots, but imagine our surprise when on passing them we found that they were French prisoners. So the Germans were giving the French our uniforms, while we walked about looking like tramps. Personally I felt very bitter about it, but the Germans would do anything to spite us. My back was still troublesome, but only on bending forward.

I had for some time teamed up with four Welsh guardsmen, with whom to share the bread. They were fine manly fellows, and as time went by, they formed a jolly good choir, and as Dai Jones had a deep baritone voice, he would give renderings of Paul Robeson's songs. The thing that annoyed them most was to be called 'Englander', but to the German mind, Welsh, Irish and Scots were all Englanders.

To give an example of the tense atmosphere among the prisoners, one night the old sweat of the Gloucester Regiment, in the next bunk to me had been out, then wandered in, when a man burst in and grabbing him by the throat shouted, "You thieving bastard, you took my bread ration," whereupon he beat him until he admitted he had taken it and ate it. The man had to be dragged off him, and he slid to the floor almost unconscious. His face showed the punishment he had received for a long time. He was shunned in the hut by everybody and he would sit for hours, staring into space.

Time passed, with one of the most severe winters ever known, so some Germans indicated, and quite a few men with frostbite had been to the fat medical orderly to have the bad bits cut off with scissors, have paper bandage put on, then back to work, if they could! I recall one evening, when a Lancashire man lying by his bunk started passing some disparaging remarks about some Scottish regiment, when a Scot in the hut walked over to him and gave him a punch in the mouth, saying, "Shut your mouth." He had to, after that. Everyone was on edge and it paid to watch what one said.

CHAPTER SEVENTEEN

The hard men

One evening, we were all startled when a Scot, who had the reputation of being a Glasgow razor slasher, by his own boasting, rushed into the hut and seeing Ginger, a tall weed of a lad, grabbed the hut broom and shouting hit him on the head with it, splitting his scalp and causing it to bleed profusely. The Scot was a dangerous man, who was subsequently overpowered, and thrown out. The reason for his action turned out to be that a Pole had left some bread hidden in a stack of bricks for the Scot, and when he went looking for it couldn't find it, and as Ginger was close by, he assumed that he had taken it. The next day, however, the Scot found the bread among the bricks, where it had been all the time. Ginger was taken by a guard to have his scalp stitched, and said he had fallen over and struck his head.

Round about February, good news came, with the arrival of Red Cross parcels, which arrived via the Stalag. The issue was one between seven men instead of one parcel per man. It turned our heads to see tins of stew, corned beef, fruit, tinned and dried, rice pudding, a large tin of 'Klim' powdered milk, dried eggs and bananas, raisins, biscuits and scented soap, a packet of tea and real coffee. The box was like an oversized shoe box in size, packed with items we had dreamed about, but there were problems in sharing the contents, resulting in a couple of spoonfuls each, but tea, coffee and cocoa were easier to share by mucking in when we brewed up. It was great while it lasted and it was good to see the Germans' eyes when they searched the boxes and saw the contents, especially the coffee, which they hadn't seen for years. Someone unwisely muttered 'England kaput', but it did show them that sending food like this meant that England was far from finished. We were to discover later on that a tin of cocoa would fetch us three white loaves in barter with the Poles.

We were naturally disappointed at there being no cigarettes in the parcels, but the Poles used to leave some home-grown for us to find, called 'Makorka', and it was terrible stuff, far too strong. One puff and I would stagger, with my head spinning and my lungs on fire. Old newspapers were scrounged on the work site, when collectively we would tear off strips and make small paper funnels and with the rubbed tobacco pushed in, hold it upright and set light to it. The paper burning would catch the tobacco, then we would blow out the burning paper and puff away. I used to soak the tobacco and squeeze the juice out of it, but it was still dynamite. The Germans' favourite cigarettes were

Turkish, called 'Juno'. They were great cigar smokers so the work squad, when going to and from work, would keep a sharp look-out for cigar butts in the road. Suddenly there would be a pile up of bodies scrambling for one butt, causing the guards to blow their tops, with civilians looking on.

The work on the construction had slowed down on the site, so the Germans decided that some of the men could be better employed down the coal-mines in Bleckhammer, not far away, so tables were set out and 700 men queued in the compound for the unlucky ones to be chosen. If you were sent to the right, you were not nominated for the mines, if to the left, you were, and as we all had an idea, from rumours, what the mines were like, nobody wanted to go, apart from being separated from our friends. Ahead of me I saw one prisoner sent to the left. He had two frostbitten thumbs, done up thickly with paper bandages, and protesting strongly, he held them up to the guard, who whacked them, and he fell howling to the ground. He still had to go. Fortunately, the quota was reached before my turn came, though it could have been one way of getting rid of 'Propaganda'.

The guards were constantly being changed, and Schmidt's turn came to go, giving me a sigh of relief, hoping that he landed in hell. We hardly knew how the war was going but the fact that it hadn't ended told us that England wasn't beaten, not that we thought she ever would be. The Germans could never understand our unshakeable faith.

Up to now, I've shown a gloomy picture of how things were, but being the first prisoners of war, nothing had been organized properly, also, unlike 1914, the Germans had conquered Europe and Norway, so there was no come back on whatever they did. Every camp was an island, the Camp Commandant was always king, for good or evil. I am not gifted as a writer to be able to express properly the emotions, mental anguish and physical suffering, the discomfort of men trying to live together in such adverse conditions; the tensions, the fights, those who never lost their sense of humour, come what may, those who cracked up; and not forgetting the body smells, which from some, was overpowering. Another irritation was the men on the lower bunks complaining about the straw dust falling on to them every time the man in the upper bunk moved. Looking back, I feel I would chance anything rather than go through all that again. Freedom is sweet, and never appreciated until it is taken away.

One Sunday afternoon, a new guard came up to me in the camp compound, beaming all over his face and said, "I am a square-headed bastard, good-morning." I must have looked amazed, so I said "Yes" with a nod. Smiling at being understood, he wandered off, repeating it to others, with some even congratulating him, which pleased him all the more. We soon found out that Wagger had been at work, playing tricks again. Eventually the guard discovered what he had really been saying, and everyone was glad when he was eventually posted.

During March, a sad thing happened. Because our freedom was nil, and the slightest information from the outside was mainly rumours or wishful thinking, I do believe the following to be true. A Corporal Green and his friend from the Cameron Highlanders, whom I had only seen occasionally, were found outside the camp in deep snow whilst attempting to escape. On being recaptured, the Commandant had them brought into a room with six guards, who beat them to death. In their fight for life, the top of one of the Commandant's thumbs was bitten off, and Corporal Green died of bayonet wounds. This story filtered out via a German. It may or may not be true, but my enquiry at the Commonwealth War Graves Commission resulted in the information that he had been a prisoner at Stalag VIIIB, died, no known grave and his name is on a column of the missing at the British Military Cemetery in Dunkirk. At the time of this story, a man brought to me what purported to be Corporal Green's kilt and asked me to unpick it, with yards of material for him. I managed to roughly cut waistcoats of sorts to wear, to help keep the cold out. I cannot imagine any Scot leaving a camp without his kilt, and this gave further credence to the story.

Now back to the Glasgow Scot, who most people avoided, because of his aggressiveness. He continually boasted that, as one of the razor gangs, he enjoyed cutting off ears. One day a long trench had to be dug by a line of men who were spaced out at intervals, but I was not placed near him. Next to him was an Irish guardsman who had the nickname of 'Mixer'. He was a likeable chap, slow of speech, with a grin always on his face. The Scot told him to do his section of the trench and Mixer replied, "Do it yourself," whereupon the Scot gave him a terrific clout, knocking him down. Mixer jumped up and started walking up and down, singing an Irish song. Everybody was watching, including the guard, when Mixer jumped on top of the Scot and a real fight began. First it went one way, then the other, until with bruised and bloody faces, the Scot gave in, leaving Mixer still with a grin on his face, battered though it was. The guard didn't interfere, but he took the Scot away. He was sent to a 'Straf-Lager' and on his return three months later, he was a much subdued character, and maybe a little wiser. Mixer was the hero of the day, having rid the camp of the Scot, and he revelled in his sudden popularity, still with the same old grin.

There was a feeling that the weather might break, but in fact, it snowed from October 1940 until May 1941. I was heart sick of it and it was very hard to keep warm on an empty stomach. There had been no change in our circumstances, we still slaved for the very minimum of food, and I often thought of the Egyptians who built the Pyramids. Red Cross parcels were few and far between, but improved as time went by.

One evening during *Appell* a tall German officer was standing next to the Commandant. He had no rank or insignia that I could see, and in very good English he introduced himself as the camp interpreter, to liaise between the British prisoners and the German side. Up to now, we were all getting nowhere fast, and this was affecting work, and relationships in the camp were deteriorating. He told us that the Commandant was being replaced and that any grievances were to be reported to him, when he would do his best to put things right with the Commandant, but could make no promises. It was hard not to give a cheer, but plenty of muttering went on in the ranks. One reason why the Commandant had been so hard on us was that his only son was killed at the Albert Canal by the British, and I wished the Commandant to be in the place he most dreaded to be!

Our clothing was in an awful mess, no tramps on the Embankment could have looked worse, and the bug situation had become so bad that in the wood joints of the bunks, they built up in layers, completely covering the wood. We couldn't get rid of them and to squash them all made such a stench that we left them alone. The new German interpreter told us that we were to refer to him as Dolmetscher and approach him any time. When he saw the bugs, he was appalled at what he saw, and as soon as the new Commandant took over, he was shown it by the Dolmetscher and immediately insecticide was sprayed on all bunks to kill the bugs. We asked for new straw to sleep on, showing him how flat and thin our palliasses were, but the Commandant refused. We showed him our clothes and he said that he would do what he could to help us, but it wasn't easy until the Commandant had settled down. He was a younger man and as strict as would be expected, but with no screaming sessions, and with much shorter parades, which was a blessing for us.

One morning when the squads were ready to go to work, the Dolmetscher called for everybody's attention and asked if there were any tailors and boot-makers amongst us, as a workshop was going to be set up in the camp to repair uniforms and boots. Hands shot up, including mine, and he went round taking names and numbers. He asked me where I had worked as a tailor, so I promptly said "Savile Row, London." Very impressed, he said, "That is the best." My instinct was to volunteer for nothing but this was different, an inside job would be heaven, whatever it was, compared to the hard work and conditions outside. I said Savile Row, never having been there, and I was not a real tailor, never having made anything new, but I thought that I would be ideal here. Obviously records were looked into, as at my first interrogation I had said I was a tailor when asked my civilian occupation.

A small room adjacent to my hut was turned into a workshop and I got the job, to start on Monday. A rotund, moonfaced guard, who was in charge of the stores was to be our boss. On arrival for work, I found the room equipped with a good treadle sewing-machine and bench, complete with cottons, scissors, hand and machine needles and a tape measure. My friends were two boot repairers with bench, foot lasts, awls, hammers, nails and leather knives, a leather sewing machine, balls of wax and hemp. Whoever had worked out our requirements had done it with typical German thoroughness. We three knew each other by sight, and they were moved into my hut, so that our guard had us together and handy for him. I saw no cloth with which to work and when our guard came in, he sorted us out regarding our work and told us a few dos and don'ts. For instance, the only time we would be allowed out of the 'shop' was for toilet purposes, so no walking about during working hours. He had lists of all tools, etc., which were checked every evening before lock-up. It was strictly forbidden to do work for any guard without his permission and I had to give a short demonstration on the sewing-machine which satisfied him. Our hours of work would be the same as those of the camp work force, but looking through the windows at the snow outside, I gave a sigh of relief to think how lucky I was to be inside. The added comfort was the issue of a small amount of coal each day for the combustion stove, to which was added rubbish from our work. Our mates in the hut called us lucky bastards, but knew that we were there to help them.

Our guard watched us for a while like an old hen, but once he became used to us, he only looked in now and again. Old tattered uniforms were brought in from the Stalag for me to use for patching and I worked all day attending to many men's repairs. They collected them after work, borrowing old trousers from the pile to wear during the day. Priority was given to repairing the three uniforms which we ourselves wore, whilst our boots were also patched up, mine being almost ready for dumping. We soon christened the guard 'Gibbs Nix', because every time we asked for something, that was his reply. He was on a good thing and he knew it, he had no intention of breaking any rules and being sent back to soldiering.

About this time, Wagger cut some holes in the lid of a Red Cross parcel box, and stuck coloured soap paper on the insides, then late at night he draped his blanket over the table, laying the lid on it, with a stub of candle inside. From somewhere he had acquired a battered old mandolin, so he sat by the window until he saw the patrolling guard approaching. He lit the candle in the lid, with small coloured lights showing to good effect, then sat under the table, hidden by the blanket, tinkling on his mandolin softly saying "BBC calling" over and over again. When he saw the guard looking through the window, mutter and then run, Wagger ripped the lid to bits, hid the candle stump, then went to his bunk wrapped in his blanket. There came shouts of command and the door was unbarred and unlocked. An officer and four guards burst in and hounded us out in the snow while the guards, with torches, ransacked the hut looking for a radio which wasn't there. We cursed Wagger, standing out there in the snow, but having found no radio, the officer called the patrolling guard forward and after a scream up slapped him hard across the face, then we were allowed back into the hut, more like icicles than men. We pleaded with Wagger to confine his tricks to before lock-up time, but had to admit that he had done a good job, as the officer had to dress himself fully before showing up.

In the workshop we were going flat out, so many men were asking for repairs that we could hardly cope, so I worked out a quota for each day. It was hard work of a different kind, working in poor light, ending up with aching eyes, but I was glad to be there in the warm. As well as my own, the men's clothes were all lice-ridden. I would pick them off and lean over, dropping them on the hot plate, where they would swell and pop, filling the shop with the smell of burning 'corpses', at which my companions would protest. They were Gunner David Rosbotham, from Northern Ireland and Marine Tom Connelly, who was a long service man of 30 years, stationed at Chatham. He was on the staff as a blacksmith and sent with a party of sixty men by destroyer to Calais on the 23rd of May 1940, only to be captured on the 26th. He always maintained that all the old timers were rounded up by the government to get them all killed off, saving on their pensions. The clothes were so threadbare that I couldn't do a proper neat cut out repair job so I had to stitch patches over the holes and tears, which looked OK and kept the cold out, for which the men were grateful.

One day the men returned from the mines, many a sorry tale was told, and they looked terrible. I could see the strain on their faces, and it was a sad aspect of the life of a prisoner of war. First it is rammed into you to be soldiers, then it seems in a flash, a sudden transformation takes place, which leaves you bewildered, ending up in the enemy's backyard, with all the mental confusion that goes with it. Safety and protection in the mines was the last thing on the minds of the Germans. They had plenty of prisoners with which to fill any gaps. There was one tall lad I remembered who, whilst down the mine, was holding oily rags on the cable that pulled the coal skips, and sadly for him, some loose strands of wire snatched the rags and his hands and wound them round the drum. Both hands were mutilated, he lost all his fingers.

With spring came the first letters and one evening came the unfamiliar cry of 'Mail up' by the camp Sergeant-Major, causing a stampede which almost swamped him. I hung around, expecting nothing, yet half hoping I would get something, but of course I didn't. My heartfelt wish was to get a letter from Annique. The letters were like a blood transfusion to the men, who had become desperate with worry about their families. The letters were read over and over again, until every word was memorized and the topic of conversation was of home for days to come.

News came to us via the Poles that Hitler had invaded Russia. It seemed to me incredible that having the bulk of Europe in his pocket, it was the worst thing he could have done. I knew that Russia was a massive country and I wondered where all the men were coming from to take it. Time alone would tell, and I could see the self-satisfied looks on the faces of the guards. Hitler was indeed their God.

Tom Connelly was a tall man, broad of stature, with a military moustache and a fierce eye, a Roman Catholic who was forever crossing himself and mumbling as he fingered his rosary. David Rosbotham was an Orangeman from Belfast, a dedicated member of the Orange Lodge, a Protestant, who detested Romans as he called them, resulting in Tom and himself always involved in arguments about religion.

Hot summer was with us again, and a contingent of Indian Army prisoners arrived, looking very downcast. The Germans, apart from hating everybody, detested coloured people and treated them like dirt.

The three of us had settled into a routine and coped with as much work as we could, but the work piled up, especially the boots, with men temporarily wearing clogs and asking every day for their boots back. The workshop wasn't smelling too good either, so I ignored 'Gibbs Nix' and occasionally had a stroll around the compound for fresh air. We got together and decided to ask 'Gibbs Nix' if an extra man each would be granted, so as to get the work down, especially as the numbers in the camp had increased to about 800 men. 'Gibbs Nix' was a big jellyfish and terrified of the officers, so it took some persuading to get him to our way of thinking, but he did see that it would enhance his position with more men under him, so eventually we were allocated two men, one tailor and one boot repairer, namely Rifleman John Butler and Percy Green. So there were two more men not working for the Reich.

John had been captured at Calais and I showed him how to use the sewing-machine. Percy Green, of the Royal Sussex Regiment was a nice bloke, and the five of us got on well together, except for the arguments about religion. I listened, but refused to get involved, as tempers soon began to fray and I thought it silly. The situation was that Butler was a Roman Catholic from Kilkenny, Eire, which suited Connelly. Rosbotham was for ever going on about the siege of Londonderry in 1699, which in the main was done with good humour, though a bit heated at times, when I would chip in and cool it down. Then Rosbotham would sing Protestant songs, of which he had an apparently endless repertoire, simply to annoy the others. Percy Green was a quiet good-natured man, who just listened and smiled. I used to get infuriated with Connelly who, when a religious argument was in progress, would get out his beads and start muttering endless Hail Mary's. We would pull his leg continually about the Royal Marines, as he was a father figure to us, and at one time, when we went a bit too far, he stood up, raising himself to his full height and said angrily, "Do you realize that you are insulting His Majesty's Jollies?"

He would often talk of his world travels and later, was to give very interesting lectures about the countries he had visited in his 30 years' service. One story was that he had had a watch repaired in Shanghai and it went well for months until in England, having it seen to again he was shown a cog made from wood, copied from the original. A marine's yarn perhaps?

Rosbotham was an orphan who had been brought up in a home, and it must have been a poor one, as he could neither read nor write, and I used to write his letter cards for him to send to an uncle in Belfast. He knew a lot about his country and was very proud of it. In time, I was to learn about Irish history from ancient kings to Oliver Cromwell and the Black and Tans, but behind it all, I could sense the bitterness between the North and South of Ireland.

If an emergency arose, 'Gibbs Nix' would bring in odd pairs of jackboots for repair and it surprised us all to see that the soles were fixed with wooden nails, square in shape and knocked into round holes. They did work, on the principle that the damper they got, the tighter they held. Lice was the deterrent for clothes and even 'Gibbs Nix' would never stay a moment longer than he had to, with this in mind.

Mail became more frequent, and this gave some of the men a lift, except one man in my hut, a sergeant, who received a letter from his wife, telling him that she wouldn't be around when he returned home, as she was going out with a New Zealander, not a coward like him. He read it out to us all, then screwed it up and threw it. During a rearguard action in France in 1940, withdrawing from a village in a Bren-gun carrier, the sergeant saw his Colonel fall wounded and stopped to pick him up, whereupon both he and the Colonel were taken prisoner. The Colonel recommended the sergeant for the Military Medal for his bravery.

Hunger still gnawed at our stomachs and work seemed the best way to take our minds off it. The rations remained the same and our only hope lay in a more regular and larger supply of Red Cross parcels, which we prayed for daily.

Connelly was referred to as 'Old Tom, the Marine' and he had a passion for snuff, asking in his letter cards for as much as 2 lbs. to be sent to him. He seemed to be ignored, as this never arrived, and also he must have liked his beer, because he used a horse's girth belt around his large stomach, but now he tucked in a spare foot of belt.

Boredom creates strange activities, so a group of old soldiers who had served in India pre-war formed a 'Shit and Shankers' society. It was apparently an old soldier's pastime in the British Army. We younger elements were ignorant about this, but in the Woolwich Depot, before the war, I had heard of it. When the court was in session, there would be seated at the head of two tables pushed together the 'Grand Master', with six men either side. The court session would open with the ritual by the Grand Master, solemnly warning the court that any misdemeanour would incur some punishment, nodding towards the 'Holy Dido', an army leather belt lying on the table in front of him. Incantations would be said, then the session would start, with the 'Grand Master' beginning to roar with laughter and the court would follow suit. Then he would slide a hand over his face, becoming solemn as a judge, the court doing the same, but it is difficult to start laughing in a group then suddenly stop in a flash. I know I would be on the floor. A culprit when caught would receive punishment decided by the court.

Walking round the camp one evening I saw this performance going on through a hut window, I saw one offender with his trousers down receive six whacks from the 'Holy Dido', and as curiosity killed the cat, I opened the hut door to see more of this funny business, I moved inside and that was my undoing. There were shouts of "Grab the shitty outsider" and I bolted for the door, but I was not quick enough and twelve pairs of hands lifted me from the floor and stretched me on to the table, where I was unable to move. A trial was held, and the 'Grand Master' said that I had wilfully interrupted the working of the court, whereupon a vote was taken, with the court shouting "Aye" to guilty, then the 'Grand Master' pronounced the sentence, that I would be stripped naked, 50 hairs pulled from my genitals and then I would be tossed into the snow outside. With shouts of one, two, three, up to fifty hairs were pulled from the tenderest spots, then I was carried bodily to the door, swung three times, then into a high bank of snow, my clothes following me. After an uncomfortable time getting my clothes back on, I went off, a sadder and wiser man. I wondered why, afterwards, only the court were present in the hut, now I realize why. I think a kind of madness prevailed in different forms, and this was one of them, a means of fighting boredom.

I should have mentioned this item of months ago. There was a German newspaper printed in English and distributed among the Stalags and work camps. Our quota was about a dozen copies between 700 odd men. Paper being very scarce, the papers often didn't circulate very far, the paper being put to a more pressing use. Some of the items were of interest, but most of it was subtle propaganda. The German authorities started the paper too soon, when British prisoners were at their lowest ebb, ill treated and starved, forced to do heavy labour, so it wasn't very well received. The Germans were trying to convince us that it wasn't us they were against, it was really Churchill, and that the Germans were really quite decent chaps, and respected the British soldiers. On reading this, there were many cries of Bullshit and worse.

The title of the paper was 'The Camp' and I was fortunate to get a copy dated December 8th 1940, inasmuch as I was feeling so low and alone, with no family ties or anything to hold on to, that when I read the following poem I felt uplifted. The more times I read it, the stronger the message came through that all would work out all right in the end. I had to keep it, so I tore the page out and kept it with me always, and in quiet moments I would read it again, and bearing in mind our circumstances, I leave it to the reader to judge 'Courage'.

No. 23   December 8, 1940   THE CAMP

COURAGE

Sir,

I submit herewith a poem which I sincerely hope you may be able to accept for publication in 'The Camp'. The poem was inspired by your very much appreciated article 'Pride', which appeared in the edition of a fortnight ago.

Yours sincerely,
(Signed) N. Farrer, L/Cpl

It is easy to be nice boys, when everything's OK,
It is easy to be cheerful when you're having things your way.
But can you hold your head up and take it on the chin,
When your heart is nearly breaking and you feel like giving in?

It was easy, back in England, amongst the friends and folks,
But now you miss the friendly hand, the joys, the songs and jokes,
The road ahead is stony, and unless you're strong in mind,
You'll find it isn't long before you're lagging far behind.

You have got to climb the hill boys, it's no use turning back,
There's only one way home, and this is off the beaten track,
Remember you are British, and that when you reach the crest,
You'll see a valley, cool and green, dear England at its best.

You know there is a saying, that sunshine follows rain,
And sure enough you'll realize that joy will follow pain.
Let COURAGE be your password, make fortitude your guide,
And then instead of grousing, just remember those who died.

They died to earn your freedom, 'twas not too great a price,
If only you are worthy of so great a sacrifice.
They bore their cross in silence, they sought not wealth nor fame,
And you must try to emulate and glorify their name.

I still have the poem, framed and hanging in my front room, the original, and in 1990 it will be fifty years old and full of memories.

An Army bandsman named Rolls formed a committee of other POW bandsmen, with a view to forming some kind of band, with 1941 slipping by, to see if something could be arranged for the coming Christmas. The Dolmetscher was approached to see if permission could be granted to buy some musical instruments with the useless 'Lager-geld' we had, also a room where men could have music practice after working hours. This was a very ambitious project, as the attitude of the Germans was to give as little as possible to the cursed Englander, but the German love of music played a part in permission being granted, as well as a guarantee that work output would not be affected, and he said that provided enough prison camp money could be collected, musical instruments could be purchased in Gleiwitz.

A meeting was called and everything was explained and it was decided to have a general collection throughout the camp for money for the instruments. Sheet music came from the Red Cross, also a few books started to trickle in.

Old Tom was for ever down-grading the Army, being the only Marine in the camp, and he never had a good word for soldiers, saying, "If you yawned with your eyes shut, they would whip the fillings out of your teeth." I thought that was good, coming from a Marine, so I decided to play a trick on him.

One night, I had a look and saw that the 'Shit and Shankers' society were in session so I went to Old Tom and told him that a man had some snuff for him in the hut, giving him the number. So, thanking me, off he went quickly. The other three came with me and watching from a vantage point, we saw Old Tom go in and a second later, there was a roar of "Grab the shitty outsider," and Old Tom tore out of the hut, being chased by the 'Court'. He shot past us, with bulging eyes, taking refuge in another hut, only just escaping the 'Court'. We were in hysterics at the sight, with Butler lying on the ground, too weak to stand. Old Tom didn't speak to me for days, until I pointed out that I had seen a Royal Marine run like hell from soldiers, then he thawed out and returned to normal conversation, easing up on his comments about soldiers, or 'pongoes' as he called us.

CHAPTER EIGHTEEN

Foolhardy

One day I landed myself in hot water, with almost serious consequences. A German sergeant came into the shop with a pair of trousers, a flat iron and a bowl of cooked potatoes, and ordered me to press the trousers. I had a smattering of German by now so I told him that I did not press German trousers. He flew into a rage and said, "Do them," but I still refused, as I would not do any favours for a German. He left the shop, leaving the trousers behind, together with the potatoes and the iron. Connolly and Rosbotham wolfed down the potatoes, then with Percy Green, they ran out, leaving Butler and myself.

The sergeant returned with a Hauptman (Captain), who went to town by first sending a stool flying with a kick. Then he shouted so much that tears of rage were running down his face, then he drew his pistol and pointed it close to my face. I stood to attention, watching his finger trembling on the trigger, with the sergeant standing there watching. I felt very angry when I received a kick on the shin, then he put his pistol away and very menacingly gave a threatening gesture by slowly waving a finger in my face and saying, *"Passen sie auf mench,"* and went out. I understood exactly what he said, that a prisoner of war will obey all German commands, or be shot.

The sergeant, looking very stern, said, "Now will you press my trousers?"

Blinded with temper, I said, "No, bollocks!" He picked up his trousers and the iron, looked at his empty bowl and walked out.

Butler said to me, "You know Bill, you should have done them, that officer will be back, why don't you go and hide?" I told him there was nowhere to hide, and rather apprehensively I sat down and waited. No one did come back, so for reasons of his own, the sergeant didn't go back to the Hauptman. Afterwards I found out that quite a crowd of prisoners had gathered outside the shop window, attracted by the shouting of the Hauptman. When Connolly and Rosbotham returned, I told them what I thought of them for eating the potatoes and Connolly said it was a shame to see them go to waste!

Christmas 1941 came and went, with nothing much organized socially, the only relief being an issue of Red Cross parcels to brighten our lives, and in our small workshop we mucked in together during the day and went our separate ways in the evenings.

The two huts of Indian Army soldiers were on their own, and suffered

178

intensely from the cold. I soon found out on a visit that they would not eat meat in stews, or bully beef, etc., so I took dried fruit, biscuits, or flour content food and did a deal with them by swapping. On entering their huts, the formality was of mutual respect, whereby I would have to go round and shake everybody's hand, then do a deal. In time, the cold, the harsh conditions of the weather and work took its toll and when the Germans couldn't get enough work out of them, back to the Stalag they went.

The 'Kink' not being in Canada and England with the Empire still battling on, spite against us took several forms, one of which was to stack the Red Cross parcels in the cookhouse boiler rooms, when in large print, in both German and English was printed 'Store in cool place, keep away from boiler rooms'. The result was that on issue, tins of food were blown and meltable items in a sorry looking mess. A protest was made via the Dolmetscher and it didn't happen again. Then a prisoner was caught taking a tin out of the camp, which gave the Germans an excuse to have fun opening all the tins when issue came round, and tipping the contents into our bowls, all mixed up, but they soon tired of it, so all tins were punctured and packets ripped open, preventing dealing until things reverted to normal.

Mail was coming in more frequently and was used as a weapon against the men as a camp punishment whereby a prisoner upsetting a guard or two would be sufficient reason to make it known on evening *Appell* that mail was in and would be withheld for two weeks, once even a month. This naturally upset everyone, to the extent that it caused more trouble instead of reducing it, the Germans not understanding the British temperament.

We heard odd scraps of news via the Poles, who must have had radios, and the blitz on England became known through prisoners losing homes and relatives in the bombings. We also heard about the disaster in Malaya and Singapore and my thoughts immediately turned to my friends out there, and wished them luck.

At long last, there was good news for us when new uniforms and boots arrived, but as they came in assorted bits and pieces and sizes, with not nearly enough to go round, the men who wore clogs had first choice of the 50 pairs of boots that came. This was a great morale booster, as later on, shirts and socks arrived so that by the year's end, almost everyone was kitted out. The work soon knocked the newness out of them and we were hard at it repairing rents and tears, also doing alterations to make the uniforms fit. Boots took a terrible knocking from day one, there being no dubbin available. However, our lot was slowly improving, and it was comforting to know that we were not forgotten by our country. Some men started to receive parcels from home containing pullovers and underclothes, but little did the kind-hearted relatives realize that some of these items were bartered for bread, eggs and butter to the Poles, who with bartering the goods among themselves were doing a thriving business at great risk.

Our daily food ration never changed, so the hunger pains were always there, despite all the extra from the parcels, but the least number of men sharing a parcel was three, the most seven and never once was I issued with a parcel for myself. In my hut, one man blew up into an enormous size, with a puffed up face and slit eyes, and with a laugh he commented that when he did go back to normal, he hoped that one part stayed as it was, just to please his wife! Another chap had a nasty looking abscess come right under the crotch, so the Germans sent him to a convent for treatment. When he returned two weeks later, he said it had been the most embarrassing time of his life, being treated by the nuns, but that they were very kind people, who fed him well and washed all his clothes, including his uniform.

Late summer 1941 a spate of boils and carbuncles broke out in the camp, to such an extent that work was being affected and any prisoner who didn't work received a reduced food issue, as our earnings from the construction firm were used to pay for board and keep, etc., and they didn't like paying for non-working men, no matter what the cause. A British Army Medical Officer, a Captain, was brought to the camp to treat the sick and he immediately insisted on having a room for treatment. Palliasses of straw were laid out for patients, and paper bandages were issued for use but no anaesthetic, as it all had to go to the Russian front for German casualties. I joined the sick queue, when the doctor looked at my ear, his comment being, "There is nothing I can do for you to stop the discharge, it is like a time bomb and I hope for your sake that it doesn't go off." While I was there, I saw one man lying down on his front with an enormous carbuncle on his lower neck. It had a large hole at the top and one on the side. It looked terrible and I shuddered at the thought of the suffering he was going through as I watched an orderly raking it out, and I'm sure many other painful things were done in the course of the doctor's work. Eventually the Germans complained that the doctor was having too many men off sick, so only the very bad cases were allowed off work. After a month, the doctor had to go and on leaving, he had his head bent forward, as he himself had a carbuncle on his neck.

Handling the dirty clothing as I did, it's a wonder that I didn't contract some skin disease or illness, because most men's underwear had long since gone, including my own, until the time arrived for the issue of new clothes. Some men were lucky inasmuch as they received parcels of clothing from home regularly, others, like myself, had to make do with what they had.

The year seemed to drag by endlessly, and on the approach of Christmas, preparations were well in hand for our first concert. In the empty hut allocated, many willing hands in their spare time had knocked up a rough stage and somehow by scrounging, some old music stands had been acquired. Regular collections in the camp raised enough 'Lager-geld' to purchase, through the Dolmetscher, enough musical instruments to form a small band. Coloured paper and sheets of thin cardboard were bought to make stage clothes and suitable attire for the band and players, the band named, I think 'Rolls Roysterers'. Practice went on every evening with the band, a clarinet, banjo, accordion, guitar, saxophone and drums, so it was a good start. Men with any talent at all came forward and eventually a concert party was formed. Blankets were found from somewhere to use as curtains for the small stage, everything being somewhat crude, rough and ready; but to have a band, a stage and a Christmas show forthcoming was, under the circumstances something of a miracle in itself, and mainly through the efforts of the Dolmetscher on our behalf. He was a good German and an educated humanitarian.

The general rule was to conserve what we could from the Red Cross parcel issue for Christmas so that the enjoyment of the concert and the saved up extras would go to make up some form of Christmas celebration for us.

I noticed that some of the guards were older men, but they were not soft by any means, and also German soldiers convalescent from wounds received on the Russian front would do a spell of guard duty.

The day arrived and we were all looking forward to our first camp concert. The Commandant and other officers were in the front row of chairs and the hut was filled to overflowing. The mood was great, so at 7.30 p.m. on Christmas Eve, the lights dimmed and the curtains were drawn, showing a well-lit stage and the band looking good in paper outfits. They started by playing 'Smile darn you smile', with cheering fit to lift the roof. The show consisted of small comical sketches, singing groups singing the latest songs and special favourites which we all joined in.

The Welsh choir sang beautifully in good harmony, to an appreciative clap from the Germans. Some of the solos were very touching to a hushed audience, and the old sweats had a field day with renderings of 'There was a Chinese maiden', 'Gunga Din', 'The green eye of the little yellow God', 'Eskimo Nell' and others, causing shrieks of laughter. They would also sing sad barrack room ballads with numerous verses. The concert was by some standards crude, but a great success, and when we all stood and started singing the National Anthem, the Commandant jumped up and stopped it, so the band struck up 'Land of Hope and Glory', with the Germans looking round puzzled when our singing must have been heard all around the camp. Here were no beaten Englanders who could sing like this, and I'm sure that some of the Germans that night thought and wondered about our morale.

Being Christmas Eve, we were locked in one hour later, to allow for the concert time and back in the huts relived the laughs and jokes of the concert, showing how everybody's spirits had been lifted. But underlying it was the nagging thought of this, our second Christmas here, and how many more were we to spend behind barbed wire. The concerts were a summer event too, so with an increase in band numbers and instruments, quite a presentable band grew, and some summer evenings they played in the open to give some relief to the monotony of prison camp life.

As German was gradually being learned a little by most prisoners, albeit terrible to the German ear, the Dolmetscher left, while a few prisoners did learn to speak the language well, and acted as interpreters for the men in general. We in the workshop picked it up from 'Gibbs-Nix'. Also on evening parades, our own interpreters would liaise between Commandant and camp Sergeant-Major.

One evening, I heard a whistle being blown intermittently and saw the camp Sergeant-Major hopping around the camp perimeter on one leg blowing the whistle with no escape, the 'Shit and Shanker' court there, making him do his punishment. I heard that one night, because one 'captive' lashed out with his fists, he was held under a freezing cold shower, fully clothed, until soaked through and pleading to be let out.

The depression of being a prisoner of war, cut off from the world behind barbed wire was felt by all, and conversation often turned to how much longer, with many talks of the possible chances of escaping, but it all seemed so hopeless with guard patrols wandering around the huts all night. Also there were guards with dogs patrolling within the outer spaced double wire walls on the camp perimeter, plus the guard towers with machine-guns and searchlights making certain that death was the reward for the brave or the foolhardy.

To try to escape from the British work site in British uniform meant that chances were virtually nil, every man being watched most vigilantly. I believe that the Englander, of all prisoners of any nation, was the least trusted and the most counted. It was practice now, apart from withholding mail, to shut the concert hut for a period of time as punishment for any misdemeanour committed by a prisoner, but all this built up more resentment.

A directive from the Stalag hierarchy decreed that facilities be provided for sporting activities, so a field close by the camp was allowed to be used for those energetic enough and willing to have a game of football on Sunday afternoons. In the course of time, when bodies became stronger, football and Rugby teams were formed, which says much for the enthusiasm of the men, plus the advent of Red Cross parcels, irregular as they were. No matter how much the Germans tried to stop it, bartering still went on, and this was one reason for collective punishment. Men sometimes lost eggs which were hidden in battledress blouses when being smacked by the guards. We reluctantly forwent the pleasure of cocoa, chocolate and some toilet soap in our deals with friends doing deals for us outside. Bread and butter was most desirable, as quantity was more important to hungry stomachs than quality, plus eggs when possible.

The Poles wanted tea and coffee, and to the best of my knowledge, were always fair in their dealings with us. But one man in my hut, after using his tea until it was clear, dried out the tea leaves, placed them back in the packet and resealed it, then flogged it for loaves of bread. The Poles complained, saying "Brookie Bondy nix good, Lyons better." Men were told to stop it if caught fiddling the Poles, as we relied on their goodwill, and fair play was essential. Cunning was used in fooling the guards, bread would hang inside trousers and any old head gear could hide a few eggs or butter underneath, with the guards thinking mainly of pockets for concealment. I expect in the case of the bread, the lice had a good feed in advance!

One day a German guard came into the shop, and I had an experience similar to the previous one. He had with him a pair of trousers, a flat iron and a bowl of boiled potatoes. He said that he had a weekend pass and was anxious about his family. With the other incident still fresh in my mind, I thought it wise to say, "Yes, I will do them." After pressing the trousers, John and I found some fat lice and carefully poked them under the crotch lining, then handed them over the wire with the iron and the bowl. The following week he saw me and gave a hard look, but said nothing. I hoped that his weekend came up to scratch!

When the warmer weather approached, there was a German guard, a small ginger-haired man, who would on a fine evening sit near the wire and give us some entertainment on his full size button accordion. He was a master of the instrument and played beautiful music to a large appreciative audience of prisoners, who gave him a great ovation on completion of his skilled recital. He was eventually sent to the Russian front, the mincing machine of the German Army and a year later, he returned to Laband. He was carried out strapped to a chair with just short stumps where his legs had been. He gave us his final performance on his beloved accordion, playing as beautifully as ever, after which he was given a great send off by the large number of prisoners who appreciated the thought behind the act. When severely disabled, he came out and played for us and I for one wished him well.

More bother occurred over the withholding of mail again as a collective punishment for all, and this time it was to last six weeks, with a camp rumour circulating that the Germans had burned them. If they didn't, I was certain that they were quite capable of doing so, and the married men used to take this holding back of mail to heart, and would get depressed. I did receive an occasional letter from my sister and some cigarettes from my mother, for which I was very grateful, but not a word from my father.

One day I spoke to a prisoner in transit from Bleckhammer. He had been a naval rating on the destroyer *Campbelltown*, which had rammed the dock gates at St Nazaire. He had lost half a foot in the action and told me that in brilliant searchlight, when the swastika flag was lowered, the skipper peed on it in full view of the Germans!

Large groups of Russian prisoners began to appear. We all knew that we had roughed it, but these poor devils walked at a snail's pace, they were emaciated, walking skeletons in rags, many of them barefooted. Whoever said that Germans were members of the human race?

A man I liked very much was Mick Walker of the Rifle Brigade, a regular soldier, tall, smart and a real good fellow. He would barter food for boot polish and if anyone criticized he would say, "I'm a Rifleman and I will look like one." One unusual feature about him was that he had one blue eye and one brown one. Someone had acquired a battered old bugle and one evening Mick said to me, "Watch this." Smartened up, with side hat at the correct angle, he marched quick step to a corner of the compound in full view of the guards and with drill bugle movements he sounded 'Retreat' to perfection, then marched back amid cheers to the hut. The German guards turned out and watched, too surprised to do anything except watch and listen to a small ritual of the British Army. Mick got many pats on the back for a good performance. He had served at Calais and we had a mutual respect for each other.

We had a whip round, and in the greatest secrecy a radio was bought from a Polish worker, it cost a lot with items from Red Cross parcels, but everyone was hungry for news as well as for food. Good news in England's favour could indicate to us when the war might end. A committee decided that the best place to hide and use it was in the concert room, as there were always men going in and out of there, whereas in a hut, if found, thirty men could be incriminated, with possible death as a result. The view of the Germans was that any news received by us from whatever source was a very serious offence.

A new prisoner joined us in my hut, still dressed in desert khaki drill. He was a South African Boer, and after a couple of days, suspicions were aroused when another South African prisoner challenged him about his unit, etc., and as to where he was captured. His enquiries resulted in him telling the camp committee that in his opinion, the Boer was a German plant. The radio being uppermost in our minds meant that hot tempers prevailed and it was decided to wring a confession from him after lock up, and from somewhere a rope was found. We were locked in earlier than usual, with guards wandering around the compound. The Boer was missing and next day so was the wireless, although cleverly hidden, the hole was left uncovered, and German humour prevailed to the extent of having chalked on the floor the outline of a wireless, knobs and all. Strangely no mention of it was made at the evening parade.

Sudden swoops were made by the 'gentlemen' in trilby hats and leather coats arriving at speed in large limousines, who methodically searched the huts by tearing and tipping everything about, including palliasses. This resulted in a shambles of dust everywhere as we grabbed handfuls of crumbled straw to stuff into our palliasses, ending up in arguments when some finished up with hardly any, and everybody taking as much as they could for themselves. I wondered at these times if I would ever be a normal human being again. The Gestapo certainly set a good example when, after these searches, we would find Red Cross food trampled into the floor, dirty and totally uneatable, and any civilian clothes from home ripped to pieces.

The 1942 Christmas concert took place, but this time it was better thought out, with no delays between turns, and the band more professional in their style and performance. The sketches were very good, thought up by the brainy ones, as well as the comedians. The territorials deserved a lot of credit for this, as many came from all walks of life, giving more than the usual barrack room stuff of the regulars, and they came into their own on the stage. The emphasis was always on music and laughter, they being the main morale boosters. Some of the 'pretty' lads were dressed up as girls in paper frocks and with make-up, etc., looked the part so well that they were escorted back to their huts after the show! Top hats were made from cardboard and I helped out making caps from cloth and cardboard, with various requests for civilian trousers and other items for the stage shows, but on sight, the Germans would have confiscated them, so I don't know what happened to them. Also, I had to be very careful as 'Gibbs-Nix' had almost caught me twice by suddenly coming in. I never heard of any escapes from Laband, as the place was riddled with spies and informers in the civilian population. The Poles were very afraid of them.

One day he came in with a guard, telling John Butler and myself to pull a hand cart to the village and collect some stores for the guards. After a couple of stops, loading up, we entered a general store and whilst the guard was busy with the shopkeeper, John and I positioned ourselves by an opened sack of sugar with a scoop lying on top. John, hiding behind me started to fill up my trouser pockets with sugar. A minute later the guard saw what we were up to and I tried to warn John, to stop him. He hissed at me, "For Christ's sake keep still, the sugar's going on the floor." The guard with a roar of rage unslung his rifle and I braced myself for a bashing, then the shopkeeper, laughing his head off, stopped him, making a joke of the whole thing. When we were leaving, he was still chuckling his head off, which set the guard smiling, so we were lucky not to be reported and returned to a work squad. We had a long hard sweating pull back, which no doubt purged our sins in the eyes of the guard, as he said nothing to 'Gibbs Nix'.

With 1943 upon us, depression became a serious illness with some men, who couldn't see any end to the war. New prisoners didn't seem to say much except the setbacks experienced. Rumours were not in England's favour, and the Germans seemed invincible, conquering most of Russia too. The winter was severe, as usual, with the usual crop of frostbite but the atmosphere among everyone in general was good, the concerts helped with the addition of a piano and a good pianist. We were all in the same boat, making it a leveller whatever one's station in civilian life, more evident among the territorials, some educated with good positions in life.

Another rumour which went the rounds was that when Germany won the war, all prisoners would be castrated and used as slave labour to rebuild Germany's bomb damaged towns and cities, also we would never see our homelands again. What seemed to back this up was on the evening parade, the Commandant repeated the warning that any prisoner caught having sexual intercourse with a German woman would be shot. In my hut one character ran up and down naked, shouting, "They're not whipping my lot out." I'm sure that we were all mentally off balance, not having seen the real world for so long, and not realizing that another two years were to pass before we did.

Comradeship was very strong now, with the common desire to annoy the Germans as much as possible, but thieving was still rife, and it was fatal to leave anything lying around. The Red Cross sent packets of seeds and all round the camp small plots of vegetables were growing, but how to cook them was a later problem, except tomatoes, which grew like bushes and cropped well. But when tomatoes had grown as large as apples and were just turning red, they would be stolen, much to the annoyance of the grower. A constant watch was kept until lock up, but ripening ones would be gone by morning, taken by the guards. Carrots also were pulled and eaten raw, so most men gave up.

One sharp-eyed prisoner noticed a new guard on gate duty, and the clamp supply of potatoes for the winter was situated just between the guard and the coal dump, so he took the room bucket and cheekily asked the guard for hut coal issue. He was allowed through, so out of sight, he dug in the clamp, nearly filling the bucket with potatoes and topped it up with coal, whereupon he thanked the guard and returned to his hut. This started a stampede and a queue of men formed with buckets, with one man allowed in at a time. Eventually the top of the clamp fell in, with few potatoes left as some of the men had been back three and four times. From the guardroom a Feldwebel (Sergeant) started roaring like a bull, frightening the life out of the young guard, who went off at the double to the guard block. All hell was let loose, every man on parade with guards ransacking the huts. Potatoes and coal found was tipped outside and eventually restored to a re-made clamp of layers of straw and earth, with the coal dump returned to its original size. After two hours standing listening to a tirade of abuse and threats, we were finally told that if the stocks of potatoes ran out before the allotted time, we would have to go without, but as a punishment, for two weeks we were locked in our huts each night two hours early.

To counteract this, a Royal Engineers electrician went to every hut very quickly, with look-outs posted, and tampered with the fuse boxes, so that when the time came for lights out in the camp by a master switch, they all stayed on in every hut. The Germans, not knowing what had happened, went very erratic, running around shouting and placing a guard at every hut. Doors were opened while fuse boxes were examined, but the conclusion was for electricians to be brought from Gleiwitz, who corrected the boxes, also padlocking the fuse box doors, the whole business taking until the early hours of the morning, with the Germans looking fed up with the whole disruption.

The football enthusiasts made emblems of their favourite teams, which were placed outside the huts, decorated with what they could find, a stone grotto, a few flowers, a team name plate. The men had so little that anything done at all was good effort. Photographs of these were taken and the odd guard could be bribed, human nature being what it is, and as did the others, I acquired a set. Some of the guards had succumbed to the temptation of bartering, as some of the contents of the Red Cross parcels had never been seen by some. For them the risk was very great, and if caught, apart from severe punishment, there was the one way ticket to the Russian front, a dreaded posting. Not that we were inundated with Red Cross parcels, quite the opposite. We were still sharing irregular issues, but collectively we could get more to eat, especially white bread, by doing deals.

John and myself used to crush biscuits to a powder, mix in some dried milk powder and dried egg from the parcels, then add raisins. When turned into a dough it would be put in a tin and baked on the hot ashes under the stove, then 'Presto', we had a cake.

As in all armies, there is always the wide boy, the old sweat on the fiddle. Such a one was the guard who we nicknamed 'Johnny Pedlar', the name of a current popular song. He was a pleasant character, always looking over his shoulder and in the thick of bartering. Myself and others wanted mainly white bread, eggs and butter if possible. Our hut was a swapping point in doing deals with items from Red Cross parcels. 'Johnny Pedlar' would come on duty, looking very plump, and come into our hut and unload thin white loaves, or whatever he had. The time came when he was heavily in debt to us, as he was taking our stuff but bringing nothing in return. No matter how much we pestered him, it was always 'tomorrow'. We thought that a change of guards might be taking place, so when 'Johnny' looked in the hut door, we grabbed hold of him and his rifle went flying. Many pairs of hands held him whilst his jackboots and trousers were whipped off. He was terrified when we threatened to throw him into the compound. So nearly in tears, he promised us faithfully to bring in what he owed us next day. To see that he kept his word, someone held on to documents from out of his tunic pocket as a weapon. He paid us in full, but after that his enthusiasm seemed to fall off. I think that all he could see in his mind's eye was the firing squad.

Health problems built up in the camp again, men with stomach upsets and ulcers, plus a general state of being run down, so as work was being affected, a Medical Officer was sent for, a Major, to see to the sick. In addition to the paper bandages, there was now a small supply of medications from the Red Cross, which was a great help. The Medical Officer seemed to be a surly sort of man, one day in the compound a prisoner passed him without giving acknowledgement, so the Major called him back, and tapping the crown on his shoulder said, "What do you think this is, an effing Marmite cube?"

The weather was very hot and mid-summer and I happened to be in the compound at the moment when in marched through the gates 200 French Foreign Legionnaires. They totally ignored the guards, obeying only their own NCOs and came in perfect drill order, a formidable looking body of men, dressed in desert kit. They were no sooner in their allocated huts when, stripped to shorts, they washed everything, including the greatcoats which they had with them. They dug their own latrines, their NCOs relaying orders from the Germans, who seemed to make no personal contact with them. Here were the truly professional soldiers, hard, with great self-discipline and I'm sure that wherever they had been taken prisoner, the Germans paid a heavy price.

I became very friendly with one of them, and helped him out with the odd bar of soap, cigarette and tea, etc., and surprisingly, all of them fitted in and made friends with us British during the time they were at Laband. He told me that as a 17-year-old, during the Spanish Civil War, he had seen his father, mother and sister shot up against the wall, but he escaped over the border into

France, where he was given a choice, join the Foreign Legion or be sent back to Spain to his death.

Before leaving the camp six weeks later, he gave me a photograph of himself as a young legionnaire. It was the only one he had, and I was reluctant to take it, but he said that I was his friend and it would be a memory of that friendship. There had been a strong bond built up in that six weeks and the legionnaires were seen mucking in with the British in the huts, sharing what we had and with their departure went a sad feeling of parting with friends, with many handshakes and mutual respect. I still have his photograph and wonder if he survived the war.

Parcels from home became a regular thing, but some civilian clothes were confiscated and shirts had the neckbands cut off, thus ruining them. Even bottles of beer began to appear. None of us in the shop received parcels, but we did any deals with some of the guards. They found it safer with us in the camp all the time, the temptation being too great for some who, when going on leave, would ask for cocoa for the *kinder* (children). But we squeezed them for all we could get as we were still to them 'Englander swine', though they were nice when they wanted something. Also I don't recollect Old Tom ever getting his snuff. I heard of one snooty character, a dentist's son, who had a collection of 15 pairs of shoes and boots, with parcels coming all the time. He wouldn't part with a thing to help anyone in need, and I hoped that one day he would lose the lot.

A purge was started, when it was announced that a mass check of all prisoners would take place in the compound on the following Sunday. Rumour via the camp Sergeant-Major was that some RAF men had swapped identity in the Stalag with soldiers, and they had managed to get out to working parties, as close as possible to German airfields. On the day, long lines of men queued to tables piled up with documents. With a slow methodical check each man showed his identity disc, and all his particulars were gone into, but faces didn't always compare with the 1940 one, as many men had changed a lot since then. Standing for so long started some men playing games, saying their names were Buck Jones, Tom Mix and all the film stars' names that could be thought of, causing the Germans at the desks much confusion, many rows and arguments. But the final explosion came when one chap said his name was Mickey Mouse. The German investigator's roars could, I'm sure, be heard a mile away and it caused the check-up to collapse, with some of the men laughing their heads off.

During the check, one man upset the apple cart when he was asked his civilian employment. He said that he was a bird frightener, but this didn't match his 1940 document, so he was asked to demonstrate, and he did, by running up and down screaming, flapping his arms like a chicken. Again, a German almost burst a blood vessel when he saw that he had been conned. However, two men were found to be different to their documents and were taken away. There were lots of head tapping by the Germans, convinced that all Englanders were mad, as men were laughing and enjoying themselves at their expense.

It was now late summer 1943, and the camp had slowly transformed itself into a truly Commonwealth community with all sorts, tending to make us BEF boys a bit of a curiosity to some, who were at school when we were captured in 1940. Times were changing for the Germans too, as more wounded were doing guard duty on short spells as convalescence from the Russian front, thus releasing fit men for active service. These guards were very sharp and it was unwise to get involved with them — in other words, they were trigger-happy.

Plans were going ahead for the Christmas show, with the object of putting everything into it and making it a super show. A Scot who had worked in a distillery before the war made a crude still, using hundreds of the solder blobs on the empty food tins, first a sealed coiled pipe from the tins soldered together, one end fixed to an empty milk tin and the other joined inside the bottom of a bucket. He was quite a skilled man and he showed us how to prepare hooch from potatoes, raisins, sugar and yeast. Obtaining these items was a problem, but then, so was everything else. It is difficult to beat the wily British soldier when he's up against it however, and the items were finally obtained. Once when out with the handcart, we stopped at a house, and while the guard was inside, I asked the Frau for sugar, and with a smile, she returned with two kilos and a bottle of red wine, so we had one sympathizer.

I had never seen this done before, but with the ingredients put in as Jock directed into a urinal bucket, which I thought would give the brew some body, it fermented and bubbled away nearly full, giving off a strong rotting smell. I kept it covered in the workshop, when one day, a spot visit by a high ranking German officer took place. On entering the shop he barked at 'Gibbs Nix' saying there was a foul stink. Angrily he turned to me and asked what was in the bucket. I politely said, "My dirty washing sir." I couldn't think of any other answer.

He went purple with rage, shouting at me, "Foul, stinking, Englander swine," among other things. I was worried in case he kicked it over, but he then stormed out in fury, with poor 'Gibbs Nix' following, white as a sheet and shaking like a jelly. When I then whipped the bucket into the hut safely. 'Gibbs Nix' returned, a sick looking man in fear, but I told him that my washing had been done.

One day when returning to my workshop, I was passing the window of the sick hut, and stopped to watch an operation. The Medical Officer, seated at a table, was in the process of removing the crushed ends of two fingers of a Russian prisoner who was seated next to him, his arm being firmly held by one orderly. He had a cloth over his head, covering his face, and his shoulders were gripped by another orderly. There was a tourniquet on the poor chap's arm. I could hear his groans, but he never moved, and without any anaesthetic, there never was any for anyone. After removing the damaged bones to the knuckles, the MO cut the skin into flaps and with a curved needle stitched them over the remaining parts of the fingers. I stood away and waited, my guess being right, the guard took the Russian away with his arm in a rough sling. He wasn't allowed to lie down for a while and recover.

Fever gripped the camp, and in every hut brews were fermenting away, until each one began to smell like a Hoxton pub, and it's strange that none of them were discovered. The time arrived for us to distil our brew, so straining the contents of the bucket, we set the Klim tin on the stove, filled with liquid, the lid firmly on, with the pipe coming from it coiled down into the bucket filled with cold water, condensing the steam as it went through to drip into a bowl set underneath. I kept a look-out while John kept filling the tin. I said to John, "How's it going?" He mumbled something and I found him tipsy, with none in the bowl, proving how strong it was. I took over and although it was a slow process, we had about a litre and a half of raw spirit, so we mixed the bottle of red wine which we had kept in with it, to give colour and flavour, then hid it so that only John and I knew where it was. This was our Christmas drink, a total of three bottles.

The summer was scorching hot, so John did a deal and obtained ten bottles of beer. It was necessary in those days to eke out everything we had to make it last, so we each had a bottle that night in the darkness and gave Old Tom one while we were looking at the dry storm of endless lightning and rolls of thunder. Old Tom kept talking and droning on, sending us to sleep, so we retired to our bunks. The next morning we found ten empty beer bottles looking at us, and in fury we turned to Old Tom, who admitted drinking them on the grounds that the thunder would have turned them! This was blatant greed and stealing from his mates, and I had to restrain John from thumping him, but he was virtually an old man and had done a despicable thing. He lost out in the long run because we never shared anything with him again.

The big day arrived, Christmas Eve, and we were all keyed up for the concert in the evening; so after food issue, the hooch was taken from its hiding place so that we could have a drink before it started. My group of friends consisted of John Butler, George Maybanks, Aussie Ned Kelly, Kiwi John Bushell, an 'English' South African, whose father was very rich, and myself.

By now we had found a way of opening the shop without the key which 'Gibbs Nix' kept, so our party started there. Old Tom, Rosbotham and Green had gone to get into the concert early. Maybanks brought a small accordion so he started off singing Welsh songs, then to the bottles we went and in our mugs we drank a toast to a rapid end to the war. John Bushell put a bucket in our circle and promptly threw up in it. He explained that when drinking spirits he always did that, then he could drink all night. I thought it would be charming to be in a pub with him. In our weakened state, we soon became inebriated and I think we sang ourselves hoarse, every song we could think of, with the last drink sinking to John Bushell's 'Now is the hour'. The first to go was George Maybanks who went mad, shouting that the guard on the gate was taking his wife out and that he would kill him, so we dragged him down and sat on him until he started snoring. The next was the South African, who tottered out on wobbly legs, then we got George and his accordion back to his bunk to sleep it off. We all went our different ways after handshakes all round and greetings of Merry Christmas. I wandered around from hut to hut and every one had its own concoctions, some of which I am sure was poison. I was given a drink here and there and was becoming very unsteady on my legs, with everything that I looked at seeming to move.

In one hut a table had been placed on a table with a stool on that, when a drunken paratrooper climbed up and standing on the stool shouted "This is how we do it." He dived, crashing to the floor and struggled to get back up and do it again, but he was restrained. Then our eyes met and with a hard stare he said softly to me, "I'm going to kill you, you bastard." I had never seen him before, but looking into his eyes I saw a killer, so I left the hut, wanting no trouble. Outside, by chance, I saw the tall lanky New Zealander, John Bushell, so I quickly explained to him about the paratrooper, when we saw him leave, looking in my direction.

John said, "I'll leave you, and you go into that empty hut and we will see what happens." I wasn't happy, as there was only one way in, and the paratroopers had a wicked reputation, so I knew that I would be like a stick in his hands. From inside I saw a shadow flit in the dark door opening, knowing that he was stalking me, when I heard thuds and John Bushell's cheerful voice saying, "Come out Bill, you old bastard, I have put him to sleep, best leave him there." I was very grateful to him and thanked him, but it was a case of mistaken identity. Apparently I reminded the paratrooper in his drunken state of someone in his past, because whenever he saw me after that, there was no sign of recognition.

I found my way to the concert at the tail end, now feeling very unsteady on my legs. The boose in the huts had built up over the weeks so many of the men were very merry, the Germans not tumbling, and someone on the stage giving direction, was having everybody open their arms wide, shouting out, "The German eagle has spread its wings, the German eagle has spread its wings, the GERMAN EAGLE SPREAD ITS WINGS AND SPLIT ITS EFFING ARSE-HOLE." All the German officers were seated in the front, not grasping what was going on, but the audience were laughing their heads off, when someone jumped on the stage and with his right arm held in the Nazi salute and two fingers of his left hand flat under his nose, he goose stepped the length of the stage. The Commandant jumped on to the stage amid the cheering and shouting, which died down when he started laying down the law, partly in German, partly in English. At the conclusion, with a theatrical flourish of his arms he said, "Na alzo I must now disappear." According to British humour, this should have been accompanied by a bright flash and a puff of smoke, but the result was that everyone was in stitches, some on the floor, holding their sides. The hut was cleared and it was a long time before permission was given for it to be used again.

The drink by now had really got hold of me and I remember leaving the hut when the freezing air hit me, and the next thing that happened was someone shaking me in my bunk and looking at a face. The man said, "Well, aren't you going to thank me?"

I said, "What for?" with a fat head. He told me that just before lock up he tripped over me in the snow, away from the huts. My trousers were folded up, lying with my boots, and I was curled up, out like a light. He carried me back, so once again I was grateful, twice in one night, for my life being saved, as with the intense cold, I would surely have frozen to death.

The cold was severe, with the large thermometer fixed to the gate entrance showing before lock-up 40° Centigrade below zero, and at night, the patrolling guards, fully dressed in winter gear, would step into huge felt and wicker-made boots, have a large cloak over their overcoats, with rifles slung upside down, gloved hands resting in a large fur muff hanging from their necks, plus balaclavas and ear muffs, while we still had the same blanket issued in 1940.

John Butler had a nasty accident one morning. He jumped from his bunk, and with the stove alight, he went behind it and stretched upwards, when his 'dick' touched the red-hot flue pipe. He jumped back with a shout, leaving skin sizzling on the pipe. For a time he walked about with his penis hanging outside his trousers, fixed into a bag of ointment. The blokes had great fun telling him of their past erotic sexual adventures, causing him to get painful erections. When fuel for the stoves ran out, bed boards were broken up and used, spreading out the remaining ones to lie on.

Well 1944 had arrived, and most of the men I spoke to seemed despondent, feeling that the war would never end. Some of those who were 40-year-olds in 1940 now looked older than their present age, and the 18- and 19-year-olds were reaching and passing their manhood behind barbed wire. How much longer? was on everyone's lips. When will the second front start to finish it off? Russian prisoners were now seen in masses, so we didn't know what to believe. Were the Russians winning, as the Poles indicated? It seemed hard to believe. The one indication that something was happening was the occasional drone of bombers going over, very high up during the night.

Spring came and I was approached by one of the German under-cooks privately and asked if I could make him a winter coat from a chequered blanket. I 'smelled' food, so I said that I would, if the price was right. He promised sausage, eggs, butter and bread. A secret meeting was arranged to measure him up in the kitchen, so I brought with me a chap I knew who was by trade a tailor's marker and cutter out, on the promise that I would give him a third of everything I received in payment. The measuring was done and the coat cut out and I commenced stitching it together in the evenings. Each night the cook would come to see how his coat was coming along, so I purposely left parts undone and the patch pockets off to hang out the time, getting from him hunks of sausage, butter and white bread. He began to protest as the days passed, until in the end I had to finish it. He was so pleased that he brought some more sausage, eggs, butter and a white loaf. I was scrupulously fair, having the tailor over each night to share a third of whatever I got, which pleased him very much. I had squeezed the cook for every bit of food I could get out of him and he knew it, but he had his coat.

There was a new guard on the gate who should never have been called up. He would walk up and down in a world of his own, with music, paper and pencil, humming to himself, occasionally stopping to write down music. Several times the German sergeant shouted at him, but the crunch came one day, when he left his rifle leaning against the gate post and wandered off singing and writing down music. I happened to be passing at the time, when the sergeant came out and caught him. He exploded on seeing the rifle, and the unfortunate guard was doubled away for surely severe punishment. I used to see a lot going on, as I would often go out for a quick walk round the compound for exercise, and also to get away from the continuous bickering about religion.

Some high spirits took place on the point of lock-up one night, when some men shinned up on to the roofs of huts and stuffed up the chimneys, eventually having huts filled with smoke, and men shouting through the windows. The guards went round frantically letting everyone out, thinking that the huts were on fire, but when they found the real reason, the chimneys were unblocked, getting a bit rough with everybody in the process.

Ned Kelly, the Aussie came into the shop one day, beaming all over his face. He received many parcels from home and so had plenty to barter with. He told me that he had found a willing guard who was well bribed to bring a mother and daughter, who was 15 years old, to a secluded area near the work site, and with suitable rewards, Ned had sexual intercourse with the girl, while the guard and the mother kept a look-out. It was now very hot weather, and he said that the German 'Sheila' was worth every bit that it cost him.

There was a commotion amongst the guards one day, when on assembling in their compounds they split forces in two lines facing each other, the farthest distance apart, when with many orders being shouted, singly they marched to each other and on passing, the Nazi salute was given with loud cries of 'Heil Hitler'. If it wasn't so serious for them it would have been hilarious, because after a good time sweating it out over and over again, they then had a go at doing the goose step. Some of the older men looked fit to drop and I could see it was hard drill instructors who had been brought in to do this. There must have been a reason for all this, and my own reasoning worked out that the Germans were losing the war, as none of this had happened before. I never mentioned that also, in collective drill, they sang marching songs. I always liked the singing, and thought it would be a good idea if it was introduced into British Army training. We heard later that for the German soldier, the military salute was now forbidden, the Nazi salute only to be used, and as always, some wag lifted his right arm to a guard, saying *"Shizen zo ho"* (shit so high), for which he took the risk of getting shot. I think the audacity of some of the Englanders prevented the guards from reacting quickly.

194

Some replacement prisoners from the Stalag brought stories of repatriations and I thought lucky devils, but of course, most of them were dying men. A story circulated regarding a prisoner named Gordon Rolls, reputed to be a rich racehorse owner. He offered £1,000 and a legally binding document ensuring him a job for life on repatriation, if any man would swap with him, the swap to be faked. Such is the price of freedom, there were no takers.

All sorts of news items crept in, such as the fact that fifty RAF officers were murdered, Arnhem, and the Russian armies pushing the Germans back, so the tide was turning, also whole towns being destroyed. Hope made us believe the good bits and discard the rest. My feelings went back to 1940 and I thought — you started it all so I hope you get driven into the ground. Going back a bit on this subject, I remember at the time of Stalingrad every German soldier wore a black arm band.

Something started to happen in Laband, when men were given an hour's notice to move and be gone. This was very upsetting in regard to the loss of friendships, but there was an old map in the camp and it showed Upper Silesia to be in line of any Russian advance. John Butler went with a few others, then some time later another group went, including myself. It depleted the workshop, but I thought I had been lucky, so I couldn't really complain. So with some quick handshakes all round I was gone.

We boarded a train with wooden seats, and after some changes and a long tiring journey, we arrived at night at a large Stalag at Teschen, in Czechoslovakia. Names and identities were checked, German fashion, about six times, then we were taken inside to a hut crammed with British prisoners, so finding a spot on the floor and securing my few belongings, I went to sleep. In the morning I was sent for and joined a group of thirty men, including those from Laband. Teschen stank and was full to overflowing with humanity, but as I was only there for about a week, I saw little of the place.

The group of us were interrogated and I thought it strange that there were so many Irish names, but they came from different parts of England, having been born there, and had the accompanying English dialects. One man told me that they were being sent to a newly formed Irish Stalag and that he didn't want to go, as it meant breaking up friendships, and that this German scheme smelled of trouble. I did some hard thinking as to why I was moved and not David Rosbotham, but not all of the groups were Irish, so it looked to me a case of thinning out the work force at Laband. Then the question arose, why Teschen, and not my parent Stalag VIIIB, at Lamsdorf? I thought that I would try to tag along with this bunch, although I had no Irish links, and get out of Teschen, where eveyone appeared to live and look for the soup issue each day, also it looked as if Butler could have passed this way.

We were interviewed one at a time. When my turn came I found my interrogator was an immaculately dressed German officer who was American, speaking with no trace of a German accent, yet he spoke German fluently. With a slow drawl he asked me where I was born and questions relating to my parenthood, etc. I told him that I had been born in Cork, when he told me that I didn't sound like an Irishman. I then told him I had been taken to England as a baby. He didn't believe me and rather menacingly said, "I will send for your documents and call you again." I began to wish now that I had never started it, but it was too late now, and to admit to lying could mean Straf-Lager.

I settled in to the routine of the Stalag, queueing up midday for dishwater soup and a piece of black bread, hating the place and the atmosphere, determined to get out of there somehow. I was sent for a few days later and the same officer went for me, real nasty, asking lots of questions as to why my statement in 1940 showed that I was born in London and not Cork. My explanation was that in Lamsdorf in 1940 the civilian who took my details spoke terrible English and as I was half deaf, the mistakes in the records were his fault, not mine. He was not convinced and with steely eyes he told me that he wasn't satisfied and concluded, "We will meet again Mister English/Irishman." I had my feelings, but I felt an icy hand clutch my heart as I knew that once these bastards got an idea into their heads, it could fester into them thinking I was some kind of spy. Why did I want to go to an Irish Stalag when it was designed to turn the Irish against the English? Well I had made up a cock and bull story so I had to stick with it, furthermore what was I landing myself into if I got to this Irish Stalag? It was the unknown.

Several days later we were assembled near the main gate in the early morning, with our belongings, and we heard that our destination was to be Stalag IIIA, Luckenwalde. The German/American officer came along with an armful of documents, paused at each man, checking details, but when he came to me he said, "Ah, the English/Irishman. I will come back to you." When he spoke to the man next to me an argument started.

I heard him say to the officer, "I am an Englishman and I want to go back to my old camp." He was a tall man of the Irish Guards, and spoke with a strong Irish brogue.

The officer shouted at him, "How can you be an Englishman with a name like Patrick Fitzpatrick?" In the persistent argument, the officer lost his temper, shouting, "I'm fed up with English/Irishmen and Irish/Englishmen, get the hell out of here." We were then marched off to the railway station. My bacon had been saved by the man next to me and we had a good laugh about it and the Germans in general. Our train journey, in a seated carriage, took several hours, with one change, when we arrived at our destination. One Stalag seems pretty much like another, with the latrine pong wafting everywhere and when checked in, we were split up into different huts, which were large, holding about 200 men or more. There was no soup issue until next day but fortunately I still had some Red Cross food with me and cold stew from the tin goes down well on an empty stomach.

It was strange at first, living with Irishmen from every corner of Ireland and the UK, who only had Irish names, but to the German mentality any foreigner with a German name was automatically German. Try telling a Welshman or

Yorkshireman with an Irish name that they are Irish. It doesn't work that way, yet into this Stalag were also brought men from every part of Britain and dialects to go with it, many with no Irish links.

I was very interested in this Stalag. It was just south of Berlin, and although packed solid with prisoners, it had a new feeling about it. There were men here from every campaign and battle, from Norway onwards, up to the most recent and so there was a wealth of conversation in talking about their experiences. I noticed that a lot of the men were tough characters and the Germans had unwittingly brought a source of trouble together, all in one place.

The guards were very trigger-happy and that was the reason why so many of the windows in the huts were broken, because at night regularly the camp lights would go out as planes passed overhead on their way to bomb Berlin and on the slightest provocation, the guards would fire at the windows, so it was wise to keep one's head down. I searched everywhere for a bunk but any spares were without palliasse and bed boards. The boards were used in making 'blowers', a crude clever contraption whereby a piece of board was used as a base, and a large 'Klim' milk tin was lined with clay and fixed on one end. Linked to it a short trunking acted as an air flow, and attached to the other end a fan was enclosed inside a circular casing. When turned at speed with a bootlace around a hub, the fan would force air fast into the clay-lined tin, and one small piece of coal or a few small pieces of wood could boil a can of water very quickly. It was ingenious, simple to make — all from empty food tins — and one of the cleverest ideas ever thought up in a prisoner of war camp. It also showed a profit, when for a cigarette, anyone could use it.

I looked for Butler but couldn't find him among the thousands, so I assumed that he never came this way. The British compound was surrounded by other nationalities, with single wire walls separating them and patrolling guards inside, very alert, who needed little excuse to shoot. From what I heard from others about the forming of the Irish Stalag, men were interviewed by the Germans and asked why they were fighting for England, their old enemy, and if they would join an Irish brigade and fight for Germany, then after six months, they would be well rewarded and taken to Ireland by submarine to freedom. There were apparently many disruptive scenes and it fizzled out when an Ulsterman in a rage tipped up the interviewer's table, almost causing a riot. I was told that not one man was known to accept the offer, making the German plan a flop. They didn't understand that many Irishmen were regular soldiers in the British Army, dedicated soldiers. Others were married in England, with families, etc., and I knew one man from Limerick who was a London policeman, married to an English girl, and had two children. That is how the story was told to me.

The Germans now took a hard line and we were treated no differently than in any other Stalag. The food issue was no different, the long queues for a ladle of soup and a piece of black bread continued, with the occasional Red Cross parcel. I soon began to detest the place. It was depressing and I somehow wanted to get out. I was told that to get out to a working party, the best bet was to see the camp RSM. It also crossed my mind to ask him if he knew of John Butler being there.

I know it was wrong to volunteer to work for the Germans, but I felt that I had to do something more than hang around in this human cesspool, or I would go mad. I found the camp RSM's office and asked about going to a working party. He said that lots wanted to go, and when I enquired about John Butler, he said that his lists showed a Butler working on a farm at Pritzwalde. He told me to come back the next day, and he would see what he could do.

The next day I was told to be ready to go at a moment's notice, as three men were required at Pritzwalde and I would be one of them. Early next morning three of us, with a guard, set out and I said goodbye to the seething mass of humanity, with its continuous struggle for survival in Stalag IIIA. There was a train change in Berlin, and I saw some of the damage inflicted by the Allied bombing raids. It was very extensive, and I marvelled that any trains ran at all, as the station was a mere shell, with skeletons of buildings all around outside, like fingers pointing to the sky, and what were once roads were now paths, winding their way through high banks of bricks and masonry. On one part of the station was a large bomb crater with rails twisted into weird shapes, and further along gangs of men were working frantically, repairing other sections of the line.

On arriving at Pritzwalde, there was a tiring walk to the farm and it was in the early hours when we arrived. After checking in, we were each handed a blanket, then we slept on the floor of an empty room. In the morning John was astounded to see me and with a good handshake we had a reunion. He told me that for what good it was bringing him here, he might as well have stayed in Laband, but I told him about a dozen men a week were leaving there, for no apparent reason other than the rumour that the Russians were advancing in that direction.

The camp was oblong, small, with the usual barbed wire walls, guards' hut and kitchen, etc. Our huts were situated in lines with corridors, our billets being rooms holding six to eight men, with the standard bunk beds and palliasses with straw. I heard several requests for new straw had been turned down, as the existing straw had been crushed to dust from long usage. There were roughly 70 men, mostly Irish, and a good spirit prevailed among them, getting on well with the Polish workers. The weather was very hot and I was sent straight out into the fields, where I joined the line of men hoeing across the field. I enjoyed the fresh air and sunshine, but being forced to work at speed in the heat made it somewhat uncomfortable, what with my old problem, flies buzzing about my damaged ear. The hours of work were long and at the end of the day, lying on my bunk seemed like heaven.

At odd times, I was puzzled by a different sound in the sky and I watched a fast moving dot, but the engine noise was way behind, with a loud roar, so I assumed that the Germans must have some kind of new plane. Usually about midday onwards, with a throbbing roar of engines, an Armada of American Flying Fortresses appeared in waves of hundreds. It was an awe-inspiring sight to see these slow moving large bombers being attacked by German fighters and the inner sections coming under anti-aircraft fire, with shells exploding amongst them. There was a war going on up there, with odd planes being blown to pieces, tumbling down on fire, with bodies falling through the air and some coming down by parachute. These planes seemed to be easy targets, being heavily laden with fuel and bomb loads.

The bombers were relentless and never wavered. As if by a giant hand, a huge section would swing left and another would swing right, while the centre mass carried straight on. I thought those American airmen were very brave indeed and it reminded me of the Light Brigade, 'Through the valley of death they thundered.' There were often masses of foil strips fluttering down, but the guard would load his rifle and threaten to shoot anyone who attempted to pick any up. Then came the crump of bombs exploding in the distance.

The constant stooping in the fields brought on my back pain, a recurrence of 1940, resulting in many stops and stretches to gain relief. The bread issue in this camp was one loaf of black bread between five, with the food issue identical to Laband, the only extra was a soup issue at midday, which still ran through me, and now, after eating the bread, I kept getting heartburn, the acid being horrible in my throat. The German diet was a destroyer of digestive systems. One would think that being a giant farm we would have fared a bit better, but we were just as strictly controlled as elsewhere. Red Cross parcels worked out one between three and deals with the Poles went on just the same. If ever Poles remember the British prisoner of war, it will I'm sure be the bartering and fair play that existed between us which they will call to mind. The parcel issue became very erratic, the Germans saying we should blame our own bombers, who were blowing up the railway system. I was not to receive another letter.

Threshing time came and that was one job I didn't like. The machine was like a hungry monster, no matter how long the bundles of oats were tossed into its gaping mouth, the German overseer would shout, *"Los, schnell, schnell arbeit."* With sweat streaming down us we would, when the overseer's attention was distracted, toss in a couple of bundles with the bindings uncut, then with much grinding and banging, the machine would slow to a halt, with the overseer screaming with rage, having to dismantle part of it to unclog the works. This gave us a two minute breathing space, enjoying the spectacle of the German frantically clearing the machine as if the result of the war depended on his efforts, but I do say that wherever I had seen Germans at work, I found them very industrious and conscientious.

We had problems with the tiny particles of straw which collected around the waist and in the navel, which with the sweat, caused some very sore rashes. It amazed me that so much dirt would come from bundles of wheat and barley, as each day our group would end up with bloodshot eyes and sweat-streaked like chimney sweeps. I would work up a terrific appetite, with little prospect of satisfying it, but my stomach had shrunk so small, that it didn't take much to get that full up feeling after eating soup and bread.

The threshing machine was moved over to a high barn, filled to the top with barley. On commencing, we were shown how to find the laying sequence of the bundles which ran circular and lifting them with the fork was simple, but lose it and the result was trouble. About one third down, I lost the sequence and started tugging the bundles out, which seemed held in a vice, when my back gave way with a stab of pain, resulting in having several days off work incapacitated. I was fortunate in that the Red Cross had supplied a first aid box which contained pain killer tablets. Life was a constant battle, but things were changing, compared with 1940, when a rifle butt or a boot was the treatment for sickness.

On returning to work, I was put with the Polish women, potato picking, and stooping again aggravated my back. Harvesting went on non-stop, as it does in all countries, then it was on to swedes and mangolds, then sugar beet, through the autumn on to the winter. I landed myself in a spot of bother whilst topping the sugar beet. I knew it was near the finish of the working day so I put a spurt on and stopped, having done my quota. The guard, a pimply faced youth, ordered me to start topping another row, so I said that I had done my share and the other men had nearly finished, but he wouldn't accept that and started shouting, so I walked away with my hoe, slowly, to the road. The guard was screaming Halt, among other things, and I looked back and saw that he had his rifle aimed at me. I ignored him and reached the road, stopping for the rest of the group to join me, and they had seen what had happened. I could never understand why Germans always lose their cool for the slightest reason, but I had no intention of stopping and he didn't shoot me anyway, but he could have done. My reaction, foolish as it seems, was to defy them because I detested them so much.

The Commandant was a German sergeant, a very strict regimental soldier, not only with us prisoners but with his own guards, and I had seen him shouting at them on the slightest excuse. There was a Sunday morning room inspection, with everything all clean and tidy when in he came, accompanied by a guard. Looking at my bed, he ordered me to fluff it up and straighten it out. I could speak some German then, and I explained that the bed was more dust than straw and the bed of the man underneath would be smothered in dust if I disturbed it. He took my comments as a challenge to his authority and shouted, "Straighten your bed." I refused, whereupon he ordered the guard to load his rifle and point it at my chest. I said to him, "Do you ask pigs to straighten their beds? What a brave soldier you are, going to shoot an unarmed prisoner of war. Why don't you be a good soldier and go to the Russian front?" He wore no medal ribbons.

He went deathly white and shot to attention, clicking his heels, ordered the guard to put his rifle up, and without a word, turned to leave, when he spotted Butler puffing away at a cigarette. He told him to put his cigarette out, whereupon John blew smoke into his face and he then left the room. John remarked that that was close, but I felt very angry. About three weeks later, on returning from work, 'Monty' of the Irish Guards came to me saying, "You are Harding, aren't you?" I nodded assent, and he said he had a message for me from the sergeant Commandant, who left that morning. He said, "Tell Herr Harding that I volunteer for the Russian front, I am now a good soldier." Monty asked if I understood the message and the reason for it. I said that I did. I felt a bit moved over this, as I had obviously stung his pride in the room with the guard as witness, and I guessed his chances on the Russian front would be very slim. Inside me, I wished him good luck.

Guardsman Montgomery had a withered arm, from wounds he had received. The story was told to me by his friend. Whilst holding a position in Italy as his Company withdrew, he kept the Germans back until he received a machine-gun burst in a shoulder, but his Bren-gun accounted for many of the enemy. He was recommended for the VC, but for personal reasons he was awarded the DCM instead. On my enquiry to his regiment it was confirmed that he was awarded the DCM.

The winter was very severe and in the farm workshop John had an accident whilst moving a thin piece of wood on a planing machine. His fingers dropped on to the plane cutters, scooping out the nails from some of them, including the bone ends. He was taken to hospital, where X-rays showed three finger bones were scooped to points and was told that as small pieces of quick were left, there was a good chance of the nails growing, but they may stay loose and be deformed. He was then returned to the Stalag.

The cold was so intense that frostbite was certain if ears were not covered, but by now many had balaclavas from home and I had acquired a scarf from someone who had several, also everyone had boots now, and even though they were old, they were better than clogs. No matter how I tried I couldn't get warm outside. I felt no face, hands or feet from the moment I left for work. The ploughed fields were as hard as concrete and in trying to dig out the sugar beet, sometimes the pickaxe handle would shatter. The poor horses were as lean as greyhounds with their ribs showing through and in trying to pull the heavily laden farm carts loaded with sugar beet across fields with deep ruts, I have seen them bent down to their knees struggling frantically to move the carts forward. One incident took place when apart from the Polish drivers using canes or whips on the poor unfortunate animals, one Pole in a rage swung a long handled shovel across the back of a horse that was bucking in terror but couldn't move the cart. A prisoner went over and uppercutted the Pole, knocking him flat on his back. The guard roared with laughter, but had the driver been a German, the prisoner would most certainly have been shot. The horse stood trembling badly, head down, when the Pole received a warning and a threat not to do it again. We all manhandled the cart to the road, but the horse looked finished to me.

We were all put out on tree felling and lopping branches, then on trestles, we had to saw the trunks into metre lengths, then they were carted away to be cut into small cubes which were then turned into charcoal. This was used as fuel for the fires on lorries and trucks, it gave off a gas to feed the engines, instead of using petrol. I have seen lorries going with a fair turn of speed on this system, so evidently it worked.

One prisoner, when swinging his axe into a tree had it skid on the frozen sap, only to cut into his own shinbone. It was a hard life, but we had to stick it out while we waited for the day when we would all go home. If only I wasn't so starving hungry all the time, it was sheer torture working with a stomach crying out for food. We made a huge fire with the surplus branches from the trees and the warmth was very welcome. In the mornings it was interesting to see the many animal footprints in the snow around the fire, feeding it every day, it was kept alight non-stop for three weeks.

This hard graft was playing my back up, and making me feel pretty miserable and I decided that somehow, hook or by crook, I would get back to the Stalag, but the problem was how! I was fortunate enough to get a package of 100 cigarettes from the Regiment and I thought it was very good of them. I decided to smoke little and hang on to them — it was food I needed.

One day we were told that there would be no work that day and we were taken to fields farther away, where many Polish men and women were being spread out thinly over quite a large area, with a small copse included. We were given tins with stones inside and with rattling and banging the tins, shouting, etc. we walked forward, shrinking the large circle all the time. Spaced around and in between were farmers, families and friends, dressed in their best and armed with sporting rifles and shot-guns. As the circle became smaller, I saw many small animals running around frantic, and they were shot after running outside the circle. Most were rabbits and some foxes. While this was going on, the Schnapps flowed like water, but there was nothing for us, we even missed our midday soup issue because we hadn't worked for it. The brushes of the foxes were cut off and presented to the women and two farm carts were filled with the dead animals showing a big clear out.

The new Camp Commandant arrived, a young weedy looking officer, the opposite of the projected image of the 'Master Race'. I was now dedicated to leave this camp, as I had become sick of the place, too small and confined. I knew that the Stalag would be worse, but I wouldn't be half frozen working there for some soup, and besides, I needed a change and new faces. Escape was useless, especially with all the bombing going on and the Germans would no doubt take it out on any prisoner who was recaptured.

CHAPTER NINETEEN

On the move

It was now February and the work in hand consisted of moving farm equipment ready for overhauling, preparing for when spring arrived. I was lifting a very awkward piece of machinery when I felt my back give, and with a yell I let it go and fell over. The guard came over and saw that I was in pain and I went back to camp. It was sore, and as in the past, it was a case of rest being needed. The next morning the guard came in and told me to get up for work, but I said that I couldn't, pointing to my back. He said nothing and I stayed there all day. I knew now that I might have a chance of returning to the Stalag. On the third day the Commandant came to see me and told me to get ready to go and see the doctor.

I went out slowly, stooping, to a farm cart which was taking some Polish women with baskets to go shopping. On arrival in Pritzwalde, the driver stopped at a market-place and the guard took me to a civilian doctor in the town, where there was a rather nice looking receptionist and I went through a partition door to the doctor. The guard stood in the doorway, getting on famously with the receptionist, but where he could also keep an eye on me. The doctor was a very friendly man, who spoke good English, which he was pleased to air fully.

After examining my back and finding the sore area he said, "One week off, then light work." I told him I wanted to return to the Stalag and he told me that only a very bad visible injury or illness could authorize my return to the Stalag.

I said, "Do you like English cigarettes?" He said that he did, so, watching the guard, I slipped a packet of ten Players over the table, and the doctor, quick as a flash, put them in the pocket of his white coat. I then said, "Stalag."

But he whispered, "I can't, I've had orders that we doctors can be shot for sending back prisoners of war who can work."

I then said softly, "If the guard knew that you had English cigarettes in your pocket, what do you think would happen?"

He went a deathly colour and whispered, "Oh no, don't!"

I repeated, "Stalag," on which he filled out a form, with his forehead beaded with perspiration, then called the guard from his flirting session and gave it to him, telling him that I was to go back to Stalag, unfit for work. The guard became angry but the doctor stuck to his decision.

As I followed the guard out, I whispered to the doctor, "Thank you," but he looked drained. God knows what he thought of Englishmen now, and I reckoned that my cigarettes must have felt like red-hot cinders in his pocket, but for me, well spent. Anyway, the general conversation now was that with the Russians coming this way, it would be safer in the Stalag, and others were trying to find ways of getting back. Three days later a guard turned up with a prisoner from some other place, and the three of us went on our way to Luckenwalde Stalag IIIA.

Our journey commenced at the Pritzwalde railway station, which was plastered with propaganda posters, some showing Churchill holding a Tommy-gun with the words 'Gangster kinder murderer', with bombing planes in the background. I thought then how the wheel had turned, when the *Luftwaffe* had mercilessly bombed Warsaw, Rotterdam, London, Coventry and many other cities. They started it, so let them squeal now that they were on the receiving end.

The guard was middle-aged, but was a no-nonsense silent type, with a watchful eye. The civilians seemed pale and drawn, not like the arrogant shouting, spitting ones that I remembered from 1940. Our train came in and it was early morning, but there were many delays, causing the guard to have a long talk with a railway official, so we alighted after a long ride to a local station, when a short march brought us to a barracks complex. We were immediately handed over to an NCO with a face like a pig and lots of mouth to go with it, who had us splitting logs with sledge-hammers and iron wedges. He got annoyed when I couldn't swing the hammer but my back was tender so I let him shout.

We were then taken to a Schnapps distillery, just outside the barracks, and on the way I passed long pits full of silver sand, and men in full marching order, huge packs and weapons, being doubled up and down in an exhausted state, near to collapse, driven on by tough looking NCOs. It looked to me like a punishment camp. At the distillery there were horse-drawn carts loaded with sacks of barley, which Polish workers had commenced to unload. We joined in with them, finding the sacks of grain shoulder high marked 200 kilos. On gripping the large ears, I bent forward to lift the heavy sack and found it difficult walking upwards on springy boards into the building. It was a struggle, and when I reached my third sack, I knew what was going to happen, as half-way up the boards my back gave way and underneath the boards I went, sack as well. 'Pig face' went into his best performance of a lunatic, but I would have none of it, pointing to my back and shaking my head.

We were doubled over into the barracks and with lots of mouth and hassle we were pushed into a small room and the steel door was clanged shut. Outside the door, I had noticed a large barrel combusion stove, the flue pipe of which went up and through the wall into the room a few inches below the ceiling, to the opposite wall and through it. There were no windows or ventilation of any kind, but a tiny space at the bottom of the door was all that let any air in. There was a spy hole with a shutter and a light bulb. The room was roughly four paces by three and seven feet high. It was also entirely of concrete construction.

There was a third occupant in the room, a foreign worker with a continuous rasping cough, who kept bringing up blood, which trickled through his fingers. He never spoke or moved and I was convinced that he was dying. I could hear the stove outside being filled and the sounds of laughter, then with a roar like an underground train, noise came through the flue pipe, which slowly turned to red-hot, giving off a terrific heat. Now and again I could see an eye looking through the spy hole. All the time we were in there the flue pipe stayed red-hot with the stove outside being continually filled.

As time passed, I hammered on the door asking for water, but the shout from the other side of the door was, "Shut up, swine," with a glaring eye at the spy hole. The foreign worker had blood running from his mouth as he coughed non-stop now, and the other prisoner's watch showed that we were locked in there at 12 midday. The heat was unbearable and the room practically airless, so I stripped off and laid on my clothes by the bottom of the door, trying to get a breath of air. I must have gone to sleep, because the door opened, the flue pipe still red-hot, and with several soldiers taunting us, we were let out. I mustered up enough strength to make it to a wall tap, where I drank my fill and ran the water over my head. The other prisoner was similarly distressed. Returning to dress, I saw the foreign worker slumped forward, his front streaked with blood, still breathing, but judging by the amount of blood he had lost, I felt he was close to death. Our guard turned up and feeling drained and weak, we went off to the railway station, where the clock showed 12.30 p.m., so we had been in that sweat box for 24 hours.

There was a long wait for the train, with crowded platforms, when suddenly the guard went rigid and hissed to us "SS!" Coming towards us, walking arrogantly with everybody making way for him was an elegantly dressed SS officer in black, looking like a messenger of death. He was well decorated, with an epaulette and silver lanyards on one shoulder, giving him, I thought, a lopsided look. He wore immaculate breeches and boots, with a pistol on his belt. As we passed him the guard raised his right arm and shouted, "Heil Hitler," with the SS officer totally ignoring him. I glanced back and saw a small pistol holster in the small of his back.

The train eventually arrived at Berlin in the evening and whilst the guard was making enquiries, I was amazed at the destruction, which was more extensive than when I saw it last. The station was a broken shell and as far as I could see was rubble. It was now dark, and the guard seemed anxious to get moving to wherever he was supposed to go, so walking down a shattered road in the town, I heard the throbbing of engines overhead. Sirens started wailing, then I heard a swishing sound, followed by explosions and a rush of air from not far off. The guard ran us, together with other people, down into an air raid shelter. It was a tube like interior, fairly long and the guard settled us at one end, backs to the wall. The lighting was dim, and as the bombing became intense, with loud explosions, movement in the ground caused the lights to jump on and off. This raid went on for a long time, with the civilians very angry and shouting, shaking their fists when one of them noticed us, and threatening violence, some made towards us, making me think that my time had come. Then the guard, with a roar, fixed his bayonet and stood in the on guard position, shouting an order which made them stop, but looking very menacing to me. They were after blood, but for once I was grateful to a German soldier, who did his duty and protected us, as we could certainly have been battered to death. The lot of them in the shelter were shouting at us now, so the guard loaded his rifle and I felt at that moment that I would rather have taken my chances with the bombing in the street.

Fortunately the sirens sounded the all clear, and the guard waited until the shelter was empty before we left and had no trouble returning to the station, when after waiting hours for a train, we eventually made it to Stalag IIIA, Luckenwalde, after another train change at Truenbritzen. I entered the Stalag feeling washed out, thirsty and hungry, and was shocked at what I saw. Thousands of men were crammed together, apparently with little form of order, with many nationalities. I even saw some Chinese, but they were separated into their own compounds. After being booked in, the silent no-nonsense guard went on his way and I found my way to the RSM's office to be booked in on his list to be put on the 'strength' so to speak for parcel allocations and to be told where my billet was to be.

I found my hut and a spot in a corner, and after a drink of water, I caught up on some sleep. Later, after a long search, I found Butler, who was pleased to see me. His fingers were healing, with no sign of nail growth yet. He had palled up with a man from his village in Eire, a man whose name was to become a household word after the war in the racing world. He was Arthur Thompson, who as champion jockey, won the Grand National three times.

John found me a spot among the hundreds in a massive hut, one of many, then I went down with a fever, lying there for days with a raging temperature and pouring with perspiration. When it passed I was very weak and wobbly on my legs, but John was very good, seeing me all right for water and my soup issue. The bunk boards had been reduced to three, one for the shoulders, one for your bottom, and one for your feet, covered with a near empty palliasse. Quite often someone would turn over in the night and crash through on to the bloke underneath, sometimes ending in a fight, with shouts in the dark of "Pack it in," etc.

The nights were bitterly cold, with the wind howling through the broken windows and many of us found it warmer to each roll in our blanket, lying close together on the stone floor to generate heat, and the floor space eventually became covered when more prisoners kept coming in from other camps, due to the advance of the Russian armies, plus new prisoners taken on the battle fronts. We became friendly with a chap named Leydon, a signals man taken with the Americans in Italy.

Every night, almost to the minute the sirens would wail and all camp lights would go out, then the guards would release the dogs, who were trained to kill. One evening I was out, away from my hut, when the sirens wailed so I bolted for the nearest hut. In the darkness I heard distant screams mingled with the horrible sound of dogs savaging, then some shots were fired. The next morning a story went round that some RAF chaps had attempted an escape, but apparently two of them made it over the first wire when the dogs got them. The third man got tangled on the barbed wire and in getting back down again, tore himself pretty badly, and I heard that he was hidden by some Australians in case of a search. A guard had shot dead the two men.

Purely by accident I was walking around the large compound the next day when I saw a hut with its doors open, and the Red Cross symbol attracted me to look inside, where I saw two corpses lying on tables being examined. Their bodies showed signs of having been savaged by dogs, and they also had bullet wounds. I had only a quick glance, but I saw enough to guess that they were the two airmen who died the previous night. Word went round that one was RAF and the other RCAF, aged 20 and 21, but I never knew their names. There were quite a few RAF personnel, NCOs downwards mixed in with us now, but RAF officers were separated from our compound by a single wire wall, patrolled by guards. This Stalag was a hotch-potch affair, with these wire walls put up all over the place. The British compound had adjoinging it the American, Italian, Russian, RAF officers' compounds, plus some small offshoots, one where I saw Chinese.

I became friendly with an RAAF Flight Sergeant. He was a good bloke and gave me his address in Tasmania to look him up after the war to work with him on the 'Snowy mountain project', saying that Australia needed blokes like me. Quite a compliment!

The patrolling guards seemed a nervy lot, who must have known that their days were numbered, with no sleep due to the non-stop night bombing. In my mind I felt it was wise to avoid these guards, as I had the impression that they were trigger-happy. The men who still had Red Cross food or drink would be busy with their 'blowers' also additional prisoners were now arriving in daily from other camps, so food was scarce, and I had run out and had to survive on the daily dish-water soup and black bread issue. The Australians had turned one area into a gambling den which was always packed with men having a go at Crown and Anchor, Pitch and Toss, etc. Among other things, watches and valuables were most acceptable but the general currency was cigarettes. One New Zealand padre was reputed to be head of a big racket in the Stalag and was referred to as 'Holy Joe, the fiddling bastard' by his own countrymen.

The Russian prisoners' compound was guarded and patrolled by Cossacks in fur hats, German tunics with baggy trousers. Quite a few of the German officers spoke American-English and one guard, a thin, weedy looking type with glasses just wandered around the camp freely, armed only with a pistol on his belt, talking to blokes, and was known to all and sundry as 'Maginty'.

He had a cockney accent so I asked him what part of London he came from and his reply was Bethnal Green, one of Mosley's blackshirts, I thought, called up as a militiaman.

The camp conditions were like a cesspool, with little space to do anything. Washing one's face and attempting to shave was achieved with a struggle. The huts, full of unwashed bodies, stank, the air outside stank, the latrines were full and stinking, with masses of men wandering around aimlessly with nowhere to go. Trenches had been dug to use as latrines, with poles set on trestles, and the poles were in constant use, with lines of men suffering from diarrhoea, etc., crouching on the poles doing their business into the trenches — not a pretty sight from the back end! Occasionally a yell would come from an unfortunate bloke who, through leaning backwards too much and the movement of the poles, would topple into the trench, much to the amusement of any onlookers, with no volunteers to help him out! I had an attack of the runs and I never wandered far from the poles, I dare not and soon found that someone getting on or off the poles caused them to bounce, making my heart jump in my mouth in my precarious position.

Unfortunately I went down with another bout of fever, and with a dreadful sensation in the stomach, would come the shaking, with water running from out of me, head to foot with a very high temperature. This lasted for several days and when it passed, I felt as weak as a baby and could hardly stand.

The bombing was colossal and constant, with some nights when the sky was lit up almost as bright as day. To go near a window invited a bullet and there was always the fool causing bullets to whizz into the hut, resulting in roars of protest. The sky at night regularly showed pathfinder flares hanging in clusters of various colours, when wave after wave of bombers would roar overhead. The topic of conversation was now the hope that none of the bombs would fall on us. I never had an ounce of sympathy for the Germans, they showed none when they devastated our cities. I had a few cigarettes left and resisted great temptation to smoke, keeping them to get food if and when I could. I was back to 1940, feeling weak with occasional diarrhoea.

The Americans in their compound appeared to be faring much better. Their Red Cross parcels were twice the size of ours, containing also a roll of toilet paper and cigarettes, which ours didn't. There was envy when they had fry-ups near the wire and outside their huts, but they offered nothing when asked, and I heard that when asked officially to share their parcel stocks, they refused. In reverse, I'm not sure that we would have shared either. It was survival now in this human jungle.

One day I wandered round to the Italian compound, just in time to witness a 'Tit for tat' showdown between the British and the Eyeties, who being soldiers without a cause were treated as civilian prisoners. They went out on daily local working parties and did deals with the British prisoners, white bread for cocoa and chocolate, for which they had a craving. Apparently the previous day, when at the wire on the point of exchanging bread for whatever, on a planned effort along the wire the Eyeties snatched both bread and cocoa from the British, leaving them with nothing. What was to happen now was carefully worked out, signals and a shout, the Eyeties were going to be taught a lesson. All day our prisoners had been cutting whatever could be found into the size of chocolate bars and carefully sealed them into empty wrappers. The cocoa tins were emptied and filled to within half an inch from the top with sand and blocked off with a piece of cardboard, then topped up with cocoa, then the lid carefully sealed back.

I was watching all this activity with great interest and all was ready when the Eyeties trooped in, waving white loaves and coming straight to the wire. Much arguing went on until the number of loaves was agreed upon and the dealing was done perfectly. Friends stood together when more than one loaf was involved, then the shout came and all loaves of bread were pulled in together and the 'cocoa, chocolate' let go, thus depriving the Eyeties of a repeat performance of the previous day. They soon found that they had been duped and with screams of rage rushed the wire, with our blokes waving the bread and jeering, whilst dodging a shower of stones, when guard reinforcements ran in and laid into them with cries of 'Macaroni soldaten', some of them ending up with sore heads and no cocoa. Our chaps got their revenge and to add insult to injury, sat eating the loaves in full view of the Eyeties, waving chocolate and tins of cocoa, plus the two finger salutes. Seeing the loaves brought home to me how hungry I was, but there was nothing I could do about it. I had run out of food quite a while ago now and the few cigarettes I kept were not any good now to obtain food with, as with so many new prisoners coming in, watches and rings were in demand, the racketeers intending to go home rich.

Following this exciting episode, I wandered back and saw two prisoners doing a deal through the wire with two RAF officers, and it was obvious to me that they had not been prisoners very long, judging by their tidy uniforms and peak caps. One had a handlebar moustache and was doing the deal for a 'dressed' rabbit. I didn't think for one minute that it was a rabbit, as it would have been cooked and eaten instantly. However, I saw 200 cigarettes change hands and the rabbit taken with the RAF officer remarking, "Wizard old man." I asked the two prisoners whether it really was a rabbit. One of them laughed and said, "No, it took us a week to entice the white cat from the guards' block," but for the two RAF officers, ignorance was bliss.

Back in the hut I joined a small group around an Irish Guardsman. He asked me to touch a spot on his forehead, then told me of a one in a million chance where a bullet had entered his forehead and made an exit over his right ear, leaving no ill effects.

CHAPTER TWENTY

The long road back

In the American compound I noticed a lot of activity, with German soldiers carrying and arranging tables with officers supervising. When the tables were placed together, a heavily built man in civilian clothes jumped on to them and introduced himself as Max Schmelling, the famous German heavyweight boxer, who called American prisoners to gather round. Soon there was a large crowd round him, all shouting with pleasure at meeting the great boxer who had fought in the USA before the war against Joe Louis. He invited anyone to come up and box a couple of rounds with him and he had plenty of takers.

As an onlooker, I saw another activity going on at a blind corner, which was closest to the American huts. One part of the wire had been cut and British prisoners were moving quickly into American huts and running back with packages and food parcels, making fast return journeys, with look-outs and friends taking the loot into a hut. The guard had his back to them, watching the shadow boxing. Max Schmelling stopped and gave a speech amid much cheering from the Americans and at this point, the looters had completed their thieving and returned, refixing the wire. I then saw tables brought into our compound, with a repeat performance from Max Schmelling, asking British prisoners to come forward, and as only seven men showed interest, it was abandoned.

In the meantime, the dispersed Americans had returned to their huts, to find their food and belongings gone. Cries of rage built up into anger when they came to the wire to see many 'blowers' working in full view, cooking Spam meat loaf and the culprits puffing away the stolen Camel and Lucky Strike cigarettes, shouting out, "Thanks Yanks." If extra guards had not been brought along, I'm sure the wire would have been breached, with a pitched battle ensuing, but shouts of, "Lousy Limey bastards," had to suffice.

It is hard really to describe the situation of the men in the camp, which was now packed to overflowing with all sorts, becoming an intolerable burden for the Germans. As camps were overrun by the Russian advance, so prisoners were brought here. Everyone walked about carrying what possessions they had, and those with bunks only left them with a friend to guard. A ceillih band was going strong in one hut, playing Irish melodies and singing anti-English rebel songs. The band consisted of a fiddle, a makeshift drum, an accordion and a banjo playing for hours on end. Fights were common between the different

Irish factions, with shouts in the night of "Up the Pope" and replies of "Right up him, King Billy for ever," followed by the sounds of thuds and blows, and in the morning there would be black eyes and bruised faces. I hated the place and the miserable existence. My brain felt dulled; I had been a prisoner too long and hardened to the state, and felt indifferent to the suffering of others. All I wanted was to leave this cursed country and it didn't bother me where.

One morning, close to my area, a disturbance broke out from an Arnhem paratrooper, who was on a top bunk. Buckets were few and far between, but the para took one, upsetting the Irishman who had it. The para was washing something in it on the bunk while the Irishman pestered him to return his bucket without success so he came back to retrieve it with some of his pals, using force if necessary. Then the para threw the dirty water over them and the bucket at the Irishman. They set to rush him but backed away and I saw him crouch on the bunk, ready to spring, wild eyed with froth on his lips. Guards were brought in, but he was left alone until three orderlies in white jackets went for him from different directions, and after a fierce struggle, he was taken away in a strait-jacket.

The paratroopers were very tough men indeed, and one with whom I was having a conversation told me that back in England, he took his girl to the local cinema, seated in the front circle, when he left to buy an ice-cream, and on his return an American soldier was in his seat, mauling his girl, who was resisting most strongly. He said that he lifted the Yank up and dropped him over the edge into the stalls below, then they both walked out. I asked if he was killed, and he said no, he had a broken back. An identity parade was held at his nearby camp, with no result. I had no reason to disbelieve this quiet, serious looking man. I decided that you must never take liberties with a paratrooper!

Some Russian prisoners had found a way into the British compound. The long latrines had been separated by the single wire wall into two halves, one half in their compound and the other half in ours. A very dangerous thing to do was crawling under the woodwork of the long seat board past a strong partition, when one slip meant death by sinking into the stinking morass below. They would ask around for an old toothbrush and a small photograph. A ring would be made from the toothbrush, with a face from the photograph inserted into it. The Russians never failed to find a client, and the charge was two cigarettes. One day, close to the latrines, a patrolling guard shouted halt, and I saw a Russian running to reach the latrines entrance, but he never made it, the guard was a sharpshooter who, quick as a flash, shot him dead. He casually walked over and turned the Russian over on to his back with his jackboot and, satisfied that he was dead, strolled away on his round. I walked away too. The guards were seeing their country disintegrating before their eyes and would shoot anyone, given the slightest excuse.

Another time when I was passing by the Russian compound, a crouching figure hissed and it was a Russian, trying to make contact with me. So first looking round for the usual observant guard and seeing him a good way back, I went over to the Russian, who surprisingly spoke fair English, and asked me for a cigarette. I only had a few left, but feeling sorry for this bundle of rags and bones, I gave him one, for which he thanked me most profusely, adding, "I am a Russian officer. If the Germans found out, I would be shot but I know that I can trust an Englishman, goodbye." I saw that the guard in the distance was about to turn back, so I moved away quickly. The ground was packed hard with snow and it was bitterly cold but I just had to get away from humanity for an hour. It was literally a madhouse, with floor space almost non-existent, with men packed everywhere, and I was becoming sick of the sight of them.

One morning Leyden sat on the edge of a bunk staring, and I said let's go for a walk. He wouldn't move, so I became rough with him, saying come on, snap out of it, but all he would say was, "Leave me, I've had it." So angrily I said to John, "Grab his arm," and between us we forced him outside and walked him about until he became his old self again. I had now reached the stage when on standing up, I had to hold my knees back, because of the shakes, and once steadied, I would be OK.

The RSM called a rough kind of parade, and down the ranks he took a terrified RAF prisoner, saying, "Take a good look at his face men, he was caught stealing food from a comrade." Before dismiss he shouted out, "I am not going to punish him, you know what to do." I walked away, I had seen too much of this sort of thing in the past. It also showed the tension between the Irish themselves when, as I walked through my hut towards the door, a long knife flashed by me, just missing the head of a man in front of me. The knife stuck quivering in the door frame, when the man turned angry, looking at a group of stony faces saying, "If I find out who did this, I will get him ten years back in England." I saw that he was a Company Sergeant-Major of the Irish Guards.

I would spend some time looking through the wire overlooking an open field, on which were rows of long oblong mounds, each with a board stuck in the top with number 200 on it. I watched the non-stop living skeletons moving at a snail's pace, four carrying a board with a corpse on it and four others trailing behind, who half-way changed places and carried the board to an open oblong pit, where the corpse was tipped in, then back they went for the next one. The Russian prisoners were dying like flies from starvation and disease, and this sad ritual was going on for hours each day. I heard that British officers estimated that 30,000 Russians had perished.

Then a surprise indeed. Who should confront me was, David Rosbotham, just arrived in my hut. It was a happy reunion, I was so pleased to see him, but when I asked what happened to Percy Green and Old Tom Connelly, he said he didn't know, as they had all been split up. He met John Butler but there wasn't the same warmth in the meeting, as John spent most of his time with a wild man from Tipperary. Later David came and took me to his pitch where from under a coat he showed me a bowl filled with hot barley soup, saying, "Eat that Bill." I protested, knowing that he needed it as much as I did, but he insisted, so I wolfed it down, and when I asked, he told me that if you paid dearly, at the kitchen, you could get it. He had given his watch. This may not sound very much on paper, but in that terrible place, under semi-starvation conditions, what he did was an act of selflessness and comradeship, and I shall never forget it.

Anxious days passed regarding food. We were issued a small piece of bread and watery soup daily, and this fluctuated on odd days, when none was issued, so it was a case of going without and to make matters worse, when I drank water, burning bile acid would rise up into my mouth, caused by the abominable bread made of potato flour and sawdust. Then it was announced that soup would be issued every other day from now on and one issue stank to high heaven, with small black bits of meat in it. John tried to drink his, but he heaved and slung it, but I was starving, so I held my nose and forced it down.

My old ear trouble flared up into a painful condition, with two large swellings and it was discharging as badly as ever. For some days, I was walking about in a dazed state, light-headed from the pain, so John managed to persuade a guard to take me to the Stalag hospital. I vaguely remember sitting in a chair, and a doctor saying that he was Serbian. As he had no anaesthetic, I was to hold tight to the chair whilst he cut inside my ear. I recollect a voice saying, "Leave him where he is and see how he gets on, his temperature is extremely high." Well I recovered OK and in the hospital hut, I shared a room for four. It was a pleasant week, with the swelling going down but the discharge mixed with blood continued unabated, and made a dirty mess on my shirt. I received extra soup, but that was all, nothing else nor any facilities for a bath, but at a tap I tried washing the caked blood from the shoulder of my shirt.

Close to the hut was a building from which I occasionally heard screams which set my blood to ice and I saw Russians carried out strapped to wooden stretchers, covered with blankets, blood streaked and groaning. The Russians were treated as the lowest form of life and if any needed an emergency operation they would never get it, so the only thing I could think they were doing was medical experiments. I remembered before seeing a Russian writhing on the ground, shrieking in pain and two German guards standing by laughing their heads off. So much for humanity.

I was returned to the compound and it was now late March 1945. The rumbling of guns were distant, sending a tingling through my veins, also the guards appeared to be very jumpy and they made no attempt to stop gaps being cut in the wire, so that the British and American prisoners mingled together. I saw some Americans holding hands so I asked an American if they were 'Nancy boys', he replied, "We call them Peggies."

One night I entered a hut to see quite a performance, with a guard standing to attention with right arm raised shouting, "Heil Churchill." Every time he did it he was given a cigarette by a laughing crowd, who were calling 'Louder', until he was roaring it out and a couple of men brought a German NCO to the hut windows to see what the guard was doing. He ran in screaming, punched the guard in the face and then doubled him out. One bloke said, "Another square-headed bastard for the chop." It was a dirty trick and I'm sure that with English cigarettes on him, coupled with what he was shouting, he was destined for the firing squad. It had been planned.

As the days went by, sounds of battle drew nearer, with Russian fighter planes darting about and it was now mid-April, when all the German guards disappeared. A senior British officer came into the compound and hurriedly called a parade, saying that the food supply was being looked into to keep an issue going, and that Army personnel were now running the kitchens. We were reminded that we were soldiers and still subject to military law and discipline, and any man caught seriously disobeying orders would have his name, rank and regiment and number taken. We were back in the British Army, the Germans were beaten. He also ordered us to stay in our huts until we were liberated.

The battle reached the Stalag and it was fierce and bloody. John and myself ignored orders and went outside to see running battles all around the wire, with heavy firing, shouts and screams, with no quarter given. I saw German boys firing from among the trees when a missile whizzed over our heads, so John and I thought it prudent to go back into the hut.

Russian tanks tore through the wire, then an avalanche of cheering men ran out of the huts, crowding round the tanks, which carried bemedalled women soldiers, armed with Tommy-guns. The Russians were Mongolians, not demonstrative, tall, thin, slit-eyed men who looked to me cruel types. I didn't like the look of them, especially when, ignoring protests, they started to relieve prisoners of anything they could lay their hands on, mainly searching for watches.

In the general confusion, I left the crowds, wanting to look inside the Russian compound. The first hut I went to was half brick half timber, with no windows. As I opened the door, a concrete step held back some inches of water and looking inside into the darkness, a stench of putrefaction went to my throat and I heaved and retched, then forcing myself to look, I saw a pile of rotting bodies. I quickly left there and after some fresh air I went to the next hut, which was rather large and of wooden construction. Inside was a scene that held me spellbound. It was a long time since I had seen such beauty.

At first sight, the interior appeared to glow from the walls and I looked at the carpet, which ran the full length of the hut to an altar. It was woven into intricate patterns and dyed in bright colours and made from sisal string, used for tying up British Red Cross parcels. As I slowly walked down the hut I admired life-sized murals, three to each wall, depicting scenes from the Bible, showing Jesus healing the sick. They were beautifully coloured and done by true artists. The golden glow from the walls was from tens of thousands of tiny diamond shapes cut from straw and stuck on the wall, forming all scenes and figures, etc. They were truly works of art and I stood awhile taking in the beauty of it all.

When I reached the altar, I saw that the cloth was made of woven coloured threads, fringed at the edges. The candlesticks, cups and other vessels were craftsmen made from used Red Cross parcel food tins and turned into beautiful shapes, set with coloured jewels made from old tooth brush handles, obtained from British prisoners. The large metal cross and the crucifix were truly works of art. Behind the altar was a huge mural, the full width of the hut, breathtakingly beautiful, showing Jesus with his disciples at the last supper. It was so lifelike. All the figures of Jesus showed a glowing halo over his head.

These poor wretches were starving and had nothing, so how on earth did they do this work without tools and the bulk of them hardly able to stand? Standing quietly looking at all of this, I felt at peace in a sacred place, and on leaving I found myself tiptoeing out. It seemed to me to show the ultimate in human faith and endeavour under great suffering and degradation.

On leaving I was confronted with a considerable contrast. Outside the death hut which I had previously visited was a farm cart, and Russian soldiers equipped with rakes, had dragged out the corpses and stacked them into the cart. I noticed that some of the bodies were rotting and some of them had holes in them. When the hut had been emptied, the cart was full to overflowing with horribly discoloured arms and legs sticking out of the sides. The Russians pulled on the shafts, and others pushed from the back, and a soldier held high a stick with a red rag tied to it; they moved off singing. I followed them to a half-filled oblong pit, where the corpses were tipped in, then they stood and sang what sounded like a hymn. It was a very moving experience, and as I left they were covering the corpses with handfuls of earth.

While I had been witnessing this, a lot of men had raided the Admin. offices and when John saw me he said, "Where the hell have you been?" handing me a small photo of myself taken in 1940 for registration, with my number hanging on my chest. I asked why he didn't bring the whole file and he replied that I couldn't have read it anyway.

The same senior British officer, with the assistance of NCOs called a proper orderly parade and among other things said that the Russian Army commander had stated that he considered us his prisoners and that arrangements would be made for us to be taken to Russia, that guards had been posted around the camp, therefore no one was to leave the camp, or do so at the risk of getting shot. He said that permission had been granted for small foraging parties to go out for food supplies and any livestock. The Russians had nothing to give, as their armies lived off the land as they moved along, which I suppose made them so merciless, fight to eat, drink and rape — the spoils of war. Some men had gone off to Luckenwalde and were glad to return to the safety of the camp, bringing back tales of rampaging drunken Russians shooting at everything, doors, windows, mingled with the screams of women being raped wholesale.

I discussed the situation with Butler and Rosbotham, feeling uneasy about being taken to Russia. This was the last thing I wanted, they were supposed to be our allies, but they didn't seem very friendly to me. It was now 22nd April, well into 1945, so John and myself decided to get away from this uncertain place. I could only see it getting worse, as there was no information forthcoming as to when we would be handed over to the British and the Americans. John and I decided to get away that night and somehow make our way home. We tried hard to persuade David Rosbotham to come but he would have none of it, saying that he had been a prisoner too long, and it was certain death outside. So when night came, we said farewell to David, who I was never to see again, and wished him luck, then made our way to the wire farthest from the gates.

Lifting the wire, we crawled underneath but it was a bright moonlit night, so we crawled through groups of dead Germans lying where they had been killed that day. It was a moment of great tension, looking at the dead faces. None of them had boots on and most were lying on their backs, arms still up in the position of surrender, sprayed with bullets from the crotch upwards. I could see the puncture holes on the nearest ones I passed, as their tunics lay open and their shirts had been pulled up to their chins. The only reason I could think of for this was that the Russians had to see the results of their handiwork. I had to brush past one corpse, a youth lying on his back with his trousers pulled down to his ankles, showing a large wound pad on his left thigh, his lower parts saturated in congealed blood, and a small hole in his temple where he had been finished off. His tunic showed SS insignia and his helmet had the SS flash.

We left this behind on reaching the trees, when we thankfully stood up and I can say truthfully that this was the only time in my life that I felt my hair stand up on the back of my head, for a Russian soldier stepped from behind a tree with a Tommy-gun on its strap pointing at us. My heart was thumping like a sledge-hammer, so I said to John, "Smile, for Christ's sake." So smiling we went up to him saying, "Americanski, not Angelski," as we had found out soon enough that the Russians favoured Americans rather than the British. Well fortunately it worked, as his face broke into the semblance of a smile, while we made a fuss of him, patting him on the back, etc., then we moved on, waving to him until plenty of trees were between us, then I leaned against a tree, feeling exhausted and dripping with perspiration. I had half expected a hail of bullets in my back and I was tightened up like a ball. With shaky legs I carried on with John, passing dead Germans on the way, one a giant of a man with his head half in a stream, flies crawling on his eyeballs, then I was surprised to see a dead civilian in plus fours, possibly a soldier who had dumped his uniform. Still the same, all the dead Germans had no boots on, so it looked as if the Russians were poorly shod. All of this showed what an unhealthy place the woods were, and as it was nearly daylight, we decided to look for a road and to follow the sun towards the west.

We came to odd villages that had no sign of life, and although we were very hungry, we thought it wiser to go round them, then in the distance there was the mournful sound of women wailing. As we got closer there was a large group of old women digging graves in a clearing in the woods and corpses piled near by ready for burial. We moved around them, as women with spades in that state could be dangerous.

Along the road there passed a Russian horse-drawn convoy and one farm cart held a packed crowd of women and girls who were sobbing and crying, presumably being taken to satisfy the lust of the Russians *en route*. My memory went back to the Polish girls in Laband, emptying coal wagons, weeping and being beaten, so I felt no pity for the women in the cart. Time rolled by and feeling very tired, we decided to find somewhere to snatch a few hours' sleep, and by a farm building we found drinking water but no food, also two battered bicycles, almost unusable, so after an exhausted sleep, at dawn we went on our way on the bicycles.

Mine had no back tyre, and when we got going, John went flying off, almost out of sight, while I struggled, riding on a back rim. I felt so exhausted, I could only go short distances, when with a galloping heart, I had to sit by the roadside and wait until I could go on again. John came back, telling me to hurry up, so I told him to go it alone and I would make it at my own pace, but he said no, so we moved along, with lots of rests. Passing a break in the woods my sharp eyes spotted a tiny figure with a rifle levelled in our direction, so with a shout, we sought safety in the trees and walked on for a while. We eventually came to a deserted village which showed war damage, so hiding the bikes, we entered the first house, looking for food. Water was no problem, but the riding and hunger added to my weak state. In the house was an old man in pyjamas, propped up with pillows, his head resting on his hand, lying dead. The place had been ransacked, with everything tipped out from cupboards and drawers and trodden underfoot, but I did find a hard crust of bread, which I softened with water and shared with John.

Two foreign workers walked in, young stocky looking men. We eyed each other warily then we left, wanting no trouble. I saw no more sign of life, but more dead Germans in front gardens, also one flattened horrible looking mess in the road, which was a man chewed up by tanks. Just a shovel was needed. We came to one house which had the front blown away by a shell, just showing the rooms and the staircase. Very gingerly we climbed the shaky stairs when I saw a treadle organ, so with one finger I played 'You are my sunshine', with both of us singing at the tops of our voices, which sounded eerie in the main street, with no sign of life. But who was to know what was behind the windows of the houses facing? So we decided to move on as we were not far behind the Russian Army. Before leaving I looked in a drawer and found a Hitler Youth dagger, an automatic, an army travel bag and a high ranking German officer's ceremonial belt, complete with sword knots. It was about 3 inches wide and made of woven wire in the stripes of the national colours. The front fastening clasp showed one half of the globe of the world, the other half a swooping eagle, showing the talons clutching the globe — the German hopes and aspirations! I put the items into the bag and took them, although I wasn't bothered about souvenirs as I was heartily sick of Germany and everything connected with it.

We found no food, so went on our way riding the bikes, mine making a slippery clatter on the back rim. We saw a farmhouse a way back from the road, so scenting food, and I was virtually starving, I know John was, we rode to the front door and hammered on it. A German of about 30 opened the door, glowering at us. He knew his days of shouting at prisoners had gone, as all farms had prisoner of war labour. We pushed our way in and demanded food. He said that he had none but his wife, holding a young baby and looking terrified as we became aggressive, told him to give us some bread. Then she cried out, pointing to the back window and with a quick look, I saw three Russian soldiers with Tommy-guns approaching, so we darted out the front and rode off as fast as we could, with a sigh of relief once we were out of sight. I just didn't have it in me to trust them.

We approached a town called Barby late in the afternoon, which showed signs of recent fighting, with many damaged buildings. On entering a main street we walked the bikes and dodged out of sight just in time to see a column of German soldiers, prisoners, pass by, many wounded and without boots. It seemed to be a Russian fetish, collecting German jackboots. The Russians guarded them well, with a tank slowly trundling along in the rear. Several tanks were moving about with slit-eyed Mongolian women soldiers sitting on them, with Tommy-guns cradled at the ready, very alert. Deciding it was too dangerous, we moved out a bit from the town.

We found a badly damaged hotel. No one was about, so we searched for food, but surprisingly found an unopened quarter-pound packet of Brooke Bond tea, and we managed a brew of sorts in the rubble and plaster-strewn kitchen. A few pieces of stale bread went down a treat too. In a bedroom where in one corner of the ceiling we saw the stars, was an enormous four poster bed with a canopy on the top, so I flopped on that and John found a smaller version. I sank into this luxurious bed, crawled between sheets as I was, with my head on a pillow, the first for nearly six years and I drifted off. We woke at daylight and left straight away on our bicycles, but back in town my wobbly tyreless back wheel compelled me to walk it on the pavement.

A German woman ran from a doorway and stared wild-eyed at us then hysterically cried, "You are Englanders, please stay and protect me, I was raped by lots of Russians last night, look at my front door, they won't touch me with you here tonight." I saw that the door was riddled and splintered, hanging on one hinge and I couldn't imagine drink crazed Russians taking any notice of us, so I told her that the Russians would shoot us and still rape her, leaving her very tearful. I felt a great urge to move on and I didn't want to get clobbered at this stage by Russian drunks, women hunting.

Moving on, we came to a wide river and an uproar was in progress, by a very large crowd of civilians being held back by a semicircle of Russian soldiers with automatic weapons. The cause of the trouble was an army constructed bridge built across the river, which was the Elbe, and the civilians wanted to cross to the other side. We couldn't see much from the back, so went to the river and threw the bicycles in, then forcibly pushed our way through to the front to see that the bridge was filled with heavy American army transport inching its way slowly to the other side, and somehow we had to get over. John spotted the last vehicle just entering the bridge and shouted excitedly, "Bill, there's a 15 cwt.

wireless truck." This seemed our only chance, so looking at each other we dashed through the Russian soldiers and dived into the back of the truck. Instantly there was a tangle of arms and legs, then someone shouted, "Look out!" and we stared into the face of a furious Russian with automatic weapon pointed straight at us. At that moment the crowd pushed forward into him, making him turn round and lay into them, driving them back. One man inside said, "We almost got shot up."

Inside the truck was a Major, a CSM, a Sergeant and the driver. We declared ourselves to the Major, who told us that several days earlier he had been parachuted into enemy territory and that the truck had gone in to pick him up. We were given some cigarettes and chocolate, for which we were very grateful and the Major told us that it wasn't possible to take us with him but we would be left on the other side, where we would be safe, as it was American territory. As we left them, with a wave, I felt terribly let down, thinking that they could easily have dropped us off at the nearest British Army unit.

We came across an American regiment of tanks lined up along an avenue of trees and we fell for lots of ribald shouts and comments, all in fun at two down at heel, ragged, thin British soldiers. We eventually reached a town of fair size and spotted a building showing the Stars and Stripes, with a sentry outside and enquired and found that it was the Provost Marshal. An American Army Major came out and we told him that we were starving, so the big hearty cheerful man, after a few questions, took us to the Officers' Mess, where there were tables laid out with linen and cutlery, with officers present having their meal. He beckoned a Mess orderly and told him to give us the best. We certainly looked out of place, ragged and unshaven with the officers smiling at us. Whilst we were waiting, I couldn't resist eating the white bread and butter which was already on the table and my shrunken stomach could hardly cope with the fantastic meal which was placed before us. A large piece of gateau finished it off, with numerous cups of coffee and when I rose to leave, I went bent over for a minute before I could straighten up. We went to the Major's office, as requested, and thanked him for his kindness and generosity. With a hearty laugh, he gave us each a carton of cigarettes and rations, saying that he was sorry that he couldn't accommodate us, as he had too much on his hands. But pointing he said, "That's the way home boys, good luck," and with a handshake we left him. What a great guy that man was, I shall never forget him.

With walking miles and getting lifts, we made some headway, but it was all guesswork and we didn't really have a clue where we were going until, looking for somewhere to kip down, we came across a now liberated concentration camp, with the now safe electrified wired gates, and I imagined the evil faced bully boys in blue with swastikas, who were there no more. Inside we found the place full of refugees, many of them Dutch, and we found a spot to sleep on the concrete floor at the foot of a crematoriam oven, which had its large door open, showing charred bones inside. We were too weary to look around, and after much back slapping from the Dutch civilians, we were soon asleep, with our few belongings wrapped inside our jackets. In the morning, on leaving, I noticed many ropes with nooses hanging from the boughs of trees and I was glad to leave that place of death.

Walking a few more miles, we came to an airfield, which was littered with burned out German aircraft, so entering a building, we spoke to an American officer, who advised us to stay where we were, as he was expecting transport planes in any day, bringing supplies. When the planes, mostly Dakotas, arrived, we with a motley bunch of ex-prisoners, mostly French, helped to unload them. They took off with us as passengers *en route* from Hildersheim to Le Havre. Whilst at Hildesheim an American soldier told me that, in his words, "Nine niggers were hanged this morning for raping women, not because they were German, but because they were white." On arrival at Le Havre, the pilot told us that he had heard on his radio that the Dakota following us had crashed, with no survivors, a very sad thing to happen when ex-prisoners of war were on their way home.

The Americans were very good to us, giving us a razor, soap and a mirror and meals in the queue with others. John and I wandered down to the dockside to find that a Liberty ship was due to leave shortly for England, so we asked for a lift and were told, "Be my guest." Once on board, we found others like ourselves, getting back home. One of the crew saw me looking at my automatic and told me that in England it would be taken from me, but not in America, so I did a swap for his gold watch. I didn't want the pistol anyway.

On arrival in England I felt no elation or excitement, just relief that the ordeal was over and I could start picking up the threads of my life again. Going down the gangplank, a schoolboy seeing my bag shouted, "Got any souvenirs mister?" I took out the dress belt and Hitler Youth dagger and gave them to him, glad to cleanse my hands of anything German.

A truck took a group of us to an Army camp and I started to unwind, beginning to feel at home. I was taken to the Medical Officer, who asked where I had come from, and I told him Stalag IIIA, Luckenwalde. An NCO was told to burn my clothes immediately and be ready for a medical. I asked if I could have a shower as I was dirty and he said no, he wanted to see me as I was. In the course of the examination he noticed the discharge from my middle ear, inside badly scarred — a hospital job. Malnutrition, dysentery and scoliosis. He remarked that I was very thin and an instant six weeks diet of double eggs and milk was prescribed. I foolishly never thought to mention my back, because now that the mental pressure was off, I was in a more comfortable state. The MO said it would be better for me to go home and rest until further arrangements were made for me to get treatment in hospital. I gave my mother's address to collect my belongings, see what happened when I got there.

Rosina had married a GI and had a baby son, and soon after meeting her, she moved to the United States, so I didn't have much time with her. I had my ear operation in Hounslow Hospital and after a spell at a large camp in Morpeth I was sent to Kneller Hall, home of the Royal Military School of Music and was medically discharged in 1946. Three more years of twice weekly outpatient treatment was needed to finally stop my ear discharge and restore my very distorted hearing, then my small disability pension stopped. I tried to rejoin the Army, but was refused on medical grounds and as, after a fair run living in my mother's house, because of continuous bad feeling from my father, I found myself a room in a lodging house.

After my discharge from the Army I took part in a government scheme, whereby following a six months' training course as a carpenter, I spent 3½ years with a firm as an apprentice, not receiving the full rate of pay until its completion. The building work brought on my back pain and I have had to wear surgical corsets ever since, with many hospital visits, at times almost crippled. The fevers persisted up to 1955, when during the last one I suffered a severe heart attack, and was saved from extinction in hospital. Through the years I have had several more, but wonder drugs have kept me going so I can't complain.

I visited Hoxton soon after my return to England, to find my school, the shop, Redvers Street and other places, like the old 'Britt', the Band of Hope, etc. gone through bombing, and as I saw no one I knew, I decided that there was nothing there for me. After looking in the grounds of Shoreditch Church before I left, I saw two large mounds, being mass graves of victims of the blitz.

In a roundabout way, John Knott and Jack Wright found me and said that as prisoners of the Japanese they had spent their time in Changi Gaol, and said it hadn't been too bad, but like me, one can't judge a sausage by its skin!

It took me several years to adjust, and I had long spells of depression, finding it hard to fit in with civilian life, especially when I faced resentment from some workers who accused us soldiers of coming home and taking their jobs. However, I fought my own mental problems and eventually came to terms with life, except for one thing, I must always have my bedroom door open at night. If it is closed, I will open it.

I made contact with Madame Le Boudec through the Nantes police, half hoping that my dreams would come true. I received a nice letter back, in English, telling me that she and Annique tried all possible means until 1941 to contact me, the police, Red Cross and the Germans, to no avail, so they very sadly presumed me to be dead. Not one of my prisoner of war cards reached them — if they were ever sent! I wrote back a full explanatory letter, concluding that as Annique had now married a Belgian, and had two children, I just couldn't come and visit them, but I wished them all a happier life for the future, and I never ever will forget them.

I married in 1953 and had four children and lived a happy life, with a dear wife who has put up with me like a saint, so I have little to complain about, and have always counted my blessings.

The question: have I any regrets? The answer is no, because along life's pathway there are many pitfalls and crossroads, with lessons to be learned, but I most certainly would not wish to experience it all over again.

Finally, the Queen Victoria's Rifles set the highest standards in battle alongside the Regular Army regiments, and were a credit to the Territorial Army. I was privileged to serve with them.

INDEX